M

306.73
Vitzt. V

I LOVE YOU, LET'S MEET

VIRGINIA VITZTHUM

I LOVE YOU,

LET'S MEET

Adventures in Online Dating

Little, Brown and Company
New York   Boston   London

Little, Brown and Company
Hachette Book Group USA
1271 Avenue of the Americas
New York, NY 10020
Visit our Web site at www. HachetteBookGroupUSA.com

First Edition: February 2007

"Dangling Conversation" Copyright © 1968 Paul Simon
Used by permission of the Publisher: Paul Simon Music

Library of Congress Cataloging-in-Publication Data

Vitzthum, Virginia.
    I love you, let's meet: adventures in online dating / Virginia
Vitzthum. —1st ed.
        p. cm.
    HC ISBN-10: 0-316-05784-3 / ISBN-13: 978-0-316-05784-4
    PB ISBN-10: 0-316-02124-5 / ISBN-13: 978-0-316-02124-1
    1. Online dating. 2. Online dating—Case studies.   I. Title.
    HQ801.82. V58 2007
    306.730285—dc22   2006019108

10 9 8 7 6 5 4 3 2 1

Q-MART

Printed in the United States of America

FOR ALBERTO, WHO TEACHES ME
ABOUT LOVE, PERSEVERANCE, AND THE INTERNET

*The easy possibility of letter-writing must have brought
into the world a terrible disintegration of souls. It is, in fact, an
intercourse with ghosts, and not only with the ghost of
the recipient but also with one's own ghost which develops between
the lines of the letter one is writing.*

—**FRANZ KAFKA**

CONTENTS

CONTENTS

I LOVE YOU, LET'S MEET

PROLOGUE

A girl never forgets her first e-courtship. Mine fell in the false-alarm year of Y2K, six months after I moved up from Washington, DC, to New York City.

Some folks back in DC spoke enviously of my chance to "become whatever you want," which didn't resonate. I was thirty-eight and basically liked who I was; it was my surroundings I wanted to change, not me. Yet in New York I did self-upgrade in ways I hadn't planned. I rode my bike on busy streets. I pitched stories to magazines I admired. I openly stared at the beautiful young men who congregate here like pigeons and taxis. Doing these things, on top of selling most of my stuff and moving into a railroad flat in Brooklyn with a very strange stranger, made me a braver person.

Reinvention didn't have to spring from self-loathing or secrecy, it seemed. It really could be organic, a form of becoming. And boldness was rewarded. Sometimes one of the beautiful men stared back, and looks sometimes led to conversation or dancing and then to kissing in a cab hurtling toward my place or his. I'd learn the gentleman's last name in the morning when we politely traded business cards, a Kabuki ritual of parting rarely followed by a phone call.

All this cosmopolitan action was thrilling and flattering and I did mean it when I e-mailed my friends back home that "you don't need a boyfriend here, you can date New York." (I was embarrassed when *Sex and the City* later built an episode around the same line.) And I was also forming routines and routes and the buds of friendships. The real-life stuff joined or displaced images from books and movies and black-and-white photos, and the city started to become home.

But I was alone almost all the time. I felt more like a movie camera than a person, especially with my Walkman on. When the music lined up serendipitously with street life—say, a wrinkled beggar trudging through the subway car as Skip James or Robert Johnson moaned in my ear—I could briefly merge our movies by giving him a dollar, even pushing the headphones off to hear him out. But it was still two movies. My one-night stands and my professional "networking" card exchanges (which also generally came to naught) were just slightly longer movies, gracefully performed, polite, then over. I prided myself on not being in the suburbs watching TV, but sometimes I felt equally spectatorial. I just walked more.

So I went online to find a boyfriend. I clicked into the personals from the margins of Salon.com, where I wrote a column. I figured I'd throw my dating dollar toward my struggling employer, which was starting to show up on Fuckedcompany.com as the Internet bubble began to deflate. (Salon, still going, has proved itself the Rasputin of Web sites.) Back in 2000, people still lied about online dating, but I didn't have anyone to lie to. And it didn't seem humiliating anyway; it seemed more like another bold adventure.

I searched first, checking little boxes to build my parameters: nonsmoking, age thirty-five to forty-five males over 5'10" within ten miles of my zip code. I chose Any for race, religion, eye color, and the rest, clicked on Search, and reeled before the instant man-bounty. Hundreds of them, stacked ten to a page as if in an apartment building. The pictures to the left of the headlines were little windows opening into each story. Either a witty headline or an attractive picture lured me in, and I found hordes of funny, creative, attractive, thinking, evolving men.

I'd guessed this demographic would be more populous in New York, but I'd never seen them gathered so efficiently. I'd certainly been in no room, building, or even block of the city with so many intriguing eligibles. It did seem absurd to have to computer-date in the most bachelor-dense city in the land, but here was a promising new neighborhood of Sex City, a better way to bring the relationship seekers together. You could check Play or Serious Relationship, and most checked the latter. The Salon personals seemed a not-unreasonable place to find a partner for the second half of life.

Making the profile was like a cross between going on a first date and writing a personal essay—and more fun than either. I quantified recent, middle-aged shifts in my mate priorities: warm over cool, soft over sharp, humble over certain. Figuring out how to scan and e-mail a photo boosted my pride in my technical competence. Crafting an adorable written me while sitting at my computer in sweatpants and dirty hair was a uniquely relaxed way to date. I didn't know yet that the paradoxical self-description is *the* cliché of online dating, so under Why You Should Get to Know Me, I put independent yet loving, sincere yet funny/ironic, tomboy yet sexy, and I made bettyveronica my handle. Making a big deal of my contradictions felt forthright, as if I were also admitting to my less attractive loner dyads: impatient yet tenacious, judgmental yet acceptance-preaching, critical and thin-skinned. I put my real age and my weight on a good day.

8Glass wrote me after I'd been on a week or so, opening with

Sorry I haven't written earlier, but I wanted to give you enough time to fool around with the other guys around here, 'cause I figure if we end up liking

each other (and I'm hard pressed to see how we're going to avoid it), I don't want you wondering forever, "What would it have been like with that cute guy from the Netherlands who had that featured ad, or that half-naked Calvin Klein pinup boy?" No, better to get it out of your system now.

I clicked onto his profile: he hadn't showed up in my search because his ad was hidden from all except those he contacted. He had big, dark, kind eyes, and his three photos included an older one featuring him with long hair. He seemed like what we called a progressive back in DC, an earnest sort I was having trouble finding in New York. For the "celebrity he resembled most" he put "the Holy Ghost"—check. Guys who list actual look-alikes, usually actors, come off vain and deluded, plus I'm a sucker for a blasphemer. He listed his occupation as "do-gooder"—check, social conscience and deflation of self-righteousness. Everything he wrote was witty and smart, subtle, layered, and decent. He lived in the East Village, my favorite neighborhood and only six subway stops away. It was all there.

I labored happily for a half hour over my three-sentence response. I asked if his handle meant he chomped shards like some carnival freak or if he was the eighth sibling in Salinger's family of geniuses. I also said I'd had trouble finding left-wingers in New York. I honed and honed and lobbed back my reply.

He answered immediately, pleased I'd gotten his handle's reference. And we were off. First a flurry of on-site e-mails, then the name disclosure and the switch to regular e-mail. In a few days' time, we were sharing our lives. Nick did well doing good, designing housing for the poor; he was a red-diaper baby who'd lived in New York all his life. He told me the exact bohemian history I wanted to know. He steered me to E. B. White's "This Is New York," a work whose wisdom and beauty attached to him in my mind. I told him my new-in-town trepidations: Smart people took fashion seriously. Writers slandered and gossiped instead of discussing Craft. Donald Trump was a folk hero. I e-screamed, "ME TOO!" when he shared his loathing of the city's eponymous anthem to crawling up the backs of one's fellow man, "King of the hill, top of the heap." Nick validated my doubts about the city, but told me I'd still grow to love it. Just what I wanted to hear.

Soon Nick and I were e-mailing ten to fifteen times a day. I guess the homeless were on their own those days; I know my work wasn't getting done. I'd try to log off but couldn't help peeking one last time for his name in my mailbox. He Googled me and read my columns, then e-mailed them to his friends and told me their compliments along with his. We typed long quotes out of favorite books and sent mini-essays about beloved movies and music. We agreed on politics and told self-flattering stories about our families and past relationships and kept jokes running over days. He rhapsodized about the beauty of my picture, not overtly sexual, but romantic. Drawn-out flirtation like this was a new treat: I generally would have slept with someone I liked this much by now.

Perhaps it felt so close because I "talked" to Nick from the room where nobody had ever been except the one-night stands and my cat Spud, confined inside for the first time in his fourteen years. I typed all my parental guilt to Nick, the first New Yorker I'd come out to as an overdevoted (not crazy!) cat lady. Was I not in effect a jailer, I agonized, knowing how happy Spud had been roaming the big yards of DC? Nick assured me I was anthropomorphizing and that retirement in a Brooklyn apartment was the best and healthiest life a cat could have. More of what I wanted to hear. As Nick and I shared more and more affectionate dailiness and art-discussion loftiness, he seeped into the room, settling among Spud and the photos and paintings and taped-up quotes, the stuff too precious to sell at my yard sale.

After two weeks of virtual woo, we decided to meet. He picked a bar on the edge of Chinatown. I washed my hair and got dressed, took the subway to Soho, and walked south on Hester Street, inhaling the world after too long at the computer.

The city was as erotically charged as ever, but softer now that I shared it with Nick. The fire escapes looked to me like black lace draped down the brick walls; the cobblestones, lumpy quilts thrown across the narrow streets. Nick's wit and compliments and wise observations played back in my head like music. I forgot that people on the street could see me beaming till their smiles reflected mine. We weren't eight million lone voyeurs anymore; we were all costars in a romantic comedy.

I reached the cross street, started checking addresses, and spotted a man leaning near a door. My breathing raced alongside my thoughts as I drew closer: "That's got to be him. I hope I'm not late. No way he's 5'11". I should have worn flats. He's not—well, I probably don't look as good as my picture either, though my picture's not as blurry as his. Would I look twice at a stranger this short and kind of odd-looking? If I liked his personality, yes, I would. Anyway, it's not a stranger, it's Nick." I straightened my skirt, smiled, and sauntered up to him singing: "Mystery date. Are you ready for your mystery date?"

The man who looked like a plainer version of Nick made a face that wasn't a smile. Uh-oh. I thought the singing was cute, but maybe too show-offy. "You're way too tall," he blurted.

I kept my smile propped up while my brain reeled: "What does that mean? It's bad, right? Not 'too ugly' or 'too fat,' but if it starts with 'too,' it's negative. After all the eloquent, gracious words he's typed, he opens negative? What's going on? And wait a minute, why's he's criticizing *me,* the one who's generously overlooking his misrepresentations of height and cuteness?"

I kept smiling and pointed vaguely at my boot heels. Then I struggled on and said it was great to, uh, meet him, if that was the right word after all, you know, all the e-mailing. I couldn't help noticing I was doing all the work. We went inside and sat on uncomfortably high, narrow bar stools; I hunched to look shorter. We exchanged some more close-lipped smiles and nods, ordered our wine, and then he turned and asked in a snide tone, "So how was your day, *dear?*"

What the hell did that mean? Was it a joke about our faux familiarity online? Some sort of crack about us being old and never married? Did he simply hate the way I looked and everything about me and want me to leave? I gulped down my wine, moving to an impromptu Plan B. While I'd been primping for Nick, I'd decided to slowly nurse one drink during the date. I was intimidated by his written intelligence and wanted to keep up. I didn't want to sacrifice thought processes to obliterate my fear and I certainly didn't imagine having the third "what the hell, let's make out in the bar" glass of wine with this gentle Cyrano.

But my thoughtful swain seemed an aggressive boor so far, more to be put than kept up with. He gulped his wine too, and we lunged in tandem for refills.

"What are you thinking?" is not a question that ever gets asked online. The correspondent *is* the e-mail *is* the thoughts that exist for you, the recipient, alone. That's all there is to him. I glanced unhappily at the stranger next to me and wondered where it all had gone—all our recognitions, coincidences, compliments, shared guilty pleasures, "oh my God me toos." Our relationship had been the realest thing in my life for two weeks. Now it was dissolving as fast as a dream you try to preserve upon waking, squeezing your eyes against your real life pouring in.

But our correspondence wasn't a dream. It was tangible and retrievable. Stored on two computers. More solid than speech and gestures and facial expressions and body language, in which I felt completely illiterate at the moment. Nick, what are you thinking? Our clear and well-chosen typed words were a truer expression of us than this inarticulate, hostile flailing in a smoky bar—weren't they? I gulped my wine miserably. This was the kind of ontological conundrum Nick and I might have tackled together in e-mail. We'd hit no obstacles in our perfect communication until we came to this accursed bar.

And I'd been the one to push for meeting. "Everyone who's e-dated tells me the same thing: don't dally online. Get to the

F2F—face to face," I'd said on the phone—a conduit that wasn't as good as e-mail for us, but still immeasurably better than the corporeal fiasco in Chinatown. "Everyone says the initial meeting is weird if you wait too long."

"Maybe they didn't wait long enough," Nick had protested, his voice rising wildly. "Maybe they should have e-mailed for a year. Maybe what we need is a return to courtly love."

Introduction:
Courtly Love 2.0

And thus my first inquiry into online dating: What the hell just happened? More questions tumbled from there. E-Nick and flesh-Nick were like two completely different people, so did that make his written eloquence a lie? Were my e-mails a lie? Rereading our billets-doux after the Chinatown crash, I noticed how we responded just to the sentences we liked. We both ignored so many direct questions and questionable observations. If either of us ever made a face at what we read, nobody knew. We went on way longer than is polite in speech, building to self-delighted crescendos. We never disagreed or asserted; we adjusted, collaborated, praised. There wasn't even the possibility of rudeness or boredom or misinterpretation or interrupting until the F2F.

We had fallen in love with written constructs, and both of us old enough to know better. Talking to people over the six years since then, I kept hearing a similar story, the teller always shocked looking back at his or her naïveté. It made me wonder how anyone made the transition from such e-mails to what the computer geeks call "meatspace" or RL (real life). How many courtly lovers out there only want a correspondent, like Nick?

(Not to mention the also-from-afar cybersexers.) If it were simply a matter of getting to the date sooner, how would you know whom to date? If you didn't get to know each other in writing a little, how were the dates different from job interviews? How could relationships possibly begin from this?

My next set of data came from my friend Peggy, who'd begun e-dating around the same time I did. We basically blind-cc'ed each other on our courtships. This is another aspect of these epistolary romances: lots of daters forward profiles and e-mails to an advisory board of friends. Online daters learned not to assume they were writing for one set of eyes only, long before the National Security Agency (NSA) admitted they read our e-mail.

Peggy had lived in DC for years and worried that she or a close friend had already gone out with every fortyish man in town. She got onto Match.com and found Jack, who'd just moved from Boston to teach at Georgetown. "Fresh meat!" was the subject line on her e-mail with his profile attached. He was cute, a year younger than she, an intellectual, with her same mix of idealism and bleak dark humor. "I'm a little worried that he's a player, though," she told me over the phone. "He's slept with a lot of women and hasn't had any long-term relationships. I'm afraid if I sleep with him, I'll fall in love like I always do and then he'll move on."

So she used online dating to slow herself down. She wrote a self more cautious and loath to trust than she generally is and set up wholesome daytime dates like bike rides and visits to museums. She and Jack were more confessional in e-mail, confessions that sometimes got picked up in the friendly outings, sometimes not. For the first time in her life, she was able to avoid the "drama" that had always landed her in relationships with men who weren't nice to her or who expected her to take care of them. Jack and Peggy moved in together two years later and live together still.

I'm a vicarious sort and an optimist, so I continued to take heart from Peggy's story—even as I fished the online sea with so little success, it started to seem likelier I'd find Amelia Earhart than a boyfriend. Over six years, I've met about sixty-five men, in bars, coffee shops, restaurants, and, once, at the fiftieth-anniversary Japanese reissue of *Godzilla*. I kissed a few, slept with a few, stayed friends with a few, but my longest romantic "relationship" from online has been two weeks. During those six years, I did date a few men I met the old-fashioned friends-of-friends way for longer stretches.

My terrible track record is not unique—more find frustration than find love online—but still baffling. Most of the sixty-five men were smart, attractive, sane, and reasonably close to their online representations. A few times I was interested and they weren't; more often they wanted to see me again and I was uncompelled for reasons I could not always articulate. And didn't like trying to articulate; one of the worst things about online dating is the need to come up with incisive critiques of perfectly nice people. A lot of us are picky offline too, but only in online dating do you grow to like a stranger in writing, then have to explain why you're disappointed in person. If you've been keeping a friend abreast of your dating, you find yourself switching from rapture over funny e-mails to (I've actually heard all of the following) "I don't know, his pants looked weird / she likes a stupid movie / he agreed with me too much." We arrive at the F2F more evaluative than open. I know I went into those dates less emotionally available than for other kinds of dates, and I sensed the men did too.

WHAT IT IS

To find out where this system enables, where it frustrates, and what it's doing to us, I needed to find online dating veterans whose highs were higher and lows more crushing than mine. I interviewed dozens of daters ranging in age from twenty-five to seventy. (Names and identifying details have been changed.) They are women and men; gay and straight; urban and rural; computer geeks and technophobes; married and single; parents and childless; able-bodied and differently so; thrill seekers and spouse hunters; impulsives and methodicals; success stories and—well, the f-word is so harsh, so let's just say "future success stories." Lovers love their stories and the wronged want witnesses, so people were happy to share their courtship e-mails, profiles, pics, all the artifacts of affairs documented as they unfolded. The people interviewed used a range of sites, and I explore about a dozen of those sites in the stories, including the biggest—Match.com, eHarmony.com, True.com, Gay.com—and some especially popular in New York, such as JDate and Spring Street Networks. My interviewees also used some fascinating smaller sites, for atheists, environmentalists, and "conscious" individuals.

I joined sites from covertly Christian, no-gays-allowed eHarmony.com to openly swinger Edoggers.com. I took so many personality tests on so many sites that the NSA knows just what to say should it want to date me. I submitted my online profile to a consultant who helps you better sell yourself. I talked to CEOs of dating sites about how they make their money and what they do with all the data they're gleaning from our profiles.

I online-dated through the run-up to the industry's peak year of 2003, when growth was 77 percent over the year before. Online dating has continued growing, just more slowly, into a $521 million industry. An estimated forty million people, almost a quarter of all single Americans, have used dating sites. In this young century, the stigma of online dating has faded to where single people are likely to defend *not* online dating as their computer-coupled friends harangue them to try it.

But the first thrill has also faded away. Since 2003, growth flattened to about 6 percent in 2006, which has prompted the sites to make drastic changes. Some of these changes reflect the shift in the Web overall to a more commercialized, standardized e-mall. The big sites are trying to boost profits by selling more to each customer at the same time. Smaller sites are specializing, serving farmers, parents, vegetarians, Ivy League graduates, libertarians, goths, and every race, sexual orientation, and religion. There are between eight hundred and a thousand dating sites in all; and they are changing all the time. Some of those discussed in this book will surely be overhauled or even gone by the time you read this.

HOW IT'S DIFFERENT

I've tried to separate out what's unique to online dating from dating in general and from twenty-first-century life, where we're bludgeoned by media and wired to our computers whether we e-date or not. The main differences are (1) more opportunities for creativity/lying; (2) the commodification of self and date that comes from shopping out of a human-being catalog; (3) the clearer separation of sex and love; and (4) lots and lots of dates, an essentially limitless number if you cast your parameter net wide enough.

One of online dating's most wonderful and terrible gifts is the chance for creative self-expression. Everyone gets to be a love poet, a comedian, a digital self-portraitist. The opportunity to write better versions of self and of relationships brought out the best in some of the people I interviewed. Online dating and the Web in general helped them live up to the kinder or more confident or more intellectual person they wrote, much as riding a bike in Brooklyn or pitching *The New Yorker* helped me become braver.

But creative self-expression doesn't always fit smoothly with honest self-description. Some misrepresentation is unavoidable among even the most honorable, which hardly applies to everyone with a computer. Leaving self-deceivers (like, perhaps,

Nick and me) out of it still leaves plenty of liars-with-intent. Along with the vanity-liars, shaving years and pounds, are the cheaters: studies estimate between one-fifth and one-third of all online daters are married.

Connected with the temptation to lie is the creeping commodification of the dating sites and the daters themselves. It's hard not to notice that the sites look like catalogs, and people often call the profiles "ads." Many of the sites have added an Amazon.com-like feature: "If you liked this bachelor, check out these four like him!" They're bundling in more services like professional photography, profile-writing help, and tips for how to e-mail a stranger, replacing the Web's old anarchy with a normalizing dictatorship. The sites are also grabbing more control of the steps—eHarmony, for example, does the matching for you based on its compatibility quiz, and won't let you see pictures till you've jumped through its expensive e-hoops.

Sites like True.com have added background checks and multiple-choice tests to determine "chemistry." My once-favorite site, Nerve.com, now rewards members for getting lots of clicks on their profile. These shifts sneak into the way people treat each other, starting with an expectation of truth in advertising and a shrinking from oddness. Knowing they're being evaluated like a product makes people respond in kind, so first dates are two shoppers peering skeptically and defensively at each other across the table. With so much product to choose from, so many dates you could be on instead, "settling" on any one seems foolish.

With all the niche marketing, it's inevitable that online dating would make it easier to separate sex from love. On Craigslist.org or any number of "adult" sites, people can order a liaison like a pizza. (Among users in L.A., Gay.com is in fact known as Domino's for how fast it delivers men while they're still hot.) Meanwhile, on the relationship sites, people can check boxes for seeking Serious Relationship or Just Dating or Play. And the predate e-mailing can serve as a sort of contract, where both parties hammer out desires and expectations before they ever meet.

Overlapping all those changes is a very basic one that should be unqualifiedly good. Online daters get way more dates. Go online and within a day, you can move from a months-long drought to five dates next week. And there are no doubts that it works; about fifty-three million people know someone who met someone online.

The greatest technological advance in the history of human mating, online dating gives single people a public square to find each other, using whatever criteria matter to them—location, age, beliefs, vices, hobbies, height, or income. People can present themselves as they like and search around the world at any time of day or night in a smelly bathrobe. With the public access comes the privacy of anonymous, untraceable e-mail through the site. It's an amazing gathering of the lonelyheart tribes, and one of the few sustained successes on the Internet. Online dating joins e-mail and porn in that small club of killer apps, falling psychically somewhere between the former's connectivity and the latter's fantasy fodder.

But even that obvious good of increased access has a downside, and it's much harder to pinpoint than the creativity-lying nexus. It has to do with managing one's hopes over many, many stranger-dates, which more often than not end in disappointment. I've found in talking to people that I'm not the only online dater worrying that I'm getting pickier, less generous, less likable as I do it. If it's just a matter of "not feeling chemistry," the online shorthand for all F2F disappointment, you feel shallow and "looksist." If you are interested, and your interest is not returned, well, that sucks for the same reasons it's sucked throughout history. And because the numbers are so high, courtesy declines: not returning calls or e-mails is a semiaccepted way to break things off.

A lot of people are grateful for online dating, but a different lot worry about what it's doing to us. We're asking, Is it you or is it me, online dating? Are you making me feel panicked, addicted, and more alone? Do you like me better that way?

The Web can drill straighter into our psyches than anything outside science fiction. Google, Yahoo, and others watch every click we make, all our purchases, utterances, and glances, and tailor their advertising to a demographic of one. Dating sites get even more information—the specific longing and loathing in our profiles—effortlessly, without surveys or focus groups. The sites lure advertisers with that access to desire, and they use the same data to "scientifically" matchmake, insisting they can find us better mates than we can on our own. Taking their cues from the more "aspirational" print and screen media, they do this largely by threatening us with lifelong singleness if we don't follow their tips for self-presentation, e-mailing, photo captions, and first date conversation. The laughing couples on the home pages are generally models, not real schlubs in love.

The Web has grown more mall-like in the past few years, but it also fulfills some of its original promise to pull culture forward. Blogs, music downloading and other copyright challenges, social networking, and online dating *are* changing the world more than reality TV, satellite radio, and the mushrooming of magazines about celebrity cellulite.

Online dating operates at the heart of that Internet paradox: a brilliant marketing tool can also be a refuge from mainstream consumer culture. Not surprisingly, the people who found love online tended to be more refugee than customer. No happily-ever-after said to me, "And I owe it all to that compatibility quiz." Like RL lovers, the online lovers in this book credit luck, tenacity, good instincts, and nerve. What's novel is how they rewrote *relationship* in an ongoing collaboration with their new partner. Profiles and e-mails served as rough drafts of the people they wanted to become.

PART ONE WRITING THE SELF

Who am I? What do I want? People spend their lives trying to answer those two questions, and online dating casually demands one-paragraph answers. Every individual's understanding of self, love, and life must be squeezed into a small box, with the shrinking number of characters left flashing as you type. Online daters don't generally acknowledge the immensity of the search for identity and happiness we're undertaking when we sign up. We can't. It would paralyze us. Instead we insist, "Hey, it's just a chance to meet someone for a beer or a cup of coffee. In and out in twenty minutes, no big deal."

Where the vertiginously high stakes show up is in the writing. Conversation, especially with a stranger, almost always starts out casual, but writing does not. Where do people generally write about or from their hearts? In their journals and diaries, in letters and e-mails, in stories, poems, essays, and songs. Writing is where we make sense of things, build arguments and theories, confess, declare, confront—where we take risks. By starting on the electronic page, online dating plunges us into intimacy while we try on new ways of being.

This often ends in disappointment, as it did for me and

Nick. To my surprise, it led some people closer to Who I Am and What I Want—and to a love born beyond the material world. The corny, overused *soulmate* is actually the perfect word for some of these pairs born in cyberspace.

THE WILD WILD WEB

A few years before mainstream Americans began self-advertising on Match.com, techies were creating virtual societies in online communities like the Well and Echonyc and in role-playing MUDs (multi-user domain/dungeon), MOOs (MUD object-oriented), and MUCKs (multi-user chat kingdom). I first read about these bodiless convocations in the early 1990s and was fascinated by the way cyberspace broke open concepts of "self," "meet," "friend," "know," "community," and "sex." And it wasn't just an ontological puzzle; it was downright inspiring. A parallel world where people were judged by the typed contents of their characters, not by race, gender, class, or beauty, seemed a genuine opportunity for human evolution.

Many of the pioneers were idealists. Englishman Tim Berners-Lee invented the Web in 1990 and walked away from cashing in on the "www" protocols because it wasn't about the money. He said in 2004, "There was no global management plan to make the Web. It happened because a very diverse group of people, connected by the Internet, wanted it to happen. The process was great fun, and still is. From the fact that it worked, I draw great hope for all our futures. May we now use every ability we have to communicate to build a society in which mutual respect, understanding and peace occur at all scales, between people and between nations."

What's not to like? I cheered the Webtopians, however, from the sidelines; WordPerfect was as deep as I went into my computer at the time. It was partly ignorance and technophobia, but also a fondness for the world outside my apartment. As much as the cyberconcepts and possibilities intrigued me, I didn't want to spend actual hours at my actual desk pretending to be an elf in a digital forest.

It wasn't until 1999 that I joined a chatroom, doing research for a column. At the now-vanished site Thewife.com, members chatted as they watched, in the top left corner of the screen, footage of "Christine," "a Silicon Valley housewife" living in a house full of Webcams. In jerkily streaming video (at least on my dial-up connection), Christine would type on her laptop, exercise, fold laundry, prepare meals, and occasionally masturbate. This was the height of the girl-on-Webcam craze, and Christine primly distinguished herself from her less intellectual sisters with remarks like "I'm proud of my natural B-cup breasts and I know to put the beer bottles in the recycling bin."

The chat was bizarrely wholesome, even chivalrous. Special gatekeepers expelled anyone who made explicit reference to the fact that we were all watching Christine writhe naked on the bed while she rubbed herself. Only a certain level of verbal/emoticon winking was OK. When she first logged into the chatroom each day, a chorus of voices would tell her how pretty she looked today, as if she were the teacher of some lewd correspondence class. Members jostled for her approval, doubly rewarded for a good joke not just by her typed "LOL" but by seeing her laugh onscreen.

"Christine" was a fascinating puzzle of simulacrum/reality— a friend insisted she wasn't "really" a Silicon Valley housewife, but if someone lives that life on camera and in the chatroom, is it an act? Unless she'd been brainwashed like Patty Hearst (whom she slightly resembled), we were interacting with someone genuinely exhibitionistic, friendly, libertarian, and lonely who occasionally had sex on camera with a guy who sure looked the part of the technocrat "hubby" she claimed to have.

The Wife was the draw, but the members, from as far away

as Australia, had clearly bonded. Chat went on around the clock even when the Webcam showed an empty house. When any regular would enter chat, a chorus of "voices" would greet him or her (a surprising number of hers) and ask, Did your son find out if he got into that college? Have you gotten over your flu? The typed back-and-forth about politics, books, movies, sports, computers, and Web culture was surprisingly smart and quick-witted, and the Wife held her own. "Hubby" occasionally entered the chatroom to espouse scary libertarian views ("I would rather my children starve to death than take money raised by taxes," he e-declared once, to an e-outcry.)

I bided my time like a jump roper studying the patterns, then leaped in as "Sally." Invisibility made it far less scary than standing at the edge of a conversation at a party, clutching a drink and waiting for an opening. I started to "talk" more, admitted I was a newbie (but not that I was a journalist). The regulars were kind and welcoming; I was gratified when they praised my knack for this kind of discourse. I had a little flirtation with a quick-witted man and would look for him when I signed on. One day I was teasing him and miscalculated my tone, and he called me a bitch. My face burned in front of my monitor; I typed frantically to explain myself. Suddenly he was gone from the room, and I was despondent. It had gotten real.

Some of the conversation was banal, but so is a lot of F2F conversation. I liked that you didn't have to speak until you had something to say, and that you could do other things on your computer without being rude. You could bid farewell and be answered by a chorus of *Byes!* and *Later*s and *CU Tomorrow*s or you could just disappear by logging off. Free of your body, you were part of the group's self-commemoration, a conversation that was as alive as a real one, but also recorded as it happened, unscrolling, marking our time together in a play we simultaneously read and wrote. How quickly I got sucked into Thewife.com and how hours would just slip away gave me a new respect for the power of the Web to whip up obsession and to attach strangers, especially among single people.

I liked how Sally could float theories, make pronouncements, and argue politics with Hubby in ways Virginia would have modulated to be reasonable. And yet wanting the group's approval kept me and the other wife-watchers, mostly, from being jerks. As odd as it may sound for a community bound by a masturbating blonde, there was a sense of shared responsibility for making this a pleasant haven. As in most chatrooms, members who'd logged zillions of hours were appointed by the Wife to police the chat for obscenity and aggressiveness; in MUDs and MOOs, these enforcers of the peace were called "wizards."

What's liberating about chatrooms as opposed to online dating is that the typed self doesn't stand for anything or correspond to reality. That Sally, she's a character.

CHAPTER 1

Lila and Scott: Souls First

Lila and Scott were the only two people I interviewed who didn't set out from Who Am I; What Do I Want. They backed into their correspondence and then an RL relationship in a way they call "innocent." Theirs is an old-fashioned fairy tale from long ago in Internet years—1995.

Lila was part of the second, bigger rush onto communal cyberspace via the America Online chatrooms. This was a population still geekier than most of the country, but way more mainstream than the DOS pioneers. The interface had been vastly simplified into graphical point-and-click, eliciting scorn from the pioneers who'd keystroked their way since the '80s around what was sometimes called the "Matrix," before "Internet" had been settled on. The AOL chatters had less to bond them than the first-wavers, and so their communications moved more quickly to romantic possibilities, either cybersex or starting a flirtation that would lead to an offline meeting.

When Lila first entered a chatroom, AOL was still a frontier. As in many earthly neighborhoods, some of the first settlers were gay men as well as (and including) transsexuals who first practiced cross-"dressing" online. AOL sought a family image, but M4M (men for men) was one of its most popular areas. Among heterosexuals, men far outnumbered women, and most worked or played with computers. Lila was one of the rare girl-geeks, doing logic puzzles, trivia, and then roleplay computer games.

Her real life, in Oakland, California, was ripe for escaping when she popped in her first free AOL disk. Her live-in fiancé had just broken off their engagement, days before her thirtieth birthday, but financial straits kept her living with him. Even more horrible, he remained her boss in his small company. Lila, who felt "more numb than heartbroken" in this house-arrest limbo, turned to the computer for distraction. "I liked AOL because it had games and it was sort of pretty, it was eye candy," she told me over the phone in her high, lilting voice. "It was cooler then, without all the advertisements. It seemed very creative, like a company inventing a computer game that it was so proud of."

A coworker of a friend told me about Lila and Scott. I interviewed them separately on the phone, first her, then him, with no idea what they looked like—just as they were invisible to each other when they met. Lila is smart and witty but unironic in the way of Californians, sincere and straightforward in the way of geeks. When she fondly recollects playing "advanced adventure games, and this is way before Myst," I envision duct-taped glasses, a pink pocket protector.

She spent most of her time in AOL's "30-something" group. She found herself drawn back more and more.

Somebody would post "age, sex, location" check, it was called an ASL check, and everybody, twenty or thirty people, would identify themselves. Then just by typing we'd set up an environment. Somebody would say "party time" and somebody else would say "<going to get drinks>" and you'd create this whole experience. It was less about showing off, it was about adding to the creation of this party. I still remember these people who I only knew as online presences for a few months ten years ago.

That space—remote but warm, active but undemanding—suited Lila perfectly. "I tend to be shy in person and feel like I need to put up something that doesn't represent shy." The phrasing makes it sound like her social mask is harder to drag around than most people's—a floor-length avatar that "doesn't represent shy." She says, "If I'm out with a strange group of people, my preference is not to talk to anyone, because I can't think of anything to say to total strangers. Being online and interacting with people who had no expectations was great for me."

She began to notice Scott, a new regular in the thirty-something room who "always seemed normal or nice or cool." An ASL check revealed that he lived in the Bay Area too and was around her age. She clicked into his "personal data sheet"—the precursor to the online dating profile—saw it was empty, and offered to help him set one up. He wrote back his thanks; he was new and could use the help. He revealed that he was a journalist researching a story on software games and CD-ROMs; she was eager to share what she knew. "Why not? Nobody was ever going to see me."

Lila, unlike Scott, sees the old chatrooms as more than half full of human potential. "You got the feeling people were telling the truth more than they do now. Maybe people lied, but the people who were lying were twelve or fourteen. You could tell they were kids." She says nostalgically, "People wouldn't put themselves out as anything flashy; nobody was trying to sell themselves back then."

Lila continued offering Scott tech support and then set him up with instant messaging (IM). They began IMing every day. The IMs were detailed, confessional, even a bit obsessed, but not romantic, Lila says. "Maybe we were flirting," she semiadmits, "but without intention or agenda. I didn't want to be fishing or anyone fishing for me." They talked about work and the Internet; they discovered they'd gone to rival high schools. Lila used the phrase "my boyfriend" in IM and Scott politely typed back, "Oh, you have a boyfriend?" Lila explained the in-house estrangement.

She had never talked to a man like this. "Men rarely spend the first hour of getting to know a woman pummeling her with questions like Scott did. I'd say, 'wait, let's talk about you,' but he'd turn it back to me, and I'd say, 'hey, you did it again!' It made me realize he was different from most men. He's humble; he thinks a lot of jobs are cool, not just what he does." This is not particular to online dating, but women gushing about men who ask questions is so universal, I wonder how any man doesn't know to do this.

He Says

I talked to Scott a few nights later. He has a friendly voice and, like Lila, an articulateness and ease that belie his claims to dweebery. I prefer doing interviews in person and mostly did for this book, but perhaps the phone and e-mail are better with these two. "I started playing around in the chatrooms for research and then because they were this fascinating window into society, these conversations among strangers," Scott says. "I would mostly bounce around the chatrooms and not say anything."

He calls himself a pessimist and says his hatred of male-on-female cruising probably starts with his own discomfort. "When I was dating, I thought, 'Nobody wants me to walk up to her in a bar and use some line.' Which may be more a reflection of my social ineptness than anything else." In the chatrooms, he says with a sneer, "You saw more guys than women. When a woman would pop up, you'd see three or four guys try to talk to her, like a frat party. Guys would type, 'what are you doing in here?'; 'what do you do?' I felt annoyed by those people. I know that's not fair."

I'm struck by the distaste Lila and Scott still share for virtually all dating rituals, including online dating. Lila criticizes a friend of hers who uses a glamour shot in her online dating profile: "That's like throwing out cheese and thinking you'll get a bear instead of a rat!"

Given their fastidiousness about boy-meets-girl, what did Scott think was going on during those weeks of daily e-mails and IMs? He insists, "Using a computer as a communication tool rather than just a typewriter was what intrigued me. The more we corresponded, the more I began to think about the Web as a useful tool for saying things that were on my mind, to be relaxed around a woman and not feel the pressure of the weird sexual dynamic."

For Scott, Lila was a tour guide in a foreign country, because she'd chatted and IMed before. He is a journalist, so questioning comes naturally, but his curiosity about cyberrelations blurred with his curiosity about Lila and distracted him from the dreaded sexual tension. The language he learned with Lila gave him a new way to be with women. "I felt so comfortable, more myself, more uninhibited. It was shockingly easy to be more relaxed. . . . I always was eager to see if I had e-mail, if she was online; I knew we'd be revealing more and more to each other." Their exploration of the technology paradoxically took the attention off the fact that they were using it to get to know each other.

Lila's home situation helped Scott relax. Because she lived with a guy, "I wasn't thinking it was going anywhere. I thought it was this cool friendship that was being established. Of course I wondered what she looked like and how she'd present herself in person, but she was living with someone."

She Says

Lila remembers a swell of affection when Scott logged off one day with "gotta run, I'm taking my grandmother to lunch." Lila asked, "Are you Asian?" and Scott typed, "No, why?"

Lila, who's half Japanese and half Norwegian, wrote back

to him, "Most men don't take their grandmothers to lunch unless they're Asian." When he told her no, he was a Romanian-Polish-French mutt, she says,

---

That intrigued me. He loves his grandmother, he loves the women in his family and respects them and thinks they're cool. I just liked him more and more.

So one day Scott IMed me that he was coming to Oakland for a job interview, and I said, "OK, then we should meet for coffee." He did not seem very enthusiastic. He said "Really?" not "Great, let's do that!" The night before we were going to meet, I made a joke about weighing three hundred pounds, and he said, "oh I'm getting little pieces of what you look like," and I said, "I'm kidding, I don't weigh three hundred pounds."

He Says

Lila was right about Scott's hesitation. He remembers, "When she suggested meeting, I thought, 'Why would we do that?' " He worried not just if Lila'd be pretty, but if anything he knew about her was true. "At that point, it became clear that something might happen. Immediately I started worrying she might look like a Cyclops; she might be a fourteen-year-old boy. You could tell from those chatrooms that people were presenting themselves in a way that wasn't real."

He didn't want the worlds to collide. In cyberspace they'd cavorted as innocently as Brooke Shields and that blond kid in *Blue Lagoon*. The fragile trust couldn't possibly survive Bay Area meatspace, where Scott was a skeptical reporter. With a meeting planned, he had to question the whole interlude, his first doubts about anything she'd said. Scott could not see any good outcome of this date, a double date really. Not only would Scott be meeting some strange woman, he'd also be trying to acquaint his guileless cyberself and the anxious, mistrustful geek he became on dates.

She Says

"I sat in the parking lot for three minutes deciding whether to put on red lipstick and I was asking myself, 'Wait a minute, why do I care? Because he seems like a great guy? Because I'm interested?' There was no apprehension. I had chatted with Scott about two weeks, extended IMs for nine days." She breaks off in our phone conversation and I hear papers shuffling. She laughs. "Wait, now that I look at these IMs, we were flirting!"

I tell her, thanks for your honesty, but I'd figured that out. Now get back to the date! "I went into the coffee / bookstore and there were three guys with beards. I went up to one and said, 'Are you Scott?' and he said 'No.' I went up to another one and said, 'Are you Scott?' and the guy said, 'No, but I wish I was.' So I went to the magazines and a different bearded guy tapped me on the shoulder and said, 'Are you Lila?' "

I ask what her first gut reaction was, and she answers slowly enough that I gather Scott's no George Clooney.

I turned around and thought, "Wow, that's him. And he doesn't look like an angry psychopath, he looks like a nice warm guy." And we sat down and he was very easy. He's not flirtatious. I don't remember what we said, probably superficial chatter, but there was mutual knowledge, I knew about his family. I asked, "How did your interview go?"

It was like old friends who finally get to meet. It was so great to have that interest with someone familiar. We had unfinished conversations to finish: "So, whatever happened with that?" It was somehow surprising that the guy who seemed nice really was nice and is funny and smart and cares about people. He's really a great guy.

She goes on some more about his attributes, still mushily in love after ten years.

He Says

Scott's predate nervousness focused primarily on Lila's attractiveness, and tangentially on his own (how nice to be a man!). "I was thinking, 'She's not going to be appealing,' but what if she is? Then I worried if she was too cute, no way she'd want to be with me. So I go into the store, and I look around. She'd told me long brown hair, medium height, half Japanese, half white. I see a woman with her back to me looking at magazines. I walked by once, and she turned, and I said, 'Lila?' and she said, 'Scott?' "

I'm pretty sure after talking to both of them that I know his answer to the gut-reaction question. Still, it's wonderful to hear him intone the punch line: "And there stood. The most beautiful woman. I had ever seen." He still seems unable to fathom his luck. "I'd dated attractive women before, but she was ridiculously stunning. A few weeks into it, I was e-mailing my college friends, 'I'm dating someone we don't date! I've gone way out of our league.' "

The connection they'd weaved online held in the coffee shop. "I can't remember a single thing we talked about, but I know it was easier by virtue of having spent two weeks talking online," Scott says.

I was incredibly nervous and constantly thinking of what I was saying. I just kept asking questions, which is what I do. We walked to our cars together, and I said, "Maybe we should do this again." It was left open-ended. And then I went on with my day and evening and got home pretty late. I turned on my computer, obviously hopeful, and sent her an instant message and then we just started talking for a while and then we ended up agreeing to get together the next night. I was jumping out of my skin.

There's absolutely no way that we would have ended up together if we'd met in real life. I'd never have approached someone who looks like that. The relationship happened really quickly; we went out the night after the coffee date and it was clear we were together and we saw each other every day after that. Lila ended up moving into my place within six weeks. Her looks quickly stopped being an issue.

Eight months later they got married. They had two beautiful children—"They take after Lila, thank God," Scott says, laughing—and live happily ever after in the pretty hills north of San Francisco.

She Says

For her looks to "stop being an issue" was what Lila had been waiting for without knowing it. For the first hour or so we talked, her rants against people's shallow standards led me to believe the poor thing was dreadfully homely. "I do not know of a single couple that is truly happy that met because they saw each other first and were attracted to each other," Lila declared when we started talking. "People don't recognize how much love can not be based on physical attraction; they think physical attraction equals love. . . . In my family growing up, people's looks weren't that important. It was more 'You're beautiful because I love you.'" (Scott tells me later her sisters are also gorgeous.)

It's supposed to be unseemly to complain about too much beauty, but Lila's "stunning" looks only isolated her from her own species of logical geek. "The biggest problem with dating is that the coolest guys like Scott don't go up to women like me; the jerky, overconfident ones do," she says. "People were attracted to me because of the way I looked and I was tired of that; those were people I didn't want to know. Fitting into someone's category of what's attractive has nothing to do with if you're funny or nice or anything that matters. . . . There's something grotesque about humanity that it cares so much about this one thing that has no importance in a long-term relationship."

Scott won Lila by befriending her before he saw her. Only online could this fairy tale have unfurled, and maybe only in those early days before the Internet was so thoroughly colonized for commerce, sex, and sexual commerce. Back in the old chatrooms, Lila found not just Scott but an integrity she wouldn't have known about without this chance to control for the variables of her looks and of dating games. "I have thirty-two single-spaced pages of e-mail and IMs from the nine days before we met," Lila e-mails me.

Have you ever seen movies of yourself when you weren't aware that there was a camera on you? Imagine those movies, but with your thoughts all out loud. Reading those IMs is looking at myself in such a totally unselfconscious place. Re-reading them, I feel myself blush at how uncensored I was (and I don't mean sexually). I was so curious: What will you say when you're sure you'll never meet someone? In the IM messages, I was glad to see that I was true to myself.

ROMANCE OF NOT WANTING

Lila and Scott were protected from the pitfalls of online dating by the very chance-ness of their encounter. They didn't project, assume, misrepresent, or wonder if they could do better as they got to know each other. Friendship made a more solid foundation for them than the posturing and maneuvering of the boy-girl dance. They're like a happy *Twilight Zone* about soul-love (the twist: "She turns out to be beautiful!") and suitably grateful for their luck. They lived the fantasy of "being judged for what's inside."

For the most part, online dating is not that magical refuge from hot or not. The pictures are what everybody sees first, though once they've been appraised, the correspondents can start a conversation with some of Lila and Scott's freedom from self-consciousness. For Lila and Scott, the biggest difference between their tale and online daters' is intent. And, frankly, it's a bit annoying the way they fetishize their meeting's "innocence." So if you actively search for a mate, you're what, guilty? Banished from the garden? The logical extension of Lila's insistence that lovers can only find each other without looking is that the truest self doesn't include desires for love or plans to pursue it. That's surprisingly passive for a geek, a breed known for persistence in problem solving.

Passive serendipity is the heart of Lila and Scott's story, and they're not the only ones who romanticize it. More than any other reason, people won't online-date because it's "unromantic." "If it was meant to be, it'll be"; "I leave it to the stars"; "Love has to find you, you can't go looking." Among my interviews, young go-getting women in particular insisted online dating upset some natural order: several of them e-mailed me rousing speeches about being happy without a man, pep talks they called denial later, after they got engaged. Nobody who had dated more than ten years as an adult professed belief in the stars, and most had tried online dating.

One of online dating's great contributions is to call the bluff on "I don't have time for a relationship now" or "I'm not really looking." If you've gone to the trouble to put up a profile, to throw the cheese up online, you are admitting you actually rather do want someone. This eliminates one of the most popular moves in the game—feigned unavailability. Of course, it also takes away a face-saving means of rejection. Yes, I do want someone, just not you.

CHAPTER 2

Michele and Benton: Postmodern Romance

Of course, most of us would rather appear—and be—self-sufficient than needy. There are a range of ways to protect ourselves from the vulnerability of admitting, on the World Wide Web, "I need a date badly enough to advertise for one." Total self-acceptance lies at the ideal end, with actual humans ranging down through various levels and methods of self- and other-deception. A certain type of hipster dons the armor of irony, "dating" in quote marks. She/he/we make the search for love into a wacky multimedia performance piece featuring the profile self—witty, attractively self-deprecating, full of obscure references to test your knowledge—and amusing tales of rejection and disappointment and all the freaks out there.

The site of choice for a lot of these bright, artsy, self-conscious daters is Nerve, aka Spring Street, aka FastCupid.com. To explain the name confusion: in 1997, sex zine Nerve.com started the online personals that in 2002 became Spring Street Networks, and FastCupid in 2005. But people kept calling it by its original monosyllable after the switch, as in "I met him on Nerve, where else?" Daters can join FastCupid not just through

Nerve.com but also via Salon.com, the *Onion, Esquire, New York* magazine, the *Village Voice,* and other alternative weeklies like the Boston *Phoenix.*

Nerve is my primary haunt, the place where an embarrassing number of the regulars know my name. It's the site most of my friends use, and it's where I found almost every good or OK online date I've had since 2000. It's where people are clearly joking when they use clichés, and the profiles are learned enough to send you to the dictionary and Wikipedia. Though OkCupid and Friendster also feel like my tribe, those two are dominated by people in their twenties. It's Nerve alone that has kept alive my belief I could ever find someone this way. One version of my oft-tweaked profile is on pages 40 and 41.

Nerve's far from perfect. It combines the sexual fringe with the cultural fringe, which is tough on monogamous hipsters. (The same could be said of RL bohemia, I suppose.) Self-consciousness reigns on Nerve, where the picture I see over and over is a man taking a picture of himself taking a picture of himself in the mirror. Of course that photo could mean, "I don't have anyone to take my picture; I'm either friendless or embarrassed to be doing this" or "I've conquered the technology, bought the gadgets, I'm omnicompetently masculine and setting out on a girlfriend quest alone." But I tend to read, "I'm commenting on my layered presentation of self and I'm not fully inhabiting this e-dating process."

To an extent I've seen on no other site, Nerve users share a postmodern view of multiple selves, defined by context. "There's no such thing as authenticity" and "The reader creates the text" are two postmodern tenets made manifest online. Nerve daters are less likely than users of Match.com or JDate.com to rage that people misrepresented themselves in their profile. They accept that identity isn't fixed, and that it's a blurry line between lying and playing. They're online a lot.

SEX AND SENSIBILITIES

Michele and Benton are quintessential Nerve daters: he got onto the site via feminist magazine *Bust;* Michele via Salon.com. They'd both online-dated for years when they met. They prefer it to RL dating and say it's a much better way to find their type of person—a quirky cultural outlier and a passionate fan.

Michele traces her journey online back twenty-five years to high school on Staten Island, where she felt like an exile. "I accepted that I'm always going to be an outcast, on the fringes, and these few people will like me and respect me and maybe they're not worthy of my attention but I have no choice." Michele found refuge first among the Dungeons and Dragons kids, then the punk rockers, then the computer geeks.

She got into AOL chatrooms in 1992 and put up her first Web site in 1996. She posted opinions, fiction, and journal-type writing on her site years before blogs or online dating, when zines were first transcending friends-of-friends mailing lists for the potentially World Wide readership of the Web. She found fellow travelers in many cyberniches, including a David Foster Wallace Listserv she joined in 1997. Like many in the arts fringes, Michele has a vision of romantic love that has been shaped more by public figures than her own private life. She e-mails that her love ideas come from "the media, mostly. john and yoko, sid and nancy (the movie version at least), dali and gala . . . those great couples who were involved in art together." (The list suggests a death wish that I've never seen in Michele.)

I met Michele a few years ago at a ravelike event in a warehouse—16 mm film on a cement wall accompanied by electronic screeching from a laptop, people videotaping each other dancing, an absinthe booth. We were both about forty, and in her online nightlife column, she wrote of the event,

NotEvil
"Doer profile"

ME
I am a: Woman
Seeking a: Man
Interested in: Dating, Serious Relationship
Age: 43
Location: Brooklyn, New York
Area Code: 718
Occupation: Writer
Education: College Degree
Ethnicity: WASP with ethnic hair
Religion: There are scientologists on Nerve?
Star Sign: Sagittarius
Relationship Status: Single
Have Children: No
Want Children: Maybe

MY GOODS
Height: 5'8"
Weight: 137 lbs
Hair: Brown
Eye Color: Hazel

MY HABITS
Cigarettes: Never
Booze: Sometimes
Drugs:
Self-love:
Self-deprecation:

YOU
Age Between: 37–48
Within: 10 miles
Education: No preference
Religion: No preference
Ethnicity: No preference
Star Sign: No preference
Have Children: No preference
Want Children: No preference

YOUR GOODS
Height: 5'11"–7'10'
Weight: 157–227 lbs
Hair: No preference
Eye Color: No preference

YOUR HABITS
Cigarettes: Never OK
Booze: Sometimes OK
Drugs: Sometimes OK
Self-love: Sometimes OK
Self-depreciation: Sometimes OK

TIP OF THE ICEBERG
Last great book I read: just re-read Delillo's White Noise, even better than I remembered. Our Kind by Kate Walbert had moments; Good Old Neon, best story in David Foster Wallace's Oblivion; Against Love by Laura Kipnis

Favorite on-screen sex scene: Julianne Moore and Dennis Haysbert under the disco ball in Far From Heaven; Keanu and Sandra in Speed; Liam Neeson and Diane Keaton in The Good Mother

Celebrity I resemble most: nut dispenser

If I could be anywhere at the moment: here and now

Song or album that puts me in the mood: Dusty in Memphis; Tricky; Roxy; Howlin Wolf; Astral Weeks; Ella Fitzgerald; "Shoop"; basso-butch garage rock (Lou, Iggy, Cramps, Animals)

The five items I can't live without: yellow bile, black bile, phlegm, blood, Google

Fill in the blanks
<u>see</u> is sexy
<u>below</u> is sexier

In my bedroom, you'll find: a person who likes to have sex, and is thus taken aback when people call it humankind's biggest puzzle or problem. It's not un-complex, but most things are worse than it.

WHY YOU SHOULD GET TO KNOW ME
I get excited by my work. I "take advantage of New York" — go to lots of free-to-cheap artsy, nonsensenyc.com-type happenings. But I live at a pretty relaxed pace. I'm not that ambitious. I don't have a cell phone.

I give the benefit of the doubt and I listen. My shoulder gets cried on.

Perhaps a bit out of touch. I was Private Lynndie England for Halloween, and I honestly feared that everyone else in the parade would be too — it seemed too obvious a costume.

MORE ABOUT WHAT I AM LOOKING FOR
OK with being mid-lifed but not a curmudgeon. No need to know every damn thing the kids are listening to, but be arts-obsessed enough to keep up with something and basically dig modernity.

I do well with single dads, but a kind, smart, funny, tall, childless guy would be lovely too. Both are good ways to live.

It's OK if you loathe G. W. Bush without your usual adjustments toward tolerance and understanding.

"everybody there could have been my kid." But she looked more mami than mommy: tiny vinyl miniskirt and combat boots, a T-shirt that said, "My cat has a live journal," thick black hair in pigtails, feisty attitude. She threw out names of experimental writers and obscure bands a little aggressively but was friendly in the New York way—direct and challenging. Many of her friends admit we were scared of her until her thoughtfulness and generosity appeared, often via e-mail.

Her online writing is smart, breezy, funny—and lonely. It's halves of conversations, coolly confessional, and reading her can be easier than being with the sometimes prickly Michele. One essay on the media's double standard of female and male beauty opens, "I'm a cute girl, I readily admit it. I'm not beautiful. In fact, I vacillate between thinking I'm OK and freakishly ugly. But I'm cute. There's almost no escaping this. I have features that, when put together, one must call cute . . . and yet guys aren't knocking down the door to go out with me." You can hear the sexy, empowered adult fighting with the frizzy-haired Hispanic teen misfit and with the sexist, ageist, racist world in the scolding phrase "features . . . one must call cute." The Internet has from the start given a voice to girls and women like Michele retroactively protesting how they were shushed when they entered adolescence and how much we're judged on our looks.

In 1997, Michele joined the dating site Swoon.com and met Jon, her first online boyfriend. He lived in Seattle, and Michele was still in New York. Yet despite—or because of—the three-thousand-mile gap, she says, it was a passionate and informed courtship. "He was among the first people to put up a Web site, so I could go back and read years of his online journal. It felt intimate," she insists, defending now as she surely did then against the suggestion that it was "unromantic" to meet someone this way. "We built up a lot of emotional intimacy before we actually met, which held up in person."

Their first offline meeting took place two months later. After six more months of visiting back and forth, Jon moved into

Michele's small Manhattan apartment. They lasted only ten months as a couple, with the big disagreement being that he wanted to stay home all the time and she likes to go out. But the two have stayed friends, linking to each other's Web sites and getting together to compare online dating stories. Michele worries her ex may be painting himself into a corner of confirmed bachelorhood. "He expects too much," she says, sighing. "Television has done that to people. A lot of online guys expect to be dating Jennifer Lopez and for her to be interested in how they spent all day coding in Perl. I keep telling him he's probably not going to do a whole lot better than me."

LEARNING FROM NERVE

After Jon split, Swoon swooned, and Michele joined Nerve. Thus began her first-ever stretch of heavy dating, and she made the standard rookie mistakes online. "I built up some very intense e-mail relationships, e-mailing or IMing ten times a day, and then you meet and there's nothing and it's like, oh my god, that person is gone," she says, shaking her head. "There's something about e-mailing or writing, at least for me, that fosters an emotional connection quicker. You're intellectualizing, explaining feelings, and that carries them forward. Plus, you don't get a reaction that stops you."

Michele learned, as everyone eventually does, to get to the date sooner—and also to disengage a bit. "I stopped getting so emotionally involved. I learned to do online what I could never do in real life. I learned to flirt. Even though you're having an exchange, it's not so deep or emotionally invested." The noncommittal flirting was revelatory for Michele, who fears she's too intense. Even more important, she found herself demanding more, "in a healthy way. I found myself thinking, 'OK, what's *he* bringing to the party? Is he bringing anything? No? All right, then he's out.'"

She lists her modest date criteria with a laugh. "I expect them to shower. I expect them to be able to have a conversation. I expect they'd read a book, that they could talk about pop culture, that they had something exciting to offer me, whether excitement about some project they're working on or a job, some kind of energy." Michele echoes many women—generally over thirty-five, smart, and seeking compatibility more than bodice-ripping passion—when she says, "Before online dating I was more passive about what I wanted. I felt I had to impress them."

Figuring out what you want and saying it is particularly liberating for women. Declaring one's sexual agency online is a cut to the chase, better than having to *earn* it in a public, general way. To be single and looking before online dating was to present at all times an alluring or alluring-enough surface and somehow telegraph availability. Online you declare your presence in the game simply by being there. It's much better for the nonpreeners of the world. And yes, you must pass the picture test, but Web presence expands identity out beyond the picture and profile. Michele says, "In online dating, I'm relatively guarded, but then there's this whole other backstory of me having all this stuff online, so if they know my real name, they can Google me."

When Michele explains how being on the Web for more than ten years has changed her life, the sardonic edge drops from her voice. "I found that people liked me," she marvels softly. "Way more than I thought they would. People have respect for my opinions and they like the things I write about. I get reactions I wouldn't have gotten if there wasn't a Web. I can get my writing out and people find it and e-mail me that they think it's great."

Michele says, "I like being online because I can be someone else. People think I'm someone completely different from what I think I am. I enjoy hearing the feedback. It's not deceptive, it's just accentuating different parts of my personality. Overall, my online persona is more intellectual and less playful than my real-life personality."

Apologizing for the pre-postmodernity of the question, I ask if there's a "true" or "core" Michele. She e-mails back, "my core personality is what's used to filter out the people i wouldn't be interested in, so i guess online dating brings out the core me in a way. maybe i wouldn't have thought previously about certain things, but just the exposure to so many variables makes it easier to narrow down what exactly you're looking for. which of course is connected to who you are."

Her answer reminds me of my favorite passage in *A Room of One's Own,* describing how financial freedom in the form of an inheritance delivered Virginia Woolf from "fear and bitterness," to "pity and toleration," and finally, to "the greatest release of all . . . the freedom to think of things in themselves. That building, for example, do I like it or not? Is that picture beautiful or not? Is that in my opinion a good book or a bad?"

Michele's broadband connection is her version of Woolf's five hundred pounds a year. She found the release in expressing her opinions on the Internet but also found freedom choosing men rather than going with whoever picked her. That assistant editor, for example, do I like him or not? Is that graphic designer interesting or not? Is this in my opinion a good date or a bad? More than most of my interviewees, what Michele cares about can be gleaned online. And she uses the self-creation possibilities in several surprising ways.

MARKET CORRECTIONS

Time is remarkably fluid online, able to flow magically in both directions, especially as people near forty. Whenever I hear about age-lying, I wonder, How do you keep track of a whole fake life? When did you go to the prom? What assassinations and teen idols and TV shows do you remember and do you give yourself a preternatural toddler memory or pretend not to remember things? If it works out, how and when do you confess?

If you look your age, isn't it more embarrassing to have people suspect the lie than know how old you are? And in Michele's case I wondered, Isn't such a lie kind of bourgeois? I always picture some society matron simpering, "A lady never tells," and I can't think of anyone less bourgie and simpering than Michele.

But at age thirty-eight, Michele rebirthed herself online as a thirty-three-year-old. Most sites have you put down a birthdate, so if you put down a later one, you age alongside your avatar. "Men add ten pounds and five years to what women say anyway, I've heard," Michele shrugs. To the questions about the fake time line, she says, "I figured out how it would work, if I'd skipped a high school grade. I did college in two and a half years, so I could have been in graduate school in the early '80s."

She changed her age

---

because people were starting to make assumptions about me. That I was old, dumpy, ugly. That I never went out. That I was dying to get married and have children. [She first tried to get her tubes tied while still in her twenties.] When I dated as thirty-eight, people asked me if I wanted kids way too often and way too soon. I also didn't put that I was Hispanic because I was attracting men who had this idea of a saucy sexual dynamo who would just jump in bed and didn't expect anything in return. I stopped checking race altogether.

Her first site, Swoon, asked for "the five CDs in your CD changer." "I was careful about what I put there," she says. "I listened to a lot of industrial music then, but I didn't want to come off like a goth girl, so I mixed in some indie rock, Weezer, Beck, Pavement, an old punk rock CD, because I didn't want to go out with an industrial boy. They're very morbid."

She learned—decided?—that a younger, less "ethnic," and musically marginal Michele would draw more compatible men. It's a bit of a head-fuck. Is a self-mainstreamed Michele giving in to a stereotype or defying it? Whatever the reason, Michele never had to do such white-bread self-marketing in any other Web community. In this, the first such involvement she paid for, relationships behaved more like a market and she pitched herself accordingly.

And it worked. She would not have appeared in Benton's search if she'd posted truthfully.

MEETING BENTON

Michele met Benton, a soft-spoken Alabaman recently moved to New York, when she was faux-thirty-five, chronologically forty. He was thirty. As with much of what she writes and says, mockery piles comfortably on sincerity in her account of their meeting. She recites in a kind of faux-schoolgirl, but genuinely happy rush, "We both had a ukelele and we both liked Morrissey and we both liked David Foster Wallace and XTC. All those things were in my Nerve profile and he e-mailed me, 'Are you my dream date?' and I was!"

She's always begun mating sensibilities-first. I ask if she was sexually attracted to Benton when they first met. "I knew I liked him, I knew this was someone I wanted to hang out with more. I thought I could conceivably sleep with him." She laughs. "But I wasn't sure if I'd *have* to." They found they were in the same downtown performance-art milieu and that they actually would have met IRL (in real life) two days hence. By the third date, they discovered their sexual compatibility and soon settled into one of those happy couples that don't have to negotiate outings because they like doing the same things—making no-budget short movies together, attending open mikes that one or both perform at, competing fiercely at *Jeopardy!* Michele took her Nerve profile down after a month or so.

But Benton, it turned out, prefers an open relationship. Furthermore, he's bisexual, so Michele must be prepared to share him with quite a large swath of the population. She accommodates this requirement or demand or request, though she's not exactly sure how it works. First, she says, "We had discussed matters of exclusivity because he's bisexual, so there's the dude question. Eventually I told him sleeping with dudes was OK, but not girls." But a half hour later, she says, not quite keeping the worry out of her voice, "We've only discussed that we have an open relationship and I would prefer not to hear about it if he sleeps with women. I told him if I started to feel weird I'd want it to stop."

Their policy now seems to be don't ask, don't tell, though they're together so often he'd have to cheat (or whatever it's called when it's allowed) during the day while she's at the office and he's working at home. When I ask Benton about the arrangement in my solo interview with him, he says, "I don't know if it's because of Michele or if I'm just getting older, but sex with other people doesn't seem as necessary to me these days."

Michele told Benton her real age after about six months. They both use the word *perturbed* for his reaction, upset more at the lie than at the suddenly-ten-year gap. She says she told him because "I didn't want that secret between us, he knew everything else about me." They moved in together about a year after their first date.

BEST-FRIEND COUPLES

Online dating suited Benton and Michele for reasons that reappear in many of the success stories. Intellectual compatibility is more easily gleaned from e-mail than are the squishier valences of passion, excitement, femininity or masculinity, beauty. Those who bond over sensibilities or worldviews are less likely to be derailed by false expectations. Sexual/romantic e-mails create a delusional connection that tends to fall apart IRL, often quite soap-operatically with one party raging and the other exclaiming, "You don't even know me!" Coolly discussing art, politics, philosophy, movies, or the Mets distracts correspondents from their romantic expectations as they get to know each other. This happened unconsciously with Lila and Scott, while Michele and Benton figured it out over years of online dating.

Michele and Benton represent an earlier breed of online dater: unique people who hadn't had as much luck in the meatspace of parties and bars and office jobs. The Web lets the brainy weirdos who shunned their proms find each other. People like Michele, more put off by a James Patterson fan than bisexual nonmonogamy and more impressed by a rare Butthole Surfers EP than a nice car, can find their dream date on the proper site, while more mainstream people can search from the wider pools of Match.com or Yahoo.com. On more and more sites, you can search the pool with keywords—names of books, bands, neighborhoods. The fine-grained data mining suits passionate fans, particularly domestic, lonely ones like Benton and Michele ready to gather all the books and CDs and cats into one nest.

They both have always liked collaboration with other artists as well as the shape-shifting made possible online. They'd each, in other words, had a lot of practice (much of it online) compromising and accepting other people's fluidity. Michele didn't put "open bisexual relationship" in What I'm Looking For, but Benton's roaming was not a deal breaker any more than her fudging her age was for him. Finding this flexibility filled out the identity each created online. In addition to Who Am I and What Do I Want, they found out, as all partners eventually must, What I Can Put Up With.

Like Peggy and Jack, Michele and Benton are a beacon for me in the vast darkness of online dating. I'm also someone who needs to love at least some of the same books and music and movies as my boyfriends. Nothing feels lonelier than enthusing to someone who couldn't care less, or wondering, "He thinks *that's* great?" Plus there's an appealing modesty to fans that makes them easier to get along with than Lila's "jerky, overconfident men" going on about their accomplishments. Fans are often shy about their strong feelings and refract them through gushing praise for a book or a mix tape of love songs. They're grateful somebody shares their passion rather than demanding that a stranger inspire it.

CHAPTER 3

Christopher: What Do I Want?

THE CONFIRMED BACHELOR(ETTE)

Like everybody else currently dating, I've had all my relationships end in disappointment. I have lasted a few years with a few men, three or four months with a few more; shorter than that, I lose count. I've known a lot of men a little, but I only know the very long haul secondhand. I've never gotten bored with the sex; I've never been bound by children or property so that I couldn't just leave when the relationship stopped working.

Sometimes this makes me feel underqualified for the middle-aged dating world. Divorcees coming on the market only know one long haul and are in their own way clueless, but they've passed a test I haven't. They've built partnerships that evolve over years, while I mostly know pangs, adjustment attempts, disappointment, and, eventually, relief to be free again. I feel ready to commit, but how would I know, really?

The easiest part, the common denominator of What Do I Want, *should* be "a partner/boyfriend/girlfriend/spouse," at least among those who check the Serious Relationship box. But after a certain number of years, do track records speak louder than self-reporting? The claims of the profiles of the never-marrieds about how we're ready and open and therapized and loving start to sound like protesting too much. We mistrust ourselves and so we mistrust each other.

Occasionally, I can't help wondering if I really want the Serious Relationship I've checked on my profile. Friends, not boyfriends, have mostly nurtured me as a reasonably happy adult. And if that wasn't gay-man enough, I supplement the friend support network with cats, the gym, other people's kids, shrinks, short- and very-short-term "romances," solitary forays into the city and the woods, art and writing and other public conversations. That's where my happiness has come from for years, and so the happiness I seek with a mate looks similarly patchy. The Dream Guy is a collage of friends' good marriages and scraps of art and media and experience like that one really perfect summer with that boyfriend five years ago and the way I can cry in front of that one friend and the companionable silence I enjoy with my brother.

The longer I go without a mate, the more normal it seems. Into my daydreams of the big love creep questions like Does he have to live *here,* in my nice quiet apartment? The writer Patricia Highsmith, who had lots of affairs but always lived alone, told an interviewer once that she was more creative when she didn't have to make conversation at home. A guilty thrill of recognition ran through me, and I had it again recently as I checked out the female competition online. A forty-four-year-old bachelorette on Nerve.com ended What I'm Looking For with "someone who will let me read in peace," and I yelped out in delight to my cat, who, reliably, didn't sidetrack me on some big conversation about it. He just glanced up, then went back to licking himself. I suppose you could just ask your husband not to ask you about "your day" or "how you slept," but the sheer volume of obligatory chatter within domesticity has always dismayed me.

We long-term loners aren't just looking for ways to assuage

our loneliness while keeping our space; we're also redefining "grown-up" without the familiar markers of marriage and kids. We wonder, are we stunted, immature because we still have sex with people we aren't in love with? Are there psychic costs to that? Do years of giving away the milk make it impossible to sell the cow? Could we stand docile in one stall; do we even want to trade our freedom and solitude for a life of checking in and negotiating?

Sometimes we're sure that our independence is the very reason we'll succeed at love. We've learned from others' mistakes; we'd know how to ratchet down expectations and give each other space and do this couple thing right. Other days we look at bickering couples and exhausted parents and know we're exactly where we're supposed to be. We're bravely standing up to marriage for convention's sake; we've seen through the brainwashing of the couples industry.

Online dating sites are repositories for the idealism and hopelessness, detached wisdom and baffled frustration, the freedom for growth or at least change that a single life allows. I've hashed these issues out with dozens of strange men I met online, bonding enthusiastically over our need for space, our worry that couples wear down each other's edge, the calm joy of solitude and silence. And it's not just online dates; these men and I all have friendships conducted almost entirely on e-mail, and not just with people who live far away. We've admitted that sometimes e-contact is enough. We like expressing ourselves and taking in somebody else in our own space and time.

"OK, I'M READY NOW"

I got Christopher's number from a friend I met on Nerve.com. For our interview, Christopher picks a bar where he has a crush on the bartender, in Manhattan's gay mecca Chelsea. I get there first and note that Christopher's type falls refreshingly outside the Chelsea gym-bunny mold—the barkeep looks like '60s folk-elf Donovan but thicker, burly and fey at the same time. Christopher sweeps in, introduces himself, kisses me on the cheek, and says sotto voce, "That's not him. That bartender is not good-looking *at all*. Let's go up to my apartment."

Christopher's 6'4" and looks a bit like Nicolas Cage, as his Nerve.com ad says, and a bit like Alfred Molina, which it doesn't. His apartment is dark and stuffed with brocade chairs and couches and ornate little tables. Sconces, gilded mirrors, nineteenth- and eighteenth-century prints crowd the walls, as in an antique shop. Christopher pours red wine in a pretty glass decanter, and we're soon blabbing like old girlfriends about dating misadventures.

Growing up in New Jersey and lacking "a gay support network," Christopher lost his virginity at age thirteen and jumped into the big-city bacchanalia. "I was having lots of sex in New York sex clubs and bathhouses when I was fourteen, then I started to see posters for gay cancer in the clubs warning people to wear condoms. I realized I was in way over my head, so I stopped having sex and then went to this tiny conservative college where I was closeted. A bunch of us moved to New York from college and I finally had my proper gay coming-out." Gay online daters have a head start on the rest of us: they've been agonizing about their identity, how much to reveal, how to communicate it and to whom since high school or before. They also don't have the enormous societal push to pair off; they really are making up adult relationships as they go.

After years of being the gay playboy, Christopher, who's thirty-eight now, wants to join his friends, many straight and newly married, in domesticity. "It's not that I don't feel like I fit into their lifestyle, it's that I want that one person I can depend on for everything. Somebody who's on my team." He admits this desire, which he's never remotely experienced, may be simply the path of least resistance and not from his heart. "Sometimes I think men are naturally wanderers and that the notion of getting into a relationship is straight-generated. Being a gay man is such an invitation to being Peter Pan, I see them walking around this neighborhood, the eighty-year-olds in their little ascots. I do think coupling is growing up but I question it too."

WIDE OPEN

Everybody complains about being limited to "little boxes" in their online profiles, but Christopher is especially cramped. Over and over, his answers to my questions take this form: assertion followed by admission the opposite may be true, e.g., "I can usually tell on a first date if there's relationship possibility. But maybe I need to give people more of a chance, but then again, it's hard to create a spark." Although it's obviously truly how he is, he's still suspicious of how much yin-yang he encounters online. "Everyone likes to think they are balanced. I'm conservative in many ways and I'm liberal in many ways. I'm mature but I'm youthful. Very high-end understanding of art but also love a bowl of baked beans and hot dogs. Everyone's kind of latched onto that. You go onto Nerve.com and everyone's expressing duality, I'm this but I'm this, it's like you're saying you can accept everyone because you're everything." It seems like he's heading for a criticism of that wide-openness, but then he veers. "I'm always changing my mind about things. I don't think that makes me stupid or weak, it makes me a more open person that I'm willing to adjust what I'm thinking."

It makes sense that confirmed bachelor(ette)s overrepresented on Nerve.com—would seize upon the "X but X's opposite" self-presentation. It speaks to the wide swings of self that coupledom invariably reins in. You can't be all over the place and be someone's anchor; you owe the beloved some consistency. Single people can be anything we want; if we feel like giving caviar another try, nobody's there to say, "But honey, you hate caviar," or accuse us of putting on airs. We are untethered, which can make us feel lonely, bewildered, emotionally autistic. But on the upswing, the world looks exhilaratingly open, in flux, full of possibility and mystery. People tend to write their profiles on the upswing.

Christopher wants to settle down with "a nice, normal, hot guy. That's all I ask." His goal is less easing loneliness—he likes his life and his friends and has plenty of sex—than growing up. "When you're gay you can really delay the responsibility that straight people get dragged into by marriage and children. Throughout my twenties, I had so much fun going out with my pack of friends and having sex with short-term people. But now in our thirties, everyone's settling down and having kids." Since he won't be birthing or adopting, he focuses on the property merge of marriage. "I'm thirty-eight and I'm ready for the next stage of my life. If I'm going to buy a house upstate and a car, I need a partner. I'd want to keep an apartment in the city too. My friends who are a couple who have a beach house, a million-and-a-half-dollar apartment, a car, and dogs, say, 'We don't need gay marriage, we're married in debt.' "

The financial trappings are also foregrounded because the relationship part is pure theory. Christopher's never stayed in a couple longer than a month. "I've never been in mature love," he says matter-of-factly. "The most intense sexual desire I've had is for people who didn't want me back. My strongest feelings are unrequited." More than most online daters, he's combing the Web for something unfamiliar.

MATCH.COM

Three years ago, Christopher tried his first site, Match.com, one of the original dating sites and, along with Yahoo.com, the biggest. Established in 1995, Match has been the gateway site for many an online dater. I went there after I grew weary of the emotionally cool men of Nerve. Like Christopher, I want a man who's honest, sincere, trustworthy; I'm past my youthful cringing at those words. What Match.com made me realize is that my guy also needs to be worldly, complicated, self-mocking. I'd rather be alone than bored.

There's probably a higher sincere guy–to-cad ratio there than on Nerve, and I'm sure it produces more unions, given its fifteen to twenty million members. Smart, nonmainstream friends of mine have found the loves of their lives there, including Peggy and Jack. But I didn't find anyone simpatico when I tried it back in 2001. I signed up again in 2004, paying thirty dollars for a month's membership, hoping other artsy people had been chased off by the playahs of Nerve. Perhaps at forty-two, I'd outgrown my need for hip. I opened my first few "Your newest matches" e-mails of twenty profiles apiece with cautious hope.

But rather than experiencing Christmas-morning joy unpacking my score of bachelors, I felt like I was being crushed by rolls of sod. Online clichés like "enjoy fine dining," "good times with a special someone," "as comfortable in jeans as in a tux" unfurled like identical lawns from identical houses, burying my hopes that some creative oddball had snuck in. More men than not characterize themselves as "normal" or "average" on Match, a rush to the center of the bell curve I found cumulatively heartbreaking.

The site seemed even more like a mall than before in all its fluorescent inevitability. Match had added more tests and features like Who's Viewed You, more photos of same-race hetero couples laughing too much, more perky articles on why a smiling photo "gets more results!" Many of my interviewees ventured onto Match and returned to Nerve.

Christopher noted that "Nerve has more downtown people, hip, artistic, whatever," than Match, but his biggest complaint with the gigantic site was "a lot of the people had been off the site for six months; people are literally unavailable." I've noticed this too; when I let my membership lapse, they still keep my profile up, and messages to me pile up in some cyber-dead-letter office, increasing everyone's frustration and feelings of rejection.

SITE SHOPPING

After three months, Christopher left Match for Gay.com, Nerve.com, and Gaydar.com. A lot of profiles on the gay sites push against stereotypes; "straight-acting" is such a cliché that Christoper's Gay.com headline, "Gay-acting, indiscreet," is a joke everyone will get, along the lines of a hetero friend who put "religious, not spiritual" in her ad to mock all the "spiritual, not religious" singles online. Besides these little jokes, he's relatively straightforward about what he wants, though his Nerve and Gay.com ads are skimpy. On Nerve, Why You Should Get to Know Me has only "Because I'm a nice and fun guy"; More About What I'm Looking For: "the same." These days, Christopher's only answering ads that have Relationship checked.

The site he uses the most is Gay.com, established in 2001, where a "premium membership" includes porn and the ability to see pictures of members' members. "Pay more, see more" is a clever lust-driven sequence that's made Gay.com the largest of the gay sites and fourth biggest of all sites. Christopher calls the gay sites in general "more cruising-oriented than relationship-oriented. I log on to Gay.com and get someone saying, 'hey want to play?' while someone on Nerve says, 'hey want to go out?' On Nerve, guys always check Relationship." I tell him that in heteroville, Nerve is the cruisey one, and he says there's a great divide between our worlds. "Girls are relationship-driven, guys are sex-driven. Look at lesbians, look at gay men, and look at straight people, Mars and Venus." Christopher gets a kick out of his profligate life on Mars even as he longs for monogamy, one duality he hasn't put into any of his ads.

Christopher's been online dating for three years but not steadily. "I'll maybe go two months without a date, but still checking the sites out, every day if I'm bored, once a week if I'm busier. A lot of it's voyeuristic and just killing time." He considers his dates failures if they don't "fill the boyfriend position." He's never had a problem getting laid, so he's not impressed with what the computer's dragged in: "Fifteen just-sex hook-ups and twenty date-dates. Five of the dates ended up with sex that night, a few more on subsequent dates."

He has trouble finding love seekers amid the booty callers and admits wishful thinking can pull his eyes off the prize.

I hooked up with this guy last month from Gay.com. He'd been on me for months but I wasn't feeling him; he seemed like someone who wanted a fuck buddy right then and there, not relationship-oriented. But I said yes in a weak moment. I was bored, wide awake, nothing to do, he's been sniffing around for six months, I tell myself maybe there's a possibility of more than a hook-up.

So I go down to his place in the West Village with a six-pack of beer. He was so uptight, he insisted on meeting outside rather than go past the doorman. I was hoping he wouldn't reject me out on the street— that would be mortifying! I met him on the corner, handed him the beer, we start chatting. First he wanted to make sure I was a match, meaning it was workable, that it was not such a not-match that we couldn't get it up.

I've envied gay men their freedom to scratch the itch sans social niceties. I've picked up men I knew not at all, but somehow I can't quite bring myself to procure sex over the Internet. I'd (a) need more of a connection than "OK, you're cute enough" and (b) wouldn't want to risk being rejected as such a not-match he couldn't get it up. A gay friend of mine was deemed insufficiently hot for an Internet-arranged threesome and sent home; he seemed unbelievably sanguine as he laughed his way through this, to me, rather devastating tale.

Even for a thick-skinned, down-to-business gay man, handing over a six-pack like some minidowry on a street corner seems the worst of both worlds. Christopher explains that this guy would find meeting in a bar too public, too much like a date. And he didn't simply have Gay.com deliver like Domino's because "he was such a closet case he was uncomfortable with these tricks coming up past the doorman. Because I was with him, they let me right in, instead of me saying, 'I'm here to see Joe Blow in 2A.' I guess it's less obvious, but then again, I walked out an hour and a half later."

Once inside, Christopher's impression of Joe Blow as a major "clo-mo" (closet homosexual) was not dispelled. "You'd have thought his apartment was a straight guy's, it was decorated total Ethan Allen–click-here-now Web site." Their foreplay was watching Larry King interview Martha Stewart. "He was cuter than his picture, he has a very hot bod, I have to give him that. But the whole closeted thing is not appealing to me, the inhibitions. When we were done fooling around, he jumped out of bed and put his clothes on. It was obvious that he wasn't comfortable after the release, with being gay. He's in sales in IBM, which is a closeting position; he seems to lead a double life."

One pull toward the hook-ups has to do with confidence and self-knowledge. As confused as Christopher is about himself as a boyfriend or husband, he's absolutely sure of his sexual identity. "I am a versatile bottom, but on the profile I say versatile. Because it's not just what you're into, it's what you're into that night, and how much you like the person. I'm not just going to throw the back door open to any stranger. I need to be comfortable with a person in a way I'm not comfortable with most strangers. On a first date, I'm usually just into kissing, mutual blow jobs, some *frottage* as we say in France. I'll tell them in e-mail, 'kissing, sucking, you know, body. You're generally not going to get into my ass on the first date.' "

He knows himself as a versatile bottom—and as a friend. "I'm more contemplative about my friendships, we talk about what bothers each other; there's more of me at risk. If a guy doesn't want to get with me, I hope he can say it nicely, but it doesn't matter. It's just a hook-up." Of his best friend Jay, the straight guy who introduced us, he says, "I can open up to him. He's been through my shit with me and I've been through stuff with him. I don't consider it vulnerable, because it's a secure friendship where I'm not fearful of it being taken advantage of. A boyfriend's going to say, 'I met this guy and so let's just be friends.' That's not going to happen with Jay because we already are friends."

FRIENDSTER

Christopher has also joined Friendster, the "social networking" site that connects people in more tangential ways than online dating. That many wanted a less targeted community was proven by the quick ascendancy of Friendster, launched in 2003 and now twenty-seven million members strong. Imitators followed, with MySpace and Facebook both surpassing it in number of members by 2005. These sites approximate discursive, real-world socializing, which merges shared enthusiasms, friends in common, and job networking with the momentum of sexual attraction. As in real life, to get a date is often why one approaches a stranger, but Friendster recognizes other connections too.

Christopher has gotten grimly efficient on Nerve.com and Gay.com, but he actually has fun on Friendster. He has two profiles, his and Marie Antoinette's. Marie's favorite TV shows include *Trading Spaces* and *Queer Eye for the Straight Guy* ("help my Louis"); About Me says only "pawn turned scapegoat." Christopher tells me, "She only speaks French to her courtesans. I have a whole group of people who communicate with her."

A current member must invite you into Friendster over e-mail. When you accept, you become part of each other's Friend Network, with your pictures displayed on each other's home pages. Clicking in, the profiles look much like those on dating sites, with pictures, age, seeking what, location, and so on. But the emphasis is on favorite books, movies, music as well as "affiliations" and "schools," and a high percentage of Friendsters list themselves as "In a Relationship" and only seeking "Friends" or "Activity Partners." Your page also includes a spot for your Friendsters to write you "testimonials," which is a little high-school-yearbooky but also a nice outlet for affection and creativity. We don't have many places on- or offline to tell the world what we like about our friends.

In the first flurry, people searched Friendster, with name or e-mail address, to look up and link to old friends—and then check out their friends' friends. All the connections are displayed, with helpful arrows between Friendsters of Friendsters when you click into a home page: "You are connected to Joe through Jane through Sam"; "You have three friends in common." You choose a level of visibility, to people one, two, or three degrees removed or to all members. I swapped testimonials with a few friends after I joined, then searched a friend's friend's profile to check the age of a local musician on whom I had a crush. He was, as I hoped, older than he looked, so I wangled a real-world introduction, then followed up with a Friendster e-mail. Such a contact is less out of the blue than a regular e-mail and doesn't raise the question of how one's address was obtained.

You can also click Gallery and see, if you entered Dating Men, all the men around your age who live near you. My Gallery includes gay men, which again makes Friendster more like real life. To see shirtless men with chic haircuts mixed in with the schlubbier heteros reminded me what a narrow cross-section I target on Nerve, Match, et al., and how much I prefer the chaotic inefficiency of real-life socializing with gay guys and women and old people and little kids and pets (who have their own social networks, Catster and Dogster). There's more playfulness on Friendster—fake profiles of "Elvis," "Rock and Roll," "Grilled Cheese," and neighborhoods. Friendster's attempt to purge these "fakester" profiles kicked up fascinating semiphilosophical debates about identity, play, and community control.

Contacting someone on Friendster feels less demanding than on mate-hunting sites. Differences aren't necessarily red flags or the core of a "to-change" list: they're just intriguing. I've never written to a stranger on Friendster, but a guy will write me every few months. The first stranger-Friendster to contact me was David M., one degree removed from me via three friends: from Boston (where I'd spent my twenties), DC (most of my thirties), and New York (thirty-eight on). Looking at the three stacked arrows, three separate lives connecting us, I felt the Web living up to its name. An invisible community had manifested. It had to mean something that David and I knew the same people, and sure enough, we've ended up sustaining a long-distance friendship between New York and Texas. I socialize with several other men I only know from Friendster, and I've used it to pursue a few women I have friend-crushes on. All the online dating sites theoretically offer the possibility of friendship if there's compatibility without "chemistry." But it's more likely on Friendster, where people are also plugging their bands, looking for jobs, and writing people they know from RL.

CORRECTIONS

Christopher doesn't know why online dating's not turning up a husband. He makes some half-hearted complaints about "all the lies about the great physiques and the ten-inch cocks," but it hasn't gotten to a third date with the guys who actually look like their pictures either. So he's trying to adjust What I Want, trying to be fair, to compromise, to transcend his shallowness. "For a while it had to be a rich dude; now I'm over that. I can compensate for money, but I can't with honesty, which is not negotiable. I can't tell double-truth to make up for his lies. I also used to be dismissive of sweet. I've been more interested in people with an edge to them, intelligent and intellectual. But I've realized that there's not that many nice people, that it's sort of rare, so they don't have to be a crazy, brilliant artist anymore."

Christopher puts himself out there at the gay bars as well as the different Web sites. He is tall and attractive, friendly, funny, easy to talk to, and has a lucrative financial-industry job. He is understandably bewildered about why no dates have taken and is trying to adjust. He's sacrificed rich, he's sacrificed "edge," and he's made another deal with the dating gods that I recognize. "I've come down on height. I'm borderline freakishly tall, and my height requirement has gone down from six feet to five-eight, maybe five-six in a pinch. Hell, if I met a great guy who was five-two—I just want our couple not to be a weirdo cat-and-dog couple. If I wanted this little fragile thing I would be with a woman."

Taking stock of the three years online, Christopher says, "I tend to generally get what I want; it's ironic or strange that the one thing that I'm really out there looking for is the one thing I can't make happen, so I wonder if you're sabotaging yourself, or if you really want it? I don't think I'm doing that. . . . I remember thinking when I first got online, 'This is going to make me so much more confident as a person, what's the difference in

contacting these strangers and just walking up to a stranger?'
But of course it's not the same. . . . Online you can aim as high
as you want, and you're not going to be that crazy in a bar,
you'll shoot low or at least medium-height." (My single girlfriends and I, on the other hand, avoid scary-gorgeous pictures
online and are more open to out-of-our-league gentlemen who
show us interest in person.)

The lower risks are still risks, the losses less obvious but de-
pleting nonetheless. "To go on a lot of bad dates, sure it wears
you down. One or two *good* dates is tiring. I've strung up as
many as three dates in a week, even two in one day. I'll ride the
bike with Bachelor One in the morning, I'll meet Bachelor Two
for a drink. If I do three in a week, I need to retreat and rest. It's
draining to put yourself out there. The prep going into that is
exhausting." The word *prep* makes me wonder about gay male
grooming rituals, but Christopher says, "Oh god no, that prep is
just fresh deodorant and changing my shirt. I mean having the
chat and flirting and getting your expectations up, wondering if
he's the one or if he'll just increase your pessimism even more."

Besides adjusting his specific requirements, Christopher's
trying to shrink hope in general. "The definition of disappointment is missed expectations; if you have low expectations you're never disappointed." But without hope, why are
you dragging yourself out to all the auditions? The longer it's
been since a satisfying love relationship—in Christopher's case,
forever—the harder it is to associate the ritual of the date with
anything but disappointment. So you offset that by trying to be
casual, friendly, "just-a-beer"—and find yourself emotionally
closed.

Christopher theorizes that he may have shut himself off unconsciously over the years. He hasn't spoken to his father or
younger brother in several years and he hasn't come out to anyone in his family. "That's more common than you think. My
friend says, 'Your mother is the first to know and the last to find
out.'" With the pronoun-hopping typical of his self-analyses,

Christopher explains, "You end up like this when you're gay, they come to cities and find support networks, because their family wasn't there for them. I'm big and masculine but I'm a pretty obvious fag, and that wasn't cool. When you have to reject your family, you get so strong and independent you sort of become this one-man show. I stood for most of my life behind these glass walls; yeah, I don't get hurt, but you can't get into a relationship."

Self-definition is hard for anyone who isn't "spouse" or "parent" or strongly career-identified. The challenge is even greater for a gay man, the very words creating an opposition between expressive and strong-silent that every man must balance for himself. When he's talking about his hopes that he could integrate sex and friendship with one person, Christopher free-associates:

Being gay for me is not the defining thing in my life. It's a huge thing and it's how most people outside would choose to define me, but it's not how I define myself. Being gay is like fifth on my list. Hmm, what are the top four? First, I'm smart. I don't mean to be pompous, but I'm not stupid. Second, *personable* is a shallow word, but I have a lot of different kinds of friends. No, my job's not in the top four. Let's see, I do consider myself stylish, I have an aesthetic, oh god, I'm defining myself as gay, aren't I? But I'm not going to these circuit parties, I've never been to Fire Island, I've got mostly straight friends. Then again, my screen name is ChelseaMan, how much gayer could I get?

As little as he's written in his profile, he's gleaning self-understanding from it—and from his attempts to expect less.

Christopher is actually one of the happier not-success stories; he is learning and even becoming through online dating. Like Lila, Scott, Michele, and Benton, he has not been embittered or deformed by his search. The unhappiest online daters rage at their cybersuitors for not being What I Want, concluding "men are all liars" or "women are all crazy." All the access just isolates them in their own frozen perfection.

Not that beating yourself up for failing to connect online is healthier, but the only person you can change is yourself. The five daters just mentioned found the elusive balance between self-respecting standards and the openness to adjust. They shifted to accommodate their fellow humans rather than rage at their failure to meet profile specifications. And Christopher especially also accommodates the new circumstances that time keeps dragging us all into.

ADULT SWIM

Christopher and I have gotten similar advice from our married friends: Passion dies anyway, so don't hold out for great sex. It's better to be loved more than you love. You can get intellectual stimulation or emotional support from your friends. Stop expecting everything from one person. I've basically embraced the same corrections as Christopher, who says, "As you become more cerebral and less sexually driven, so maybe a guy's not so hot but he's a good guy and reliable and makes me laugh. The other spiritual things are there—reliability, love—if I had all those things and there was a sexual connection then I'd be fine."

When I got online, I was almost forty and fairly formed, so like Christopher, most of my online self-adjustments have been lowering my standards, uh, I mean casting a wider net, er, that is to say, embracing more of the rainbow of humanity. Ironically, I arrived at this "settling" while taking the opposite tack—admitting to the e-world, hey, this is what I like, and I'm going to go for it.

I'm surprised it took me till late 2004 to get onto JDate, "the world's largest Jewish singles organization," which many of my friends use. I'm a shiksa, but with a long history of Semitophilia: my first French kiss was with a grand-nephew of Sigmund Freud, while listening to Bob Dylan, and I've tended to chase the chosen ever since. Despite my admission in my profile that I was gentile, just by entering this party, I was shaping my identity—or, as Michele puts it, emphasizing a different part of myself, the Jew hag. It was the first time I'd used Internet dating to zero in on a population that wasn't mine.

I don't think my attraction to Jews is some creepy fetish or objectification (but I wouldn't, would I?). Nor is it guilt about my German heritage, though that does tend to come up: one JDate said of our Friday-night plan, "Great! A movie, a beer, and some reparations." It's more that Jewish guys and I tend to share a wavelength of amused self-awareness. Jewish men are often as twistedly self-conscious and overthinking as I am, but less paralyzed. They emote more yet flail less. They're ironic and successful, whereas we ironic gentiles are more likely to be bitter underachievers.

I alluded to more Jewish qualities I like in the Person I Want to Meet box on my JDate profile:

> Curious, engaged, reflexively kind chooser of mercy over justice, though you are, because all the best people are, big on social justice. Funny. Warm. Sexual joie de vivre-haver, critical and psychological thinker. . . . Dates gentiles. Because I'm not Jewish. I was raised by backlashing atheists, have a soft spot for Buddhism, but I've disproportionately dated among your people.

My two months on JDate were during the election season of 2004, so many of my e-mail exchanges featured commiserating, ranting, and tales of haranguing Ohioans and Floridians to vote for Kerry. Later in November, like an uppercut following a right hook, came my forty-third birthday. I knew I'd entered a second grim era of theocratic, imperialist rule under Bush-Cheney-Rumsfeld. The surprise was being vaulted straight to the end of middle age by JDate: most of the suitors in my inbox were in their fifties and sixties.

I was astounded at the ageism in the profiles. A vast majority of men listed age ranges that topped out well below their own, something I hadn't seen nearly as much of on Nerve or Match or Friendster, where I get e-mails from younger guys. The self-descriptions asserted over and over, "Look [ten years younger than posted age]." Most of the cute guys my age asked for women twenty-five to thirty-five. This was annoying, but I had to cut them slack, assuming they wanted to have kids.

But this would not explain why, for example, Marvin, fifty-six and with grown children, asked for women thirty to forty-five. This was typical of his cohort. He kept e-mailing and attempting IM with me in all caps, and after he also showed up in my Match.com inbox, I decided to just ask. "Marvin," I typed, "I'm curious. What's wrong with women your own age? Why are you posting for people who are not your peers?"

Marvin answered, "I JUST LIKE WOMEN WHO ARE YOUNG AT HEART, BECAUSE I'M YOUNG AT HEART. WHAT'S WRONG WITH THAT? WOULD YOU LIKE TO GO TO DINNER?"

JDate brought me to a turning point in my dating narrative. Like Michele and, who knows, maybe Marvin, I AM YOUNG AT HEART and in habit. I contemplated lying about my age as I looked through JDate at my peers ignoring me and the geezers courting me. The sheer pileup of transgressions appealed: a gentile gay man in a woman's body trying to snare nice Jewish men with lies. I opted instead to rewrite What I'm Looking For, to open the dating pool to adult swim. I decided that smart-funny-kind men over fifty were now acceptable, because I'd go out with someone seven years younger than me, so it's only fair. And surely I'm not the only one with crow's feet *and* White Stripes tickets. Opening the pool also allowed me to answer the "reparations" guy, whose headline mocked all the

Ponce de Leons on the site: "Look 51! Feel 51! Am 51!" (Not surprisingly, he's a writer, and we've stayed friends.)

To further reward myself for my honesty and open-mindedness, I amended that to smart-funny-kind-tall. I'd been trying to let go of my sexual attraction to six-feet-plus since I moved to the City of Short Men, but if I was going to go old, by gum, I was going to reclaim tall. I had to laugh at bartering inches for years with my online dating deity, because He obviously cares so little. He's an Old Testament type, more a tester of my faith than a provider.

Constructing one's online dating self often feels like arcane religious scholarship, a little bit Talmudic, a little bit Zen. You're seeking balance amid paradoxes such as "Don't sell yourself short or lower your standards" yet "Stop expecting so much and you'll be happy"; and "Keep it casual; it's just a beer and a taco," even though you've checked the Serious Relationship box. You must achieve a hope/no-hope state of mind that would challenge the Buddha himself. And into that optimistic, ungrasping mind you must never admit the bad thoughts that come knocking after every disappointing date. "I am incapable of loving" is one that we can at least take up with our therapists and can offset by loving our friends and families. We're more alone with the conclusion that Who I Am is "Someone nobody wants."

PART TWO
SHOPPING AND SELLING

Online dating isolates mate seeking from social life. Where we once found our lovers through friends, work, hobbies, or simply living out in the world, now we scroll through profiles alone at our computer. "Hmm, this one has nice arms and reads Mary Gaitskill; that could work with my apartment." We shop for the One and advertise ourselves amid instant headlines and polls, banner ads, search engines, eBay, and porn. More than ever before, we are dating in a commercial zone.

The Web's metamorphosis from oddball utopia to shopping mall is only part of a bigger, older shift toward commodification of the personal. Consumer culture rests on our disinclination to ponder hard questions like Who Am I? and What Do I Want? When doubts and questions do creep in, simple, sexy, purchasable answers are everywhere—on screens, glossy pages, the side of the bus, and fifty-foot billboards stretching to the heavens. "This is what's beautiful; this is what's hot; this is what you want and how you want to be seen."

The Web initially seemed like an alternative to capitalism's playground of created need, but geeks have to eat too. The online businesses that succeed tend to exploit the "need" to know everything the moment it happens and to buy anything immediately. And as the Internet gets more image-based, it can better whip up the "need" to look younger, hotter, skinnier. The fear-of-ending-up-alone industry includes the sellers of cosmetics, fitness equipment, and plastic surgery, and arguably everything that's marketed as helping you get the guy or girl (beer, cars, pants, lamps). Online dating is staking a convincing claim in this territory now, using its unprecedented access to single people's deepest vulnerabilities. Match.com et al. are inside our home computers, our sex lives, our romantic and life choices, perfectly situated to colonize our romantic desires.

Online dating needs to stoke spinster/bachelor anxieties, because the market is flattening. No longer is simply turning people loose to find each other on the site profitable. As I've mentioned, online dating's peak growth year was 2003. To survive, the biz has had to move beyond people access into created need. Without our scientific matching, you'll get divorced! Without our e-snooping, you'll date felons! Without our profile advice and photographic consultant, you'll never get picked out of the crowd.

CHAPTER 4

A Self-Portrait in Compatibility Quizzes

The dating sites' snake oil is basically the same goo peddled by women's magazines and self-help books. The original technology of letting people search by age, location, interests, vices, etc., and contact each other anonymously is all that's truly useful, but it's no longer profitable. The bigger sites now advertise on television and radio, and so have lured some technophobes and late adopters online, but to survive they need something more to sell. Enter the compatibility test.

This is the bell/whistle most pay sites use to differentiate themselves. EHarmony.com has its twenty-nine dimensions of compatibility and True.com its ninety-nine relationship factors. Match.com has moved through Total Attraction Matching, Chemistry.com, and MindFindBind with Dr. Phil. All the sites claim sole access to the secrets of love and call the others pretenders—Texas-based True.com is particularly feisty about how its algorithm could kick all those other algorithms' asses. Various doctors of relationshipology have hung out a shingle at the big sites, and often they have an advice column on the site—more value added.

I took various tests with what I imagine is a typical balance of skepticism and hope—plus the preemptive consolation of "it's research." My findings fall somewhat short of a testimonial.

EHARMONY

EHarmony was founded in 2000 by relationship scold Dr. Neil Clark Warren. Warren admits he personally is an evangelical Christian, but claims separation of church and site. His wife, eHarmony VP Marylyn Warren, explained in an interview with Alternet that the site doesn't do same-sex matching because "We just don't want to be involved in something we don't know anything about. We just want to create good heterosexual families."

Neil Clark Warren wrote a book called *Finding the Love of Your Life* in 1992 that argued that marriages between similar people did better than attracted opposites. Before he launched eHarmony, Warren performed "autopsies" on four hundred marriages—successful and unhappy—to find out what made the difference. He then came up with his twenty-nine dimensions of compatibility. Those include Character, Sexual Passion, Obstreperousness, Dominance vs. Submissiveness, Spirituality, Traditionalism, Autonomy vs. Closeness.

EHarmony says it's tested its own success, and it links to its scientific research paper, which argues that eHarmony couples (who've been married less than five years) are happier than other "marrieds." EHarmony couples did especially well on "dyadic cohesion," including "how often the couple laughs together, works together on a project, or has a stimulating exchange of ideas." Thank you, science, for discovering that marriage is better when the partners like each other. I selected the seven-day free trial, marking on my calendar the day I should quit to avoid the preposterous fifty-dollars-a-month fee. The 436-question test took over an hour, page after page asking me to fill in one of seven dots ranging from "not at all" to "very" to rate myself on traits like Honest, Bossy, Under-achiever, and Sensual. A handful of questions were about the importance of faith, and I testified honestly to my agnosticism, curious to see if I'd be one of the 15 to 20 percent eHarmony turns away.

But lo, I was accepted and the real me revealed. I'm loyal and dislike abrupt change and prefer honesty to dishonesty. It went on like that, as innocuous as a horoscope, up until "Communication style": "You are sincere, a good listener, not pushy and overall a comfortable person to be near . . . an individual whom most people find pleasant to be with and a calming type of person."

Well, yes and no. I listen and I ask a lot of questions, but that's not everybody's cup of caffeinated tea. "Calming" is not among the compliments I regularly receive. Boyfriends have told me, "I don't know exactly what I feel about that; I don't have a position paper, OK?!?!" and "What is this, a cross-examination?" and "If you're gonna keep dating Jews, you'll have to cut us more slack."

Then, the Warrens told me, "In communicating with others, you may support the mainstream ideas rather than new trailblazing activities. You may prefer the stable and traditional activities." I started yelling at my computer, "How dare you cast me in your own bland image? I've done naked performance art and civil disobedience and a threesome, you evangelical homophobes, so don't tell *me* I'm the mainstream one around here!"

I'd said I wanted men who were tall, local, creative, agnostic or maybe Buddhist. My super-scientifically chosen compatibles were a few short human resources directors or Methodist electricians from New Jersey whose last book read was "a murder mystery" or "*The Five People You Meet in Heaven*." Their phrases echoed those in Match, the special someones to share it all with, the equal comfort in jeans or a tux, the startling fondness for sunsets, long walks, beaches. Noting that eHarmony had deemed me mainstream, I wondered if the site had also unfairly brushed my suitors with a coat of beige. But then all the more reason to be irreverent or witty in the few blanks that allowed self-expression, and none of them was.

I somehow missed the free quitting deadline (and wrote in my journal: "What does it mean? Do I subconsciously want the big-God-Daddy site to take care of me??!?"). So I spent a month slogging through the glacial pace of eHarmony's "ice breakers." Instead of letting people contact each other, the site guides everyone through a set of steps. First comes an e-mail announcing that "Guy Whose Profile You'd Never Respond To wants to break the ice," then a few days later, "OK, now pick three questions from our boring list and send them to each other." Then answer them. Then "OK, now you list your deal breakers and if you're lucky, GWPYNRT will send you his deal breakers." And on and on. Imagine the dance of the seven veils done as a PowerPoint presentation that goes on for weeks. Presumably the fear is two crazed forty-somethings rending the fabric of society by rushing into a coffee date. I talked to several other people who'd tried eHarmony and had similar experiences: nobody they were sent shared any of their interests or lived near them or appealed to them at all.

The site suggests a yearlong investment of more than five thousand dollars because "Members who are most successful make a serious time commitment to our process. We suggest you work at this for 12 months—6 months at a minimum, but 12 months is best. eHarmony was designed to help you find a serious partner for a long-term relationship. The importance of this life decision means that meeting a variety of people and spending considerable time getting to know them is the best path towards success."

When I quit eHarmony without having so much as exchanged an e-mail with anyone, the Warrens hit me with this emotional blackmail:

If you are closing your account because you've met a special person to share your life, on eHarmony or elsewhere, congratulations. If you haven't yet made that connection, I'd like you to consider the following points:

- Research shows only 1 in 4 American marriages are actually happy.
- Choosing the right mate is the KEY to creating a compatible, loving relationship.
- Finding a soul mate on your own and knowing if you're really compatible has never been more confusing or difficult.
- eHarmony's proven method of selecting compatible matches has helped create thousands of happy, successful relationships.

Silly prideful me, thinking I could go it alone: deliverance belongs to the Warrens.

TRUE.COM

True.com is the paranoid cop to eHarmony's meddling pastor. Launched in 2003, True.com aims to protect its members from criminals, predators, adulterers, cads, liars, and even "the pain of divorce." It runs criminal background checks on all its members (activated when you send your first e-mail), prosecutes married people for fraud, and has members take a 616-item quiz that measures ninety-nine compatibility attributes.

The True test is based on a study of 112 married couples and measures "subfactors" like Attachment Style, Social Life, Sex Life, Couple Friendships, Individual Friendships, Personal Space Needs, Tactfulness, Conflict Proneness, and Intellectualism. True founder Herb Vest and former True psychologist Jim Houran make a fuss about how their research is the only legitimate matching science out there. Unlike eHarmony's claims that people are best off mating with their own kind, True says the happiest couples have a specific mix of similarities and "complementarities." Couples reporting the greatest satisfaction, for example, accounted for their discontents and contents very differently. Another intriguing conclusion in the study: men's top "areas of dissatisfaction" are "gender issues" and "sex issues" while women bitch about "division of labor" and "dealing with stress."

So what science did True's test drop on me? I'm liberal, "somewhat intellectual," have "modern gender role beliefs," "need emotional intimacy," and "having a social network is somewhat important to" me. My Ideal Partner likes himself, has "high emotional intelligence," and (I love their quote marks in this next one) "believes in doing the 'right' thing and behaving with integrity." The only thing that might be news I could use is: "You appear to be almost ready to commit to a serious long-term relationship." Almost? But most longtime singletons entertain this fear at some point—"Is that the problem? Do I not really want a mate even though I really really think I do?"

So I chalked that up to more True.com fearmongering. It was not fear of intimacy that kept me from dating the men who contacted me on True.com—nineteen-year-olds nicknamed "Playah" and "Sex U Up" from the Bronx; hardworking Christian gentlemen in New Jersey looking for classy, feminine ladies; and many, many men equally comfortable in jeans or a tux who enjoy a beach walk. My odds on True.com seem less promising than on a subway car; those guys at least live near me. And it would never have occurred to me to wonder which ones had a criminal record—I don't recognize True's vision of an Internet crawling with seductive forgers and thieves and rapist-murderers.

In 2005, True added its Sexploration quiz. This fits with True's increasingly Saturday night/Sunday morning split goals. Despite founder Herb Vest's claim that True promotes "wholesome," long-lasting marriages, the site's ads have gotten steadily sleazier and more misogynist. Lots of headless body parts, including a torso in a bikini over the caption "We're pulling strings for you." From the margins of men's profiles comes the leer, "Could he be Mr. Right—or Mr. Right Now?"

The Sexploration quiz asked me if I liked S&M, porn, or telling fantasies, how many sex partners I'd had, and things like that. My results:

> You are the Traditionalist. Don't let the name fool you! Traditionalists are full of heat that so far they've released in pretty standard ways. When it comes to sex, they're comfortable doing it, comfortable talking about it and good at listening to what their partner wants. Traditionalists do well with every sex type with a little work, but naturally partner best with other Traditionalists, Introverts and Intellectuals.

I got placed with the nerds! I'm at the opposite end of the compatibility range from the frisky Mavericks and Fantasizers. A friend diagnosed my classification. "It's probably just because you don't want to do anal or watch porn. That's the only reason you're a Traditionalist, don't worry." I assured her I wasn't worried about being classified mild-not-wild by creepy, paranoid-schizoid True.com.

Taking this test means that now I get even more True.com e-mails I would never answer, with subject lines like "I'm winking because we're intimately compatible." They're still teenagers or jeans-and-tuxers, but now they open with this generic leer.

MATCH.COM

The silliest test I took was Match.com's "physical attraction test," in which pairs of photos pop up and you click your cursor on the face you like better. Then you describe your own face shape. (Why, exactly, on a site with pictures, do you need this?) Trying to get the results of my test, I accidentally clicked into measuring my attraction to myself, which was baffling: while I'll like "her narrow, pointed-square chin" and "mesomorph face, with square chin and wide face," I won't like "her long, oval face." So overall I and I are in the bottom 30 percent of mutual attraction to my countenance, seemingly as unstable as Michael Jackson's.

Match.com unveiled more silliness in late 2005: Chemistry .com. Its online quiz claims to predict whether two people "will have chemistry." Questions include the usual importance ranking of sex, money, and ambition plus the relative length of ring and index fingers (this indicates testosterone levels, apparently) and a few optical illusion puzzles. I half-expected "Put a buttercup under your chin" and a classification on the super-scientific Butterlover scale. What they told me:

> You are a NEGOTIATOR/director
> You have a great overview of reality. You see many angles to the same issue and enjoy discussing multiple solutions to complex problems. You like to use your imagination and engage in creative theorizing. You have executive social skills, easily picking up the gestures, facial expressions and speech patterns of others,

and so on, again all about as plausible as my Sagittarius profile.

OKCUPID

OkCupid was launched in February 2004 by six Harvard math graduates in their twenties who started by writing some cheeky personality tests that spread virally around the Internet. The first was the hilarious OkCupid Test, which classifies everyone, Myers-Briggs style, as Deliberate or Random, Brutal or Gentle, Love or Sex, and Master or Dreamer with questions like "How do you feel about blind dates? (a) good (b) nervous," then "How about homeless people? (a) sad (b) annoyed." I tested as the Peach (Random, Gentle, Love, Master), certainly more appealing namewise than some of the other types: "the Vapor Trail," "the Dirty Little Secret," or "Genghis Khunt." I also took the Politics Test, Slut Test, and Death Test (I'm a Socialist, 65 percent Slut, and I can expect to die when I'm eighty-two).

The tests are bait for the dating site, which is centered on a matching system OkCupid persuasively claims is better than the others, in that it lets you decide what matters. I like OkCupid because it's smart and witty and, best of all, free. They make a persuasive argument against the other sites' "scientific" matching—and a less persuasive one that their matching works.

At a Starbucks across from OkCupid headquarters in Manhattan, I interviewed Sam Yagan, "business guy," short and dark, and Chris Coyne, "creative guy," tall and blond. At twenty-seven, they've already made a killing with SparkNotes, an online Cliffs Notes knockoff that they developed and then sold to Barnes and Noble. They say OkCupid can afford to stay free because there are only seven employees in an office small enough that they take their meetings in the Starbucks.

At the center of the site is a constantly growing database of questions by the seven staffers and by heavy users of the site. The OkCupids write some initial compatibility-determining questions, but members who have answered at least five hundred questions can submit questions too. Those "super users" also become the initial screen for other member questions, narrowing down what the OkCupid employees must vet before posting. It's more like a community art project than an arranged marriage, a throwback to the good old participatory days of the Web. Where nanny-state sites like True and eHarmony impose upon members their version of what's essential to a relationship, OKCupid lets the people decide.

The two hundred fifty thousand "active users per month"

are mostly young, mostly male, bright oddballs, with a spattering of tongue-pierced goth girls. Several Webtopian tropes run through the site: a strain of aggressive libertarianism and a fascination with polyamory, the open swinger kind as well as standard sneaking. The youth of the membership shows in the preponderance of questions like "Is open-mouthed kissing someone else cheating?" and "How many dates before you have sex with someone you like?"

Each question has three answer keys: (1) Your answer. (2) How would your Ideal Match answer this question? (3) How important is their answer to you? After you fill all three blanks, the next question pops up, and the stats at the bottom of the page change. For example, based on my 202 answers, OkCupid "knows me" 92.9 percent, a number factored into compatibility measured as both "Friend" and "Match." I'm not measured against some norm, but only in relation to people I communicate with on the site.

Like all the questionnaire-based sites, OkCupid says its "matching science" is the best, and the founders back their claims up energetically in Starbucks. Sam Yagan explains, "The idea of posing a set of questions allowing someone to state their preference, their ideal match's preference, and a weight— Chris came up with that. We applied for a patent for the question-driven matching algorithm. Other sites assume the way you answer the question is how you would want your mate to answer. We don't assume that; we let you decide." The weight members assign a question can push it up to the top of the pile; Yagan says "Do you believe in God?" is important to a lot of members and will appear fairly early when you start answering questions.

Coyne and Yagan are amusingly contemptuous of the big sites' matching science. Coyne says, "Look at eHarmony, they have a patent claim to have the best matching algorithm based on PhD studies of twenty-nine dimensions of your personality. The fundamental flaw is that they could never probably do the research enough to measure all the real different kinds of people there are out there, and they're obviously having a bunch of PhDs who probably aren't good enough to be professors at universities."

True.com based its test on a study of 212 successful marriages. I ask Yagan and Coyne if there isn't some advantage to having True's data, which maybe OkCupid question writers wouldn't think to ask. Why not learn before you get in too deep that the two of you differ fundamentally on saving money or disciplining children or how clean a bathroom needs to be? Yagan says impatiently, "You can't generalize! Every relationship is totally unique, and it's hard to generalize. Chris's wife is short. Does that mean tall people and short people should be married? Do you see what I'm saying? It's possible to presume causality and be wrong."

Coyne says, "There's no way a survey that doesn't ask specific things about what you want will be accurate. We don't claim that your match will be perfect. We claim to find you people that you claim to want that claim to want you. Like if you said, *I don't want my ideal match to be sloppy,* but then you press that that's not very important to you, we rate it accordingly low in our matching algorithm." Yagan concludes, "We don't make assumptions. We don't measure you against other people. We ask who are you and what do you want and we give it to you."

BLINDING US WITH "SCIENCE"

OkCupid's matching philosophy does seem the closest to the old Web's spirit of celebrating individuality. You *can't* generalize. But neither can you find out much that will predict F2F compatibility from a compatibility quiz. They're a gimmick in *Cosmo* and they're a gimmick online. Their diagnoses are just the standard sales mix of flattery and warning to correct or disguise the subject's inadequacies. "Learning," variously, that I'm an oval-faced, sexually Traditionalist, calming, intellectual, independent Socialist Peach NEGOTIATOR/director with about forty years left to live didn't make me feel known or seen or better equipped to find love. Nor did it find me a match.

Granted, I'm not what anyone would call a statistically significant sample. But none of the sites' questionnaires or tests helped me or even seemed close. Take this head-to-head comparison between one of my best friends, whom I talked into joining OkCupid, and my only OkCupid date, Don: OkCupid scored my friend and me a 53 percent (romantic) Match and a 69 percent Friend match. Don and I were deemed 69 percent Match and 71 percent Friend.

A funny, chatty writer, Don contacted me on the site. He flirted outrageously, buttering me up about my lovely picture and great writing and fretting that I might not find him attractive. He sent me another picture of himself, with glasses, so I could get an honest preview. He was pushing for a lunch in my neighborhood, "so I can see you in your life." He split his time between Pittsburgh and Manhattan and worked four days a week here. I ended up going down to meet him near Wall Street. He was cuter than his picture and flirty. We chatted a bit and I asked why he lived in Pittsburgh but worked here. Don gave me a mock-accusatory look and said, "Well, I *wondered* when you were going to ask me that!"

He kept the playfully annoyed tone as he answered that he'd moved to Pittsburgh last year to live with his girlfriend. "Oh no," I asked sympathetically, "and you already broke up?" No, he still lived with her. My eyes widened; he talked faster. Yeah, they lived together but they hadn't had sex in months and he was starting to look around. He didn't know exactly what he was after on OkCupid—maybe he did want an affair; maybe he just wanted to talk about it; he was confused. I listened reasonably, journalist eclipsing romantic hopeful, and asked questions. I didn't realize how pissed I was until the next day, when I expressed on e-mail my irritation about being dragged through the snow to meet a man who was not available. He mocked my expectations. "Come on, I live in Pittsburgh," he wrote, and then implied that I must be sort of desperate to consider that a date. Feh! With 71 percent Friends like him, who needs enemies?

True.com's Sexploration, the test that found I was a "Traditionalist," didn't steer me anywhere useful either. My one experience meeting another type suggests how, in general, compatibility tests on dating sites are fatally compromised by their need to flatter the customer and get them to buy more months on the site. True.com tried to finesse its "findings" when a sexual mismatch, the Maverick, contacted me across our gap. The tall, cute, young Maverick was my sexual polar opposite, according to True. Under a big arrow between our pictures, True gave this advice to Mavericks dating my timid kind:

> Traditionalists are full of pent-up energy. They're good at talking about and doing predominantly conventional sexual activities. You get to be the swashbuckler that helps Traditionalists release all that energy, and your challenge is to do it without overwhelming them. You can introduce Traditionalists to an exciting smorgasbord of sex—and it'll bring you closer as a couple.

True can't alienate us by warning that he would freak me out or I would bore him. So it hedges its way to limitless possibility as it suggests its fat arrows can lead me from my repression.

Similarly eHarmony undercuts its own emphasis on slow, careful mating with this ad for a new book in its margins:

> Date . . . or Soul Mate? How to Know If Someone Is Worth Pursuing in Two Dates or Less by Neil Clark Warren, Ph.D.; $12.99~You Save: $2.00 (13%).

True and eHarmony's have-it-all doubletalk are perfect examples of how online dating has become part of the fear-of-ending-up-alone industry. If they have the keys to love, you've only yourself to blame for not buying those keys. Extras like the tests, True.com's background check, and eHarmony's control over the process are just the beginning. Industry experts say the trend is to bundle more services into the sites, starting with profile consultants merging with various sites. True's started doing this with a profile help column by someone called "Fite" whose picture looks an awful lot like CEO Herb Vest's pretty new wife, Kerensa. Fite's advice for a photo caption includes, "One favorite is 'the Joey' (from *Friends*): 'How YOU doin'?' This one is cute under a particularly dapper shot, like one of you in a tux at a formal event." This is the value-added we've come to: present yourself with a catchphrase from TV.

None of this improves at all on the original technology. The big sites have taken a beautifully unmediated communication method and made it into a mall full of products that nobody needs but that we're increasingly scared not to try. EHarmony's suggestion that by quitting I was going straight to eaten-by-my-cats spinster hell was the most blatant, but all the big sites apply similar pressure.

They also aim to make us feel alone at our computers. Most online content providers—blogs, magazines, newspapers—have added a "place" for people to gather: interactive comment sections or discussion pages. As Lila discovered in the AOL chatrooms, those bodiless parties knit individuals into a group, sometimes more tightly than IRL. But even as they pile on the options, dating sites generally have not added such gathering places. Scrolling invisibly through the profiles is very isolating, on purpose. You are alone without your scientifically determined soulmate. There is no casual contact and no community.

As the sites butt in more and more—"say this on your caption; light your picture like this; here are ten tips for breaking the ice"—they're undermining what's best about meeting people online. It was not long ago a place to be more honest, confessional, curious, yourself but maybe a little braver. The big sites are discouraging that, warning instead that outliers will be shunned. And who can blame them? "You're fine the way you are, so be yourself" has never sold anything to anyone.

CHAPTER 5

Alice: Branding in the Youth Market

Compatibility quizzes may not do much for consumers, but they're a godsend to advertising departments. Who needs focus groups to tease out secret desires and vulnerabilities? Online daters fork over details of what they want, how they want to see themselves, how they dream and spend their money. The sites mine profiles for "skiing," "David Sedaris," "lingerie," "cruises," and send you the ads you'll fall for along with your newest matches.

Chemistry.com is using technology to fashion TiVo for humans. When I clicked into the "How You Match" tab from a man's profile, it told me to toggle a little tab between "No Interest" and "High Interest." Then it anticipated my next question:

Why is this important?

Your feedback is an integral part of our matching process. By indicating your level of interest in potential matches, you help us get to know you and what you're looking for in a long term relationship. Over time, as our system accumulates knowledge about your preferences, we will refine our matching criteria to bring you even better, more compatible matches.

What's happening to all this data? Dating sites generally do not sell the information they gather straight to advertisers and marketers. OkCupid's Sam Yagan says, "That's where our reputation lies, keeping our users' privacy. If it got out that everything you say to OkCupid, they sell, we'd lose our users." OkCupid and other sites instead guarantee advertisers that they'll get the ads in front of the right eyeballs, and the advertisers can track the click-through rates of the ads. (And even without dating sites selling ads, a spreading mass of corporate and government interests are looking at everything we buy, write, or look at online. Even the geek-beloved Google tracks what we read and write to determine what ads we see.)

As Yagan says, "The Internet has the most accountable advertising structure of all media." He lays out what OkCupid can offer advertisers. "Every member has given up a lot of information about themselves, so we're going to know, for example, if you like to use a cell phone. And we might be able to target users for ringtones. If your favorite band is going on a tour, we can sell you tickets." They see the selling and the matching as unproblematically seamless. Coyne adds, "We can ask members any question we want, and a lot of them, to determine what makes a good match. If we want to know if you like action movies, we just put a question in the database that asks, 'Do you like action movies?' and we will have the majority of users answer that and we can target ads to action movies to them. It makes matching better and targets ads better."

Does it make a difference if I answer a question thinking it's to match me to a man and it's actually to sell me a movie ticket? Yagan and Coyne insist well-targeted ads are news we all can use ("I don't want to see a tampon ad! Show me the BMW!" Yagan cries). I do appreciate free media—radio, alt-weekly newspapers, TV so long as I can hold the remote with the mute button—and ads bring them to me. And forewarned is supposedly forearmed. If I know what's going on, I should be able to just tune into dating and ignore the static of the ads. Right?

True.com CEO Herb Vest helps clarify what rubs me the wrong way about the overlap of selling and mate-searching. He explains in his honeyed but not-to-be-inter-RUP-ted Texas drawl how True.com uses data it gleans from the quizzes and the profiles. Vest commands the room with just his voice booming through the phone line from True HQ. He's sixty, very rich, with a gorgeous new wife the same age as his son. After making his fortune in financial services, he started True in 2003, now the sixth-biggest dating site. His modest golden-years goals include "protecting people from the pain of divorce" and "solving the whole love business with technology."

He says True does not sell data to marketing firms. "No, no, we don't sell e-mail lists or anything like that. I learned a long time ago to never say never, but I don't see that." Then he starts pitching a scenario he obviously doesn't see as dystopian:

I can see us using that data in other ways. For example, what TV programs they might want to watch. Products they might want to buy. Let's say you and I have a date, but I only know a little about you from your profile, so my first question is, "Where would Virginia like to go, and should I bring flowers?" We have a search engine that would go in and see your demographics and they'd come back and tell me if women of your demographic would like a small gift or where would you like to go for dinner? Do you like sports jackets or suits? In what color? The more targeted the demographics the better, but it's always better than nothing. Lawyers have been doing this for years with juries: Does this jury like facial hair? Glasses? Sports coats? They'll dress themselves and their client to please the jury. There's a book called *Dress for Success,* it talks about all this.

I suppose the sales paradigm covers some love affairs. Herb Vest laughingly admits he dressed for success on his dates with his bombshell bride-to-be Kerensa. He wore his ten-thousand-dollar watch and designer suits, because that's what her demographic would like. But outside of gold-diggers and the men who buy them, for whom does this work? A zero-sum market simply isn't where real relationships happen. Love is a renewable resource: when lovers give themselves to each other, they aren't diminished. But in the marketplace only a sucker gives it away.

THE YOUTH MARKET

I wasn't sure if my interviewees in their twenties would share my antipathy toward advertising and marketing. What does "selling out" even mean now that "indie" bands and movie directors treat TV commercials as an art form? But I found a surprising distrust, even fear, of ads among younger online daters. Aaron, a twenty-five-year-old social worker from Philadelphia, reads media and marketing studies like they're radiation reports from a nearby nuclear plant. "You need to know that marketing people have psychologists and behavioralists playing on people's inadequacies, using psychology as a way to market products," he admonishes me, till I tell him, "Dude, I'm in your camp already."

Aaron stuffs his ears and eyes against the siren songs of mass media to preserve his free will. "If I spend more time watching TV, movies, on the Internet, I fear that could mold my opinion of what's sexy, what's attractive. That's happened to a few friends. One guy I know, regardless of what party he's at, will find a skinny blond woman and talk to her. I think it's media influence," he diagnoses solemnly. Yet, for all his self-policing, Aaron admits, "I don't know if my attractions are biological or environmental, that is, media-based. I'm not able to tell because I've worked so hard to keep other people's opinions out."

Many young people who fear and loathe corporate manipulation of their desire by corporations are Webtopians. But Aaron lumps the Internet with the rest of ad-driven media. He stopped online dating because he found himself responding to images, not words. "I let the pictures be the gatekeeper. I was picking people based on their looks, and I'd notice myself grasping at straws to deny it: Hey, this person likes Morcheeba. Hey, she reads George Orwell. She works with kids!" He blames this looks-privileging on the mass media distorting his tastes and desires. He admits when prodded that he also gravitates toward physically attractive people IRL.

I ask Aaron how he feels about the concept of people "branding" themselves like companies, and he passionately denounces it as the scourge of his generation. Looking at profiles of people twenty-one to twenty-nine on Nerve.com and other sites, I tend to agree. It's like flipping through a stylish online catalog of vintage T-shirts and butt-crack jeans. The poses and headlines are types from a John Hughes movie—the sex kitten, the rock star, the brooding intellectual, the geek girl in cat-eye glasses and thrift-store dress, the class clown. The pictures are magazine-arty, the "ad copy" breezy.

And if there's one thing they're all trying to be or get, it's someone "hot." Aaron was the only person under thirty I talked to who did not use the term extensively.

MONICA'S SOLUTION

Whenever I fret about our "hot"-seeking consumer culture, someone tells me to relax and enjoy it, it's "aspirational." People trot out the a-word to explain mass media, like it's one of human nature's laws—and somehow enjoyable—to measure ourselves against airbrushed photos of teenagers; look at magazines and catalogs and TV shows full of things we can't afford; watch movies and shows that strip from life all complexity and any pain that can't be eased by money or fame. But aspiration doesn't seem all that sustaining, particularly now that we're becoming products and buyers ourselves on the online dating sites. The twenty-somethings I spoke with either described paranoia about being marketed to, like Aaron, or seemed alienated from their own desires, or both.

Take Monica—twenty-eight, beautiful, a PhD candidate. She moved to New York from Nebraska with only one sex partner under her belt. She signed up on Match, then Nerve, to look for a boyfriend peripherally but also to gain erotic experience. She's studying the sexual history of women in graduate school, "So I'm out there having all the sex I want for all the women who couldn't before!" She also wanted to forestall any regrets "when I'm fifty and married."

She also uses online dating to reprogram herself away from clinginess. She says she's always been afraid to say "I love you" to her New York boyfriends because it scares them off. "I can't imagine a relationship where I could just say what I feel. I've gotten hurt so much; I like guys and they seem to like me and then they break up with me and they all say the same fucking thing: 'I'm just not in love with you, you're wonderful, you're perfect, but I'm just not going to fall in love with you. I want to be swept off my feet.' I tell the guys, just tell me what the problem is, and they just say, 'It's not there.' I don't know how much more romantic it can be," she says, throwing up her hands in frustration.

Monica, like most of the young women I talked to, paints casual sex as feminist and free, but "desperate" for a boyfriend or husband as totally not-hot. A young woman wanting a relationship seems to inspire fear in men and contempt in other women the way sluttiness used to. Embarrassed by their boyfriend-desire, many young women defensively adopt some of the worst prerogatives of male dating—narcissism, status consciousness, instant gratification, predatoriness, lack of commitment. Use him before he uses you. And they use the Internet to put this more-alienated-than-thou, un-needy self across.

Monica calls her Nerve profile "really casual, really laid back"; she's checked Play as well as Serious Relationship. She observes that on Nerve, "Men who do online dating to find a companion are probably the nerdy, unattractive ones. The hot ones are doing it to get laid. They can meet so many women, it's a huge temptation." So given that data, has she changed tacks? She leans forward and says conspiratorially,

---

One thing I did change over the course of online dating was that at some point I consciously decided I was only going to go after really hot guys. At some point, I realized I could get a good-looking guy. I didn't have to date nerdy guys. I thought, if I have to put up with shit, I want to at least feel proud when I'm walking down the street with him, not embarrassed. So after the last not-that-cute guy broke my heart, I said, "I want to get a little more something out of this, like someone I can brag about." And the stars aligned, and everyone I've dated since has been really hot.

Monica's now dating two men, presumably hot, because "Dating more than one person seems to be the best way for me not to get attached, that's the best way for me to control that. When I focus on one guy, that's when my feelings go out of control. The second guy, the one I'm more into, thinks I'm superindependent and just not worried about anything with men, because I've learned to give that image by not calling them."

This bright, beautiful young woman reminds me of the abuse victim who's "repeating the cycle." Why has she accepted that a moment of envy or admiration from a stranger on the street and convincing her two boyfriends that she doesn't care about them is the best she's going to do? Her self-burning conclusion fits with my sense of hotness now. Its definition has "grown" beyond sexual attractiveness to encompass unattainability, rudeness or remoteness, the pitiless gaze of the underwear model. Hot can't coexist with vulnerability or even relationship. And yet it's a grail to a generation.

ALICE: BROKEN PIECES

Twenty-seven-year-old Alice is far more self-aware and less masochistic than Monica. She understands that "unattainable" makes no sense as a quality to pursue or aspire to on a dating site. But she can't quite transcend the allure of the ungettable and of not-needing. She was mortified to join a dating site at all because, she explains,

---

In your twenties, you're trying desperately to live up to other people's standards, you haven't come fully into your own. You're trying to find a job, a career, an identity, live on your own, not need help from anyone, and in doing that you become hyperaware of the way people rate other people. I think in your twenties you're closer to high school mentality than adult mentality. You're more defensive, more protected, and have this superiority complex. Each of us thinks, "I'm the person who doesn't need to online-date like these other people, I'm just going to go on and look." That mindset is protection, because most of us think we should be able to meet somebody [offline] at this stage of life.

As in high school, less-formed people are bound to worry more if they're at the right party. Affiliations and group approval fill in the gaps of self. No matter how the stigma of online dating fades as the numbers rise, no matter how ironic and distanced the self-branding, there remains something toweringly uncool about posting your picture and your hobbies on the Web. For people under thirty, there's the additional shame that most of your peers are (a) single and (b) go out. But a heartbreak and new-city loneliness pushed Alice reluctantly online.

I met Alice through a friend and interviewed her over dinner and a bottle of wine. She's self-possessed, mature, with a good job in a publishing house. She describes herself as flitting among groups, lacking a community. She's attractive in a fragmented, contradictory way—sad brown eyes and a big bawdy laugh; conservative-for-New-York clothes and bodacious curves. After graduation from college, she moved to Chicago, where she flogged a stalled relationship with a sexy loner for about a year: "He looked like Jesus," sighs Alice. Finally she gave up the ghost and moved to New York.

HOT GUYS IN MY SHOPPING CART!

The first site Alice joined and the one she dated most on was Nerve. When she first logged on and searched for local males twenty-five to thirty-five, she says, "I couldn't believe it! I kept going, 'Wow, some of these people are really good-looking and smart and funny! There are normal people; there are hot guys. This'll be like shopping! I can put hot guys in my shopping cart!' It was totally addictive—the more I went through them, the more I wanted to go through."

To fill out What I'm Looking For, she drew on "an amalgam of past boyfriends and my dad. I get along with my dad, respect him, and emotionally we're very similar. He's a musician and into books and art, he's liberal and open-minded and easygoing and has a good sense of humor." She had less fun with the self-description part. She didn't seize the opportunity for introspection like some older rookies do, as an opportunity to reflect and compose a better self. She felt she had to write a commercial and didn't want to. "It's something of an art form among my generation, but I'm not that good at it. There's a fluidity in language now, jingles and slogans are part of our language, those catchphrases, and those get trotted out in the profiles."

I ask her what she thinks about people-branding and she says, "Online it's more the branding of yourself through the music or movies you like, you create your image that way. People defining themselves through what they consume." Her easy assumption that art is just another status-defining product is anathema to my fangirl sensibilities. It matters what music and movies and books a guy loves. Like Michele, I think of those passions as windows into and bridges between people, not accessories calculated to project an image.

Advertisers clearly exploit the "whatever" cynicism and the refusal to directly express anything that now pass for irony. Alice sees the ads and the irony as organically entwined. "I think we in our twenties are more comfortable with a less earnest language to describe ourselves, a less frontal way of getting at themselves, more sideways, more blasé. It's a byproduct of irony, of consumerism. We have problems with earnestness. We have trouble writing 'I'm looking for my soulmate.' There's a discomfort with that straightforward, lay-it-on-the-line way of expressing." Alice grew up on ads that mock ads that link their product to happy, healthy love relationships and families. That content has been corny her whole cognizant life.

So Alice hedged her bets in a generationally appropriate manner. "All my profiles said I didn't expect to find what I was looking for on the Internet, because I'm looking for chemistry. I didn't take profile writing seriously. It was more like a joke, just trying to be entertaining. I asked for someone who smells good." She didn't take men's About Me sections very seriously either, because "I don't think most people have much self-awareness." She looked instead to their What I'm Looking For boxes to analyze the bachelors.

What's surprising is that her savvy didn't help her any. She sees through the poses, but couldn't write a profile that included that insight or anything else personal. I ask what qualities she left out of her own About Me box, and she replies, "Well, I'm incredibly loyal and I'm a good listener, but those don't sound that attractive to me! I think somebody fun, exciting, adventurous is more appealing." Alice, who does seem thoughtful and kind in conversation, left out the very attributes and preferences that actually would serve a relationship in favor of the ones that project hotness from far away, like a remote star.

FIFTEEN DATES

Over the course of five months and fifteen strangers, Alice followed what seems to be standard protocol: "I only met for drinks; I never had dinner till the second date. If they'd asked me out for the first date, I expected them to pay. If I said, 'Let's go out,' we'd go dutch. If I wanted to stay past one round of drinks, I'd buy the second round, or offer to."

Of the fifteen men she met, Alice was interested in two. The unlucky thirteen included one who had gone to her high school a few years before her and named all the teachers they both knew whom he'd masturbated to. "At that point, I wouldn't even let him buy me a drink; I was like 'I got this.' . . . Then there was this hot yoga guy who'd listed himself as a New York resident and at the end of the date he said, 'Actually, I'm staying with a friend in New Jersey, can I crash at your place?'

"I got the impression that a lot of people go on Nerve just to have sex." Alice was looking for something longer-term. "I thought having sex with a Nerve.com guy would rule out having a relationship. I guess that's old-fashioned. I think lots of women think it *shouldn't* be that way, so they act against it, but it's still true. I've had men admit to me that they think less of a woman who has sex on the first date." This also seems standard protocol, echoed by most heterosexual online daters I talked to and a few I slept with. Sex on the first F2F date often signals it will be the last date.

Alice admits the no-sex rule was negotiable. But nobody seduced her, despite Nerve's reputation as the sexy site.

I can be pretty impulsive, if someone had just taken me and pushed the right buttons, it would have happened! But I feel like they didn't know what to do with me, and that made it easy for me to have my boundaries. I went out with this cute black photographer and I was really liking him, but he had a few drinks and was so all over me, I got scared off. He asked me my bra size! I was like, "Dude, you're not supposed to ask that on the first date, you're supposed to sneak a look at the bra lying on the floor on your way to the bathroom!"

Two men got Alice's hopes up: she calls them both "intimidating." The first one took her out a few times and tried to seduce her. She held him off. The strategy didn't work; he just stopped returning her calls one day. She shrugs unhappily. "That's the thing, people are just going on so many dates." The other guy similarly led her on and then disappeared. "I'd wondered if he lived with a girlfriend; he'd only call me during the day when he was working and it felt fishy. I sent an e-mail asking, 'Are you disappearing on me?' and he didn't answer."

Alice concludes in anger,

On Nerve, a lot of guys are going through the motions of wanting a relationship and they're just trying to get laid. I have the sense it would take something extraordinary for them to make a real connection and continue on. I had a number of men say things to me like "I can help you with your computer or fixing that leak in your bathroom." They have no business making these projections into the future. It makes you make assumptions about the way they feel about you and it's bogus. Maybe they're just having a happy imaginary moment, maybe it's not malicious, but I have a real big fucking problem with that. I think the Nerve.com guys are not stable, nonmonogamous, probably dating other people. I don't trust them.

I hear her wrath, but I can't hate with her on the "happy imaginary moment," not completely. Even if the leak or the computer never gets fixed, the guy may have meant it when he said it. That first leap is never exactly "true"; it's always a bit of an experiment, a thrilling risk. The difference online is that declarations and gestures are based on almost no information. Before online dating, we had to wait for chance to wash eligibles onto our shores—but everybody got more time to acclimate. If old-fashioned, offline daters made promises and plans, it was usually because the nascent couple had comforted each other or resolved a difficulty or forged an understanding. Some connection had been made, some reason to open up to this one, to take the next step.

But it's hard to build a connection when you're going on two, three, or five dates a week, especially for the young hotties. Cute, personable twenty-somethings in big cities can date and hook up constantly, and they're supposed to revel in that freedom. But some of them deep down want a relationship and may end up alienated and exhausted. They may find themselves blurting out "happy, imaginary" futures to the next Nerve date who seems warm and sympathetic—like Alice.

With everything so speeded up and contingent, the gestures of relationship stand in for the real thing. "I'll fix that leak" may be an unexamined, unconscious way of saying, "I'd like a steady girlfriend." But how's a guy supposed to pick, especially when the girls on Nerve seem so freewheeling and un-needy? And all that soulmate sincerity crap is sort of embarrassing anyway . . . so they all keep dating and scoring and disappearing.

MORE FISH IN THE MAINSTREAM

Next, Alice tried Match.com. But she found that steadiness is not enough either. "You can trust Match.com guys more, but they're so average. That sounds elitist, but they were really suburban." Sincerity is pretty much all the Match.com men had going for them, and for Alice, that was one more minus. She observes, "On Match everybody says, 'I don't want to play any games.' I don't want to play games either, but a certain playfulness is required. I think the whole thing's a big joke and I don't like when people are too earnest, like on Match.com."

To try to find a just-right middle between the dull Matchies and the slick Nervies, Alice signed up on JDate. This site yielded the nicest, most presentable bachelor of Alice's short online career. "This guy had a stable income, a good job, he owns his own place, he's got his car, he's taking me to a fancy dinner. He had two dogs. I got drunk on the first date and was attracted to him and I was sure it was going to work out. But on the second date I realized there was no chemistry, nice guy, but a little too anal for me, a little too circumspect, not that cute." After she let him down, on e-mail, Alice says, "I was beating myself up for being superficial. 'So what if he doesn't have much of a chin, get over it!'"

Soon after that date, Alice quit all the sites and took her sad stock: fifteen men, no sex, two crushes who both disappeared without a word. Alice had no "at least I tried" bounce; she ended up feeling worse. "If you're using this tool, being proactive, and you still fail . . ." She trails off, unable to express the depths of such loserdom. "I haven't been in a lot of long-term relationships, so maybe I'm less tough and take the rejection harder, but the experience made me feel rejectable, disposable, inadequate."

Alice quit online dating to do things that "don't emphasize the lack, positive things like reading a book or going to the gym." She admits to some baby panic (at twenty-seven!), but like Aaron, she's not sure of its source. She thinks the media planted that worry in her brain. "You're selling this commodity, your womanhood, and online dating makes you feel like you have to hurry, hurry and catch the man." She comforts herself that she's not ready anyway: she subscribes to psychologist

Abraham Maslow's to-do list for true individuation. "He says you have to get things straight with your family, your friends, you find your career, and only then when you're OK with yourself, only then when you're a whole person on your own, can you be part of a successful relationship. Until then you're just these broken pieces."

In one's embryonic twenties, Alice says, "You're desperately trying to live up to others' standards" because you don't trust your own yet. You haven't earned the authority to accept you, much less to declare a self in a profile. You're not sure what you have to prove and to whom. What do they want of you? What do you want? Alice soft-pedals her loyalty and compassion, and leads with freewheeling and wild, though her best sex was with someone she spent months getting to know first. Thoughtful, educated, self-aware, loved and emotionally supported by her parents, Alice cannot find her own vast stores of likableness while she's online dating. The self-actualization of Lila with her beauty hidden or Michele posting essays or even height-dropping Christopher—not happening here. And it's not helping her conceptualize the couple she wants to be in either. Though online dating leads some to fantastical expectations, Alice and many of her cohort suffer the opposite. They can't articulate a trusting, contented relationship, even with a form provided.

Alice finds selling herself distasteful, but she can't see online dating any other way: she cannot connect the image making to an honest articulation of who she is and what she wants. She's suspicious of introspection, and so she looks out for answers. And there is "aspiration," clothed in the sounds and visions of her demographic. Alice has grown up on ads targeting her since birth through made-up-by-marketers stages like "tween" to adulthood. Like Aaron, she knows it, but she hasn't constructed any alternative value system yet out of the "broken pieces." I ask her who's the dream girl for her dream man, and she considers a while before she answers. "Cameron Diaz. She doesn't take herself too seriously, she's fun, hot, legs up to her neck. A girl who looks like a supermodel but can joke around like a sailor."

EVERYBODY'S A STAR

Online dating lets us into the flow of images that flooded most of the last century and every available inch of space and second of time in this one. The image that everyone chases, the god-head of consumer capitalism, is the sexy girl—the image Aaron resists. Women chase men who gaze at two-dimensional re-productions of a woman younger, prettier, thinner, blonder, bustier, "hotter" than almost all the real ones. The same picto-graph is sold to women as aspirational, tweaked slightly for the different markets as it moves down the conveyor belts through *The O.C.* and *Penthouse* and *Esquire* and *Vogue*. The hot-girl pictograph has morphed over the last century from prettier-than-most to our current ideal of Auschwitz-skinny thirteen-year-olds with breast implants. Women chase the pictograph knowing perfectly well that if we did somehow draw close, it would just get Photoshopped still further from reality. ("Spring's freshest look: two heads!")

Now we online daters can be public images too. In our profile photos, we mimic the pictograph in our poses and hairstyles. (Men are being sucked into this world now too, a depressing step down toward equality. Now we both have magazines dedicated to what's wrong with our bodies.) We write advertisements for ourselves like copywriters, sometimes with professional help. The serious online dater now employs a new industry of ama-teur starmaking: the makeup artist to paint, the cinematogra-pher to shoot and light, the consultant to write the profile, the advice columnist to walk you through the date. We all have a pro-motional campaign, we're all celebrities.

This sounds both egalitarian and glamorous for about three seconds, till you remember how Americans rip celebrities apart like hyenas chewing gazelles on the veldt. Paparazzi stalk them for magazines devoted to candid photographs of their fat rolls and morality plays about their marriages. It's much more pervasive and cruel now than when John Updike wrote, "Celebrity is a mask that eats into the face."

The more we sell our images in the online marketplace, the more embarrassed and hidden we get about our sweaty, saggy, unairbrushed selves. As dating sites adapt to the fear-of-ending-up-alone industry, they plug us even deeper into the commercial matrix. Lust and loneliness and fear keep us scrambling to stay in demand, fresh, hot. Herb Vest has succeeded wildly for a reason: he's figured out that manipulating this fear is how you "solve the love game."

CHAPTER 6

Trevor: Parts and Services

The marketplace aspects of online dating alienate and depress a lot of us. But another lot go to the Internet specifically for a more circumscribed transaction. And for those cool customers, there's Craigslist.org, a meretricious utopia where everything's up for sale, barter, or at least discussion. Anyone can sell, buy, hire, swap, or meet used furniture, sublets, roommates, employees, lovers, situations, or scenes. Nobody's getting rich off the stripped-down, graphics-free site: help-wanted ads posted by businesses in three cities have allowed the site to stay free for everyone else for more than ten years. There is very little editing or censoring. The more bizarrely specific or pressingly immediate the craving, the more likely it is to appear on Craigslist, the bathroom wall of the Internet.

Though a small percentage of lonelyhearts use it to find a relationship, Craigslist is best for hook-ups because it's the least mediated. Free, no joining, no profiles or pictures required, and posting is instant. It can be quicker than masturbating to post "horny in midtown now; who's around? your pic gets mine." And instantly get replies. Daters approach it more like an adventure: Craigslist personals users tend to have a

Yahoo or Hotmail or other untraceable e-mail account to quarantine the seething correspondence. You really don't want these people knowing who you are.

Reading Craigslist is like putting on X-ray specs that render visible hidden desires. A quick spin through "men seeking women" (M4W) yielded these messages in bottles, which are PG-13 next to the baroque pornography under "Casual Encounters":

> LADIES: THIS IS MY PROPOSAL m4w
>
> Thanks for taking the time to read my posting.
>
> I want to meet a SWF 20–32, attractive, in shape, intelligent, interesting, and fun. I am not particular about how tall you are, your hair/eyes color, nor your breasts. . . .
>
> There will be NO sex or touching of any type. I want to take you to a restaurant for a nice dinner one evening. We can talk, enjoy great conversation, food, some wine. This evening will be something that you and I will share together only once. At the end of the meal, we will order one dessert of your choosing. After you finish that, I want you to excuse yourself to the ladies room and remove our [sic] panties and hand them to me. We will then leave the restaurant and never see each other again. If that appeals to you, please write back and I will tell you more.
>
> As for me, I am not some perv or sick-o. Im an intelligent, attractive, SWM (not married), tall, in shape, dark hair, green eyes, educated, professional, well traveled, well read, and someone who will provide charming conversation during our meal. You won't be disappointed at all. And again, to make it VERY clear - THIS IS NOT ABOUT SEX at all. As I said, its more erotic if there is absolutely no touching at all. I want us to experience something very secret, erotic and a bit naughty together.
>
> This will take place in Manhattan

(I especially love "one dessert of your choosing," like the whole scenario would be dashed to bits if the cute SWF said, "How about I get the sorbet and you get the crème brûlée and we share?")

The marketplace aspect of online dating is foregrounded on Craigslist as on no other site. The odder the request, the more likely the seeker will offer compensation.

> Book author seeking one female to work with
> I have made some efforts before to find an erotic muse on CL. Here I go once again. I am a published author (male) who charted at the top of Barnes & Noble and Buy.com's online bestsellers chart.
>
> I am looking for a woman who will let me document our sexual activities together in poems or even mini-memoirs. I have made some nice money publishing before in the five digits. Yes, you will have an erotic relationship with me, the author and I will pay you as a co-author. You will get half of my advance and half of all sales/royalties made now and forever this book is in print.
>
> So if there's a woman in Manhattan, Queens, Brooklyn, Bronx or someone else interested, please email me. I am attracted to all types of women . . . small, tall, Caucasian, Black, Spanish, Asian, Indian, etc. I'm sure you won't have any problem with me. I don't look like Stephen King or Wes Craven.

Craigslist was the obvious place for me to fulfill my need for interviewees, and I took the two-birds-with-one-stone approach. Hey, they might frown on it in journalism school, but my ad is quite vanilla for Craigslist and the personal angle netted me more responses. My ad for women, posted in M4W (men for women), read the same, minus the first paragraph, and got exactly one response.

> looking for a boyfriend AND research w4m, 42
> I'm pretty and smart and nice and a writer (see below).
> Craigslist seems like the Wild West, but a few people I know are in relationships spawned here, so what the heck. . . .

> The research part: I'm writing a book about online dating, and
> I'm looking for articulate, self-aware, long-time online daters. I'm
> especially interested in married people using Craigslist and other
> sites to step out on their spouses . . .

I was quickly inundated by defenses of adultery, denunciations
of gold-digging bitches, offers to have my pussy licked for
hours, lots of suggestions that we combine interview and date
and "see what happens." (Sadly, an interview-date is not all
that different from any online first date.) I also received one
meta-date invite—a game manufacturer suggesting I help him
test a romance card game he's developing while I interview
him. He wrote with enough flirtiness and curiosity about my
looks that I assumed it was a date. All our subtexts protected
us from the usual embarrassment about the lack of "chemistry" on my part, and maybe on his. Halfway through our
lunch/game test drive, at about my twentieth use of the word
adulterer, he said in his queeny way, hand pressed to chest,
"Well, I'm the 'm-word' myself, you know." I was more re-
lieved than annoyed. It was nervy of him, but I had, after all,
advertised for cheaters.

TREVOR: PLASTIC SURGERY FOR THE SOUL

I also got a long e-mail from Trevor, a frisky fifty-nine-year-old
Brit in a sexless "for the kids' sake" marriage. He declared online
dating

an invitation to reinvent oneself as the person we all deserve to be—rather
than the sad pale approximation we see in the mirror. Craigslist is plastic
surgery for the soul. And better still—it's interactive. A place where one hus-
tler can meet another, each knowing he or she is a phony but easily hood-
winked into believing the "other" is genuine. This sets up humungous
amounts of insecurity and angst—an essential part of the online experience.

I found it strange that he called Craigslist "interactive" as if that were unusual in dating, before I learned that Trevor is a connoisseur of the dissociated date.

His opening e-mail also called the modern U.S.A.

a uniquely lonely place . . . in which the prevailing level of trust is especially low and one in which people are encouraged to experiment with their identity to a degree unknown elsewhere. You can literally be whomever you wish to be. Now—along come Craig's List, Eroticity, Adult Friend Finders and a hundred other sites offering instant connectivity and the anonymity of an old style orgy where everyone wears a mask. . . . I've met many women this way—and have fucked, sucked and fingered a few. It can now be revealed to a serious social scientist such as yourself that the following are my conclusions:

No one is ever MORE attractive, witty, or well endowed than advertised.

Most are LESS—many FAR less.

Behind many a "hot horny woman" lies a MAN.

Behind many a "hot horny priapic" guy lies a timid disfunctional metrosexual male mess.

Half the women on any site are trolling for $$$$—not orgasms.

Most are overweight—many are FAT.

Many of the most brazen guys are 14 year old virgins in the 9th Grade.

Very few emails lead to meetings (too many lies already to risk it).

And very few meetings lead to sex—or even dinner.

But . . . and this is an important proviso showing yet again that the exception proves the rule . . . the very best, the tenderest, most passionate and most talented lover I've had in many a long year was discovered right here.

Lunch?

XoTrevor

Trevor sounds like Peter O'Toole on the phone. He picks a trendy restaurant in the meatpacking district for our interview. I'm too intimidated by his age, confidence, accent, and sheer perviness to countersuggest someplace cheaper. (This is how sexual harassment works—not that Trevor harassed me, just that I felt unmanned as an interviewer by those advantages. I realize I'll have to buy my power back by footing a bigger lunch bill than I want to.) I suggest e-mailing pictures for identification purposes, but Trevor opts for self-descriptions and "I'll be wearings"; he later says he likes eyeing all the women and guessing which one's his when he meets an online date.

The man who emerges from the fashionistas at the bar is tall and elegant, with close-cropped white hair, chic little glasses, and a leather jacket. Just a bit of gut pokes over his skinny pants. He steers me skillfully with a hand on my back to an outside table where he can wave a cigarette around as he holds forth. He's a charming flirt, and occasionally brave in his revelations. I like him in person, then am rather appalled when I transcribe the tape at home alone.

Trevor started trolling both Craigslist and Internet porn around four years ago; he describes himself as "a bit of a sex addict," an exhibitionist, and a voyeur. He also goes to swing clubs and orgies. Besides Craigslist, he joined "more pornographic sites like AdultFriendFinder.com and Edoggers. Lots of pretty women, lots of hookers, some sex addicts. You have to pay, not much, a monthly fee. They have a large population from all over the world. Like Craigslist but with pictures." He's primarily shopping for one-time experiences, but says ideally he'd find a mistress. He says he's procured about twenty sex partners online, some for a night, some for a few months. He had one mistress from RL for two years, but she gave him an ultimatum and he chose his family.

Trevor talks about his online comrades like they're products or bugs on a pin. Peers of his who want companionship come in for the coldest scrutiny. "There's an age where people get needy and they want a mate, a significant other. Lots of 'exploring the city' and 'going to museums,'" he says contemptuously.

I see the lonely fifty-eight-year-old widow who likes the Met and wants a giving, warm, funny, Jewish

retired editor who does a bit of teaching at the Co-
lumbia School of Journalism and he too likes the
New York Times and flea markets and exploring the
city. They're not looking for thick cocks that go all
night . . . it's a more forgiving marketplace among
older Craigslist users. It's not about getting the best
olive oil, it's about getting any old olive oil.

He mourns that women stop selling their sex at an age well below his own. "When women reach age forty-five or so, they tend
to post a different sort of ad," he says sadly. "They don't write,
'I'm hot shit and I have a great ass and my legs go on forever and
my tits are to die for and I want you.' Sex disappears among
postmenopausal women, they don't paint themselves in a pornographic manner even if they're very sexual. It's all about the museums and exploring the city." Alice worries about the "broken
pieces" of an unintegrated self—Trevor insists on it. He says he
mostly shuns prostitutes because he wants "real" experiences,
but he just wants the pornographic pieces of the real women.

ASPIRATIONAL DATING

Trevor says of the sites with pictures, "If the photography is
stylish, I like that. I'm biased toward good photography, like in
advertising, it hooks me every time." His admiration for a good
sell extends to the written on Craigslist: "I like women who are
up-front about their sexual needs and desires and are sort of
vulgar about it, with the verbal dexterity to turn me on." And
thus was he drawn in by a Craigslist ad posted by "Jenny." He
paraphrases the W4M ad, "I'm twenty-two and I'm a grad stu-
dent and very hot and horny and looking for an older man; I'm
always thinking about sex, send me a picture and a description." I don't know how skillful that copywriting is, but it certainly targets its demographic.

Trevor explains the steps. "I usually don't send a picture right away. If you want to be seductive, you have to reveal yourself like the seven veils. It's a striptease. I wrote back to Jenny that I'm thirty-nine and tall and athletic and my cock is nine inches long and asked, 'Do you want a picture?' " They were meeting in a wonderland where people morph at will, Trevor explains. He has a folder of digital photos on his desktop: "Some of them are not of me, some are. The cocks and faces that aren't me are all pictures that have been sent to me in the course of these dialogues. I have about twenty body parts, faces, torsos, and cocks.

"So I sent Jenny a huge cock, not mine. Then she says, 'Wow, that's amazing, do you want one of me?' So I get a very shadowy picture of someone who could be a woman or a man and a note that says, 'I've got much better ones, but I want to leave them for later.' I write back, 'If you are who you say you are, I'd like to meet you, how about a drink?' " Trevor was calling her bluff; an invitation to meet generally separates the women from, usually, the men. "Sometimes after you suggest a date, you'll never hear from them again. Other times they'll pester you for more pictures of that beautiful cock—'How big is it again?' When there's too much interest in cocks, it's always a man."

But ever-game Trevor made the date "in a gloomy midtown bar. I stood there for fifteen minutes thinking, well, I've been stood up. Then a slightly scruffy, ashamed-looking young man walked up and said, 'I'm Jenny.' " Trevor replied, "No, you're not, you're Jenny's alter ego." Jenny, perhaps figuring, "well, I'm not a woman, but he's not thirty-nine either," asked if Trevor wouldn't like to fool around with him anyway. Trevor replied gently, "I'm not gay but let's have a drink and you can tell me who you are and why you do this." Jenny told Trevor that this particular ploy—be a woman up till the date—works with a surprising number of men who understand somehow that the hot, horny girl is code for a gay assignation.

Why? Craigslist M4M is full of rather impressive cock pictures (which I now know to take with a load of salt!). There are pages of amiable requests for head, spankings, rimmings, tops, bottoms, and three-ways. I wonder if Jenny's weird mix of discretion and fabulism reflects fear of being "out" about his homosexuality. Or maybe an extreme form of "down low"—sex between men (usually macho-looking men of color) who refuse to identify as gay or bisexual. Jenny and the men who read "her" mask correctly may have pushed their desires down so far out of sight that they themselves can't see the cock staring them in the face. Their ads and their fake pictures actually trump reality when their fantasy somehow makes it into meatspace.

OUTER-DIRECTED

Part of why Trevor keeps such crazy company online is to be the amused, sane de Tocqueville commenting on his adopted land of constant reinvention. He prides himself on being less fucked-up, more honest than the "brilliant con men like Bill Clinton" who typify the New World. Amid all the labile mendacity, Trevor says he gains stability from his "strong inner life," as defined by sociologist David Riesman. Trevor says he knew Riesman in college—he also drops the names of R. D. Laing and, repeatedly, Tina Brown.

Trevor summarizes the types Riesman laid out in his influential bestseller *The Lonely Crowd* (omitting the third, "tradition-directed" type). "The American character is what Riesman calls 'outer-directed,' meaning it takes its cue from the world around it, not the light inside. The inner-directed was more prevalent in the nineteenth century than the twentieth, before mass media, and that type knew strongly what he believed and followed it. Now, he said, we define the inner truth from the mirror of the outside world."

Trevor's enthusiasm for *The Lonely Crowd* leads me to check it out, and though the book is more than fifty years old, "outer-directed" is an apt diagnosis of twenty-first-century

America. Riesman describes inner-directed people as those who navigate life with a "gyroscope" of "internalized goals acquired early in life"—not necessarily altruistic aims, perhaps worldly and ambitious, but some vision of a successful life that doesn't change constantly depending on the audience. The outer-directed people, he writes, are "those whose conformity is insured by their tendency to be sensitized to the expectations and preferences of others."

That's voyeuristic-exhibitionist, how'm-I-doing? U.S.A. in a nutshell: reality television, celebrity worship, self-branding via purchases starting in childhood, everything that Susan Faludi calls "display culture." Trevor absurdly but predictably calls himself an innie "because I'm European, older" and because he's against airline deregulation. "I have a political conscience, I'm not an unreconstructed capitalist." But the only gyroscope directing his online life is a fascination with deception and a chilly, commercialized lust based on porn.

Trevor uses the Internet as more of a peephole than a meeting ground and reveals only his disguises. His e-self is nothing more than his appetites and his seductions, and his correspondents are "offerings," like HBO On Demand. Or so he hopes. He says he's grown bored with online dating, and is now waiting for the day

---

when Craigslist allows me to "meet" in live-action view; when everyone has a Webcam. I'm sure the next generation of computers will have them built in and streaming would be better than it is now. I would know so much more before the date that way. Now I'm experiencing their literate gifts, but with the cam, I'd remove that need for literate gifts; we could see each other, we could take our clothes off if we wanted. I'd see how she moves and talks . . . there's no keyboard at all, there's just a screen. . . . I could put a towel around me and we could talk. It could be the whole interaction itself for the people on Craigslist who don't really want to meet.

This isn't just the pipe dream of one unhappily married sex fiend. Many sites are beginning to explore video dating, and industry experts predict it could be standard in ten years. Herb Vest says 10 percent of True members have Webcams and he's anxious to add video chat to True's offerings. Vest envisions a scenario where "you go to a private chatroom and have a virtual date. You can see them, see them laugh, see their expressions, you can do all that before they know your real name or where you work. It's so much more economical time-wise."

AIRBRUSHING MY PERSONALITY

The less people trust each other, the more money online dating can make. Voyeurs and exhibitionists need technology. And when you're an "offering," as Trevor puts it, you'll need an advertising campaign to reach buyers, who know through their shopping that they too need help to stay competitive themselves. For research purposes, I contacted a profile consultant, and hired him to critique my Nerve profile. He's one of several such independent firms, but the profile-tweaking service is starting to be "bundled" into the sites themselves.

I contacted E-Cyrano.com and sprang for the fifty-dollar "silver profile makeover and analysis." I sent company founder Evan Marc Katz my Nerve profile (see page 40). He advised me how to improve it in a twenty-minute phone chat from his home in LA. Katz, cute, engaging, in his early thirties, started E-Cyrano in 2003 after working for AmericanSingles.com and JDate; he also wrote *I Can't Believe I'm Buying This Book: A Commonsense Guide to Successful Internet Dating*. His longest relationship has been seven months—worse than me!—but he believes strongly in the numbers game. Go on enough dates and you will find your beloved.

His profile advice underlined the great tension in online self-presentation. Are you selling yourself to as large an audience as possible or, like Michele and Benton, communicating your particularities? Should you risk alienating the many to reach the One? Katz, not surprisingly, advocates for crowd-pleasing, and he stomped on my best lines. My "five items I can't live without"—"yellow bile, black bile, phlegm, blood, and Google"—has always gotten kudos from the literate smarty-pants it's aimed at, probably the most referred-to part of my ad. My type of guy comes back with a pun on "humorous" or takes the opportunity to describe his own, usually sanguine, personality.

Katz just found it gross. I told him, hey, I'm a little gross, or at least body-fluid-friendly, so that's an OK association. He went on to critique my response to the idiotic question "Celebrity I resemble most." Referring to the photo of me next to a nut dispenser, I put "nut dispenser." Katz scolded gently, "You shouldn't say nut and you shouldn't say bile. Those are alienating and you want to always accentuate the positive. I look at the picture and see your pretty eyes, not the nut dispenser, so that just makes me scratch my head." Under Why You Should Get to Know Me, I mentioned that I'd been Abu Ghraib torturer Private Lynndie England for Halloween, and Katz nixed that too. "That reminds me of Prince Harry dressing up like Hitler. You're coming off like the Princess of Darkness."

He had decent generic advice that I already followed anyway: a profile should mix funny and sincere, specific and generic. I agreed with his general directive of "Lots of turn-ons and no turn-offs." People who demand "Please don't be" followed by a long list seem like pissy malcontents. He called my sincere bits too generic and thought my More About What I Am Looking For needed to be more detailed. He said, "Most of us men are dolts; we don't know what to say. The more specific the hook, the more likely we are to grab onto it. We want to see ourselves in your What I'm Looking For." But what does he mean by "we don't know what to say"? Are they looking for a script for the first date?

Finally, he suggested I be born later—make my age thirty-eight or thirty-nine in the headline and then confess to the lie in the profile. "Oh, like tricking them into drinking poison? Why the hell do I want someone who doesn't want what I really am?" I started ranting. He cut off my choleric sputter with, "It's only to manipulate the search results, not manipulate men. People lie online because they're insecure; it doesn't make them liars." He explained in a soothing tone that I could make ignorant ageists rethink a rule against over-forties, ease them into the idea with my pretty eyes. I didn't take this or any of his suggestions. I know "me" is a fluid concept online, but that's all the more reason to stay moored to the parts I value, including honest, funny, inappropriate, and with forty-plus years of life experience.

CHAPTER 7

Rachel: What's Wrong with Shopping?

The problem with e-dating pontification: the opposite of everything is true. It is isolating yet it connects. People are more honest and confessional online; people lie and confabulate more. It creates fussy, demoralized people-shoppers, but it's delivered true love to someone you know. One of the most puzzling conundrums involves discrimination. It can become an ugly, self-destructive habit: some online daters simply hone their skills at finding fault with profiles, e-mails, human beings. When I feel that creeping up, I quit the sites for a while.

But fussiness can also be self-actualization, born of self-esteem. Women of a certain age in particular tell me they demanded more and then found love online. Loath as I am to admit it, focused human-shopping can work beautifully. It certainly did for Rachel. A thirty-nine-year-old mother of three, Rachel posted a Match.com ad for men who were over 6'2", had all their hair, earned more than $150,000 a year, and lived within five miles of her zip code. I wanted to disapprove of Rachel's superficiality and gold-digging, but ended up impressed with her tenaciousness and optimism.

Of her criteria, I'm the most mystified by "within five miles" after what she tells me about the cruel initiation rites of Bergen County, New Jersey. In this upscale suburb of New York, so Rachel tells it, when women enter into infidelity, divorce, or both, their chests are sliced open and bags of saline inserted. "As soon as you get divorced," Rachel tells me in a long phone call,

---

you find out how many people cheat and how many women get boob jobs. Most of the women in Bergen County don't work, they spend all their time in their gyms with their personal trainers and going out to lunch with their friends, so there's all this focus on the body. Boob jobs are rampant.

The guys all work in the city and they don't want to leave their kids or move out of their houses, so they cheat. I'd say eighty percent of the people in this area who are around forty are having affairs. When I separated, I was approached by so many married men who'd say, "My wife and I have an agreement; I just need passion." I'd say, "I just got divorced, what do I want with a married man?"

It's a little bit *Desperate Housewives,* a little bit Jane Austen. Where the nineteenth-century Englishwomen practiced their piano playing or needlepoint, the Bergen wives make their bodies their accomplishments, honing them at the gym and the plastic surgeon's. Sometimes the taut flesh gets turned back on the matrons like a weapon: Rachel has a friend down the street whose cheating husband took naked pictures of her "just for us, baby" and then posted them on the self-explanatorily named Shareyourwife.com.

Rachel's own divorce was foreshadowed on her physique too. She lost fifty-seven pounds right before she left her husband. "I'd done Weight Watchers after each kid, but this was the first time I got to my goal weight. I was ready to do something for me, I was done having kids." She won the house and primary custody of their daughters, ten, seven, and four. She took her first job since before her fourteen-year marriage, helping people plan their finances two days a week from a Manhattan office. "Being a stay-at-home mom is very isolating and very selfless; I felt like a nursing cow. Losing all the weight made me feel like a woman again, and my job made me more confident about using computers."

She began seeing someone she met in real life; he turned out to be "emotionally abusive. When I broke up with him, he said, 'You better not leave me, who's going to want you with three kids?' and I started to believe him." So she began online dating "to get away from the mean guy." Friends had suggested JDate, but she found Match.com "easy to maneuver through" and immediately found people she wanted to write.

Despite the divorce and the mean guy, her Match profile positively bristled with self-esteem. Nor would she be dissuaded from her specs. Six-footers would write and beg her to give a couple inches, but she stood firm. "I'd say, 'I could meet you, but I'm not going to want to kiss you, I only like big guys.'" She also resisted the Stepfordesque local pressure to supplement. In fact, she made "What do you think about boob jobs?" the litmus test for her online dates.

This seems like an easy one for guys to get right—you either really don't like Barbie tits or else you lie. But then I thought about the demographic. A fortyish divorcee seeking a tall, rich second husband in Bergen County was as likely to be surgically enhanced as not. This was not actually a no-brainer. And sure enough, answers from the locals ranged, Rachel says, from "'Yeah, you want me to buy you one?' or 'Everyone over forty should have one' to 'A woman should do what she wants' to 'No, I prefer natural bodies' to 'More than a mouthful's a waste'"—a junior high fave still going strong, apparently.

FORTY-FOUR MEN

Rachel left her fourteen-year marriage because it had grown cold, but her belief in the institution stayed unshaken. She immediately began looking for her second husband. She reads my mind about the rebound and says, "I know, I know, people think you should be by yourself for a while after a divorce. But I just hate that. I would rather be with people. Friends or guys, but not alone."

Rachel loved online dating from the start.

On Match.com I really regained my self-esteem because everybody I met wanted to go out with me. Besides realizing that people want me, Match helped me figure out what's a good partner for me. I realized I don't want to be with someone who's mean, who's not successful, who's a slob. It helped me hone my checklist and it helped me not worry about having a checklist. I think a lot of guys respect that you have things you want too and that you can ask for what you want.

She also denies there's any supply problem: "At our age, there's a lot of men coming available; I found more opportunity dating at forty than in my twenties."

Despite my mythically long strikeout, my sisters have me mostly convinced that online dating can be great for the fair, more accommodating, sex, especially after we've gained our postyouth confidence. By the late thirties, we've realized we are as smart and competent as the guys who've been bragging to us since high school. We've come into our sexual own and made some peace with however it is people respond to our looks. We value quirky-cool less, fair and nice more.

Rachel had gained knowledge divorcing and online dating, and she's not the type to keep it to herself. Many of her financial planning clients are new divorcees with children, and now they also get a pep talk about online dating as part of her services: You can do it after your kids go to sleep! It's where the busy, successful men are! She shares happy stories she's heard about eHarmony, though she's never tried it, and she pooh-poohs fears about Internet predators. "There are more scary guys in bars than on the Internet. I don't know how to help women get past that fear that they're going to meet a weird guy. If you meet a guy in a public place, and you have intuition, you're not going to get in trouble. You can tell if he's a whack job."

She says she never met psychos or suffered online burnout or needed to take a break in the year and a half she met the forty-four men. "I dated whenever I didn't have my kids. It could be two weeks before I could meet him because I only don't have the kids every other weekend, and I wouldn't get a babysitter to go on a date." She stacked the no-kids weekends four-high on a few Saturdays. "I'd meet one guy for coffee at ten, one for lunch at noon, one for happy hour at four, and then one for dinner at seven. I'd be taking notes in the car."

Single parents have tighter schedules and less energy, but kids take some pressure off online dates. Not only was Rachel too busy to brood, she also lived with three people she loves and cuddles with and needs to model optimism for. She stayed upbeat through forty-three frogs, she says, because "I love meeting people. When I went on a Match date, I wouldn't be like, 'Oh my god, I hope this is my husband'; I was like, 'Hey, I have something fun to do Saturday night!' She adds, "I have no horror stories. The guys I met were quality guys, hardworking, friendly, and a few ended up being my clients. It was shocking to me how many guys fit my criteria." Rachel doesn't complain about obfuscation or whitewashing in the profiles: she relished the problem-solving part of reading people. "I have really good intuition and assessment skills. I'm a trained social worker. I can tell quickly if someone's in my world, even from e-mail, from the way they talk about their kids."

Her instincts failed her once in forty-four men. Most of her first dates didn't result in a second, but three of the second dates led to a month or so of dating, and once, merging the kids. "This one guy and I agreed after six or seven weeks to take our profiles off and be dedicated to each other; we were as hot and heavy as you can be with kids. He had two sons. The first time we all got together, it panicked him to see our five children together and he started acting weird. He didn't call me that night or the next day."

Instead of stressing, Rachel went to her girlfriend's pool the next day. They went inside so the friend could show off *her* gorgeous new boyfriend from Match.com. "So we're looking at Match," Rachel says, "and I see my boyfriend on Match has a brand-new profile within the last twenty-four hours. I called him up from her bedroom and said, 'What are you doing? I can't believe you would do this instead of talking to me, you immature baby, when were you going to tell me you were back on Match!?'"

Other than that, she has few complaints beyond the standard learning-curve one. "At the beginning I'd stay on the phone till three in the morning sharing all this private stuff, and then I'd meet the guy and go, 'Oh my god, I'd never kiss this guy in a million years.' By the end I'd speeded it up." Even the savviest shoppers get sucked into some epistolary romance or pillow talk before that first e-crush disintegrates on the F2F. Everyone has to learn on their own that the most fantastic words mean nothing without what Rachel calls "the good click."

She had the good click with the three men she dated for a while before she met Kevin. The last PK (pre-Kevin) match had never been married, a group whom Rachel says in general "didn't understand my life. They'd expect me to be more spontaneous." This final bachelor recognized her picture from their gym, wrote her, and they dated for three months. "Nice guy but very focused on work," Rachel summarizes briskly. "I realized I wanted more passion, more commitment; I needed a more in-love relationship.

So I stopped seeing him and thank god I did, because you know how people stay in something that's just good enough? Four months later I met Kevin."

ACT NOW TO GET THIS DEAL!

Rachel says six thousand women responded to Kevin's Match .com profile the day he posted it. None of them were Rachel's friends, as she'd e-mailed them all "hands off, this one's mine" when he appeared in her Your Newest Matches e-mail. He was forty-one and "very good-looking" and had the other specs. She took her shot immediately. "I write him this quick two-sentence e-mail and I know other women are writing him longer, more detailed things about wanting to know him. So I write him again and say, 'I think I wrote you yesterday, but if I didn't, I'm interested. If I did, I'm very, very interested.' He thought that was cute and he wrote back. We agreed to meet and as soon as I sat down, I said, 'I'm done, I've been doing this for a year and a half. You're new at this, you do what you need to do, but I know it's you.'"

Rachel is in some ways the most conservative dater I interviewed, but she's also the most feminist despite her salary requirements. She was the knight in her online romances, not the princess waiting in the tower: she roamed widely and proclaimed her intentions without coyness. The Internet was perfect for her. Mastering the computers at her office job helped raise her self-esteem above "nursing cow" and equipped her to better her life.

Kevin, the head of sales and marketing for a big manufacturer, had been married for thirteen years and raised a stepson from toddlerhood to college. He got divorced after his wife had an affair. Rachel says warmly, "Kevin had every right to cheat because his wife did, but he thinks it's wrong. . . . He's such a genuinely good man, he has an aura of goodness. There's very few men as sincere and loving and good." He passed the boob-job test by answering that women's bodies are beautiful and they shouldn't change them.

Kevin felt the good click too: Rachel was his second and last online date. Not long afterward, Rachel retired her profile, prompting Kevin to deadpan, "Did you hear Match.com is going out of business? Your quitting bankrupted them." Rachel says she knows Kevin compromised by dating her. "What he wanted was a woman who was maybe forty whose kids were grown or who didn't want kids. He raised this other woman's son and wanted to have an easier life with no kids, sleep in, travel. Instead he's got three kids and a puppy." They got engaged on Valentine's Day 2004, a year and three months after they met, and were married that summer, a month before we spoke.

Rachel in her modest, boosterish way credits Match.com for delivering Kevin. "I could retire now if I got a commission for everyone I sent to Match. When single women meet my husband they say, 'Ohmigod, you met *him* on Match, where do I sign up?' They tell me I'm their inspiration—I managed to keep my house, and on Match, I met an amazing man and moved into an even bigger house with my children." She got more than everything on her list.

The marriage, the kids, the big house and high-paying job don't always deliver the happiness they're supposed to: just look at the cheating and the divorces roiling Bergen County. But they make up what most Americans consider a successful life, and that makes them reasonable criteria for online dating. Despite her own disappointments, Rachel kept believing in the American Dream. Match.com put her in touch with the other believers.

PART THREE

LYING, aka
INTERNET TRUTH

WHITE LIES ARE THE NEW BLACK

Michele's estimation that men always add five years and ten pounds to women's profile stats rings truer the more people I talk to. Online dating, it seems, has changed the meaning of the word *honest*. Slogans like "You're as young as you feel!" become closer to true when truth is the profile lie you can get away with. "Nobody in life would ask you your age or your weight," argues a friend who knocks numbers off both. "Those questions beg you to lie."

Truth is often a reasonable balance of lies, which fifty-nine-year-old Trevor explains. "Sometimes I say I'm thirty-nine to get her to write back, but I couldn't turn up at an assignation; there's clearly no way I'm thirty-nine, and she would then not believe anything I said. Everything would be a lie." If one lie is too preposterous, and isn't balanced by another big one, the whole thing crashes down. (Trevor could be thirty-nine when meeting Jenny, who was really a man, because he still was closer to reality than "she" was.) Trevor doesn't even phrase it as "what I could get away with": the believable lie *is* the truth.

I'm not a huge fan of lying. It separates people from each other and from themselves, aka compartmentalizing. Liars tend to be passive-aggressive in their relationships: fear of being caught breeds resentment, and getting away with it breeds contempt—while the lied-to wonders, "Where's *this* shit coming from?" Even a victimless lie like age-fudging is destructive. It feeds ageism the same way self-closeting feeds homophobia and "passing" fed racism. Why should bigots get the power to shame anyone for the year they were born? It turns you against yourself to lie about something so basic to your identity.

But when in Rome . . . I still don't lie, but Internet dating has softened my self-righteousness, as I discovered on a Nerve date a few years ago. Things were progressing nicely with the forty-six-year-old Web designer who DJed and painted and was cuter than his picture. Then, over his second beer, he looked at me sincerely and said, "I have to tell you something." That statement produced a momentary illusion of shared history. It's a thing couples say. I felt weirdly close to him and I smiled supportively, "Yeah?"

"I'm really fifty-three." He watched my face when he said it. To my surprise, I felt more protective, embarrassed for him, and intrigued than tricked. I wasn't dismayed at the fifty-three part either; in fact, I was happy to learn I'd been lusting after a guy in his fifties. Adult swim was working, even if I hadn't known it. "How come you lied?" I asked gently.

"Because I was afraid nobody would go out with me." His response was honest and touching and it carved texture into the smooth surface of a first date. It gave us traction. When a lie is confessed, the liar gets to see beyond the other's social skills—her immediate reaction to the lie, her flexibility, her forgiveness, perhaps her own confession offered up in return. The lied-to can be understanding and reassure the liar it doesn't matter. Both can find out what might take offline daters months—attitudes about deception, which kinds of lies the other considers "white," which unacceptable. The fifty-three-year-old and I shared a bit of ruefulness about humankind's insecurity and vanity, and it warmed up the audition process. (Unfortunately, the lie-and-forgive pas de deux proved the best part of the date.)

Wishful profile writing extends beyond weight, age, height, hairline into the blank for "occupation," which many an administrative assistant or customer representative fills out with *artist* or *musician*. "Last great book I read" may turn out to mean "Book I've always meant to read." Many Nerve.com men use "Song or album that puts me in the mood" to advertise their priapism: they don't need no stinkin' album because they're always in the mood, heh, heh. "In my bedroom, you'll find," usually, a Shangri-La of fluffy pillows and high-thread-count sheets and considerate lovemaking.

CHAPTER 8

Holly and Charles: Better Self, Temporary Version

As profile and e-mail lies get less concrete, deception blurs into self-deception. Is it a lie when never-married over-forties say they're ready and able to commit for a lifetime? When the alcoholic declares herself sober after a few dry weeks? When we write our profiles and imagine ourselves in love, we see our best selves supported. We don't think about being challenged or questioned or drained. Of all the strange aspects of the saga of Holly and Charles, the most fascinating question is "How much of it did he believe when he was writing?"

Holly met Charles on Conscioussingles.com, a site "designed to gather together those of us who are committed to being and becoming more aware and conscious while on the path, and open a space for community and interaction." It defines *conscious* as "those who seem to share interests in healthy, holistic living, personal growth, spirituality, metaphysics, recovery, social issues and the environment." A profile search reveals these data in this order: religion (with "spiritual" being the most common response), age, astrological sign, gender, height, location, diet (omnivore to vegan), profession, seeking (activity partners to serious relationship). Established in 1998, the site costs $9.95 for one month and has about six thousand visible profiles.

If any dating site seems like a refuge from scoundrels, it's this one, with its uncharacteristic message boards providing community and support. Members actually share their fears that they won't find a partner in these discussions and wonder if it's the will of God; others encourage them to keep their love lights on. The sacred and the profane collide amusingly, as in this post questioning why there's no blank for weight or body type:

> This may offend *some* members, but anyone who's got a problem listing their weight, or were upset about it here, are typically overweight and do not want to HAVE to disclose this. So . . . how is weight really different from height? Or eye color? Or astrological sign? It's a part of who we are, and therefore we should be honest about it. After all, isn't honesty one of the virtues of being on a spiritual path? Isn't that one of the things we all strive for? If Jesus Christ were alive and using the personals, would he lie, or "lie by omission"?

A question that cuts to the heart of Internet "truth": WWWJA— What Weight Would Jesus Admit? Another reminder that even the most spiritual among us are living in a material world: the profiles do include photographs.

The site was a natural for Holly, a sweet, soft-spoken social worker who advocates for mildly to profoundly retarded clients and is committed to "doing God's work." She describes her faith as "the belief that we are all brothers and sisters of God. I try to be kind, to be a light in the world." She read about Conscioussingles.com in a magazine in a doctor's waiting room and liked that it "was open to all faiths and the environmental causes I believe in."

When she first logged on, she was living with her parents on forty-five wooded acres in a small town in Georgia. She had moved back home at age twenty-eight because the family was struggling financially: her father had lost his job and Holly needed to stay in town to keep her grant for the college she was sporadically attending. She decided to online-date because "it's a small town, maybe seven thousand people total, not a lot of guys here. My girlfriends were doing it and told me there were nice guys on there."

She was looking for "someone spiritual, open, nonjudgmental." Before Charles, she met several conscious bachelors who "were very nice and had good listening skills in person, but just not the chemistry." Holly is so nice, she practically apologizes for objecting to hilariously awful date behavior. "One guy told me he liked costuming and showed up on our second date dressed like Darth Vader with a full-sized Yoda doll, four feet tall. This was not a *Star Wars* festival, this was a dinner at a restaurant, with friends. Another one couldn't order his own food; I had to order for him. And he was a pilot."

Six months after she signed up, Charles, thirty-nine and never married, contacted her. He lived five hours away in South Carolina, but otherwise seemed perfect. Holly was impressed with his profile. "He had pictures of himself playing with children in the water in Nepal; he also had a photo of himself with Mother Teresa. I was impressed. A girlfriend said, 'Holly, I don't know how humble this guy is,' because he went on and on about his volunteer work and his travels. But I was impressed with all that and I liked that he had an environmental job in the federal government."

They e-mailed for about six weeks every day. "I fell in love with the man in the e-mails within a month. He asked about me, my dreams, goals, aspirations, interests, spirituality, work, family. . . . He wrote about the same things. We shared our lives online through daily e-mails." The e-mails weren't sexual or even romantic, but mostly about spiritual and environmental matters. They never used the phone. Their first date, at a bluegrass festival in Holly's town one Saturday in October, was the first time they spoke to each other.

They met at the Welcome Center of the chamber of commerce. Holly says, "I was already in love with the person I was writing and it felt good to see him; he looked like his pictures, the attraction was there. We were a little nervous. We ate dinner first, then went to the show and didn't get much time to talk alone because all my friends were there. He stayed in a hotel and just left in the morning without calling. When we parted that night, he just said, 'I had a nice time,' no 'Let's get together again' or anything. He told me later he was impressed I didn't press for when I was going to see him again." He e-mailed a few days later and invited her for a weekend at his family's orchard in North Carolina.

On that weekend she met his parents, siblings, nieces, and nephews and hit it off with all of them. They had several other weekends away from either of their homes; then in December he invited her to a housewarming party at his new place in South Carolina. That was the first time they had sex. Holly says slowly, "It wasn't the best; he seemed sexually inexperienced. Very grateful. He gave me a dove pin the next day and I thought that was nice. There were flowers waiting when I got home."

Six times Holly traveled to see Charles and then around Christmas, "He came to Georgia to ask my daddy for my hand." But he still hadn't mentioned marriage to Holly. In February, he took her to a fancy restaurant in South Carolina and told her he'd gotten a new job in northern Virginia, near DC. Holly was taken aback, because he'd never mentioned that he was even job-hunting. Then he said, "I'd like you to come with me, not as my girlfriend but as my wife," and pulled out a diamond ring. "He told me I wouldn't have to work," Holly says. "He would take care of me financially and I could volunteer in the many volunteer positions I hold dear. He said he wanted me to continue God's work in the world and he would provide the financial part. He said everything I dreamed of. I accepted the proposal."

But she worried about such a big omission. The job hunt was the first secret, the first gap she saw between e-Charles and

RL-Charles. Holly also worried about his physical distance during their visits.

> When we were alone, he'd want to go to bed early, almost like he wanted not to be with me. It was a two-bedroom house and he put me in my own room. He said, "I don't want you to think I'm just after sex." He'd meditate for an hour before bed, so we never went to bed at the same time even when we were married. I thought he was trying to be spiritually enlightened so I respected that. Usually we were with his family and friends, and I loved how he was with everyone, on his best behavior. His friends and family were such normal, loving people.

It's a fascinating reversal from most Internet liars, who like the way online dating keeps everyone in their lives separate. Charles enlisted supporting players to help him act the part of the virtuous man in the profile. It's this detail that makes me suspect he didn't set out to deceive but rather to change. He probably started out believing he was or could be the man he was writing for Holly. He wanted to want what he told her he wanted.

REVELATIONS

Charles told Holly they'd be living on a farm in northern Virginia, and she moved up in February, two months after his proposal. She did, despite his offer to support her, find (low-)paying work in Virginia before she moved and got her first look at the "farmhouse" he'd rented. It was an unconverted, uninsulated stable, and Holly and Charles were the only nonequine tenants. Holly could hear her neighbors whinny and sigh and stomp as she tried to fall asleep; she always smelled manure when she was home. Besides the horses, they shared the building with "one chair, termites that came out twice a year, and a black snake."

She tried not to show her dismay as she crossed the threshold. "My first feelings were, I love this man and it doesn't matter where we live. It was one room, all open, including the kitchen, with a mattress on the floor. When I walked in everything was his Buddha, his gurus, his wall hangings. A few days later, I went to put up some of my angels, and he said they didn't match his stuff and would I please ask him first." Holly insisted, saying, "This is a we, not an I," and put up some angels, and Charles stopped speaking to her for a day or two, establishing the pattern for the months to come.

They lived there for about ten months before they married in June. It's creepily apropos that Charles stabled his fiancee alongside obedient animals: he began training her immediately. "He told me how I should make the bed, that I could only watch thirty minutes of TV a day, what foods I could eat, that I had to work out several times a week." After she got her first (tiny) paycheck, Charles asked her for rent money. He refused throughout their marriage to get a joint checking account. He made her pay for her own food and for gas if they visited her friends or relatives. Holly, who is 5'5", watched her weight dip below one hundred pounds.

It was the coldest winter Holly had ever lived through, and Charles rationed the heat, even complaining when she plugged in a space heater or a heating pad. "He'd tell me to put on a coat when I was home. I'd be so cold my nose would bleed. If we were living in the Depression, didn't have the money, I could understand not having the heat on, but we were not in poverty." She found out later he was making in the mideighties at his federal job and owned several properties.

Charles's job took him overseas for several weeks at a time, and she began to look forward to him being gone so she could turn up the heat and eat. "I didn't see him much when he got home because he was online and in bed early. We didn't talk like a couple. I went to several marriage counselors and ministers, but he didn't go with me. He'd say, 'I don't want anyone knowing our business' or 'You're the one with the problems, not me.'"

As if that weren't enough domestic bliss, they also weren't having sex. Charles had Christian friends who had abstained for six months before their marriage, and he suggested they follow suit. Holly accepted this on spiritual grounds, even as the religious connection, so important to both of them, was feeling shaky. "He went to a 'self-realization fellowship' that had six gurus including Jesus and some men with Indian-type names. I wasn't happy being there, and he didn't invite me on their retreats." So she started attending a church on her own. The other big bond—family—was unraveling too: "When he said online he was all about family, he meant his family. He wanted to always spend time with his family over the holidays instead of taking turns."

But she still loved the man from the e-mails and believed that was the real Charles. What she was seeing, "I chalked up to stress. I know how hard it was for me leaving home for the first time, my family, friends, work I loved, everything I knew, going to a larger city near DC, a new job, new home, new friends . . . beginning a new life. I felt like he was going through the same thing, so I was very patient and understanding of the circumstances. I loved who I knew he could be. Couples make it through affairs, so I figured I could make it through a hard winter."

They went ahead with their preparations for a June wedding. "Two weeks before the wedding I gave back the ring, but he said all the right things. He bought me Dr. Phil's book *Relationship Rescue,* which is pretty sad two weeks before your wedding. I went through the [interactive workbook] by myself, he wouldn't do it with me." Holly's prayers that it would all get better once they were married were quickly answered in the negative. "I figured on our honeymoon I could have dessert, but he said it was a luxury in life. I wanted to go horseback riding and he said, 'No, I've planned what we're going to do.'"

Then came the sex revelations. They finally were having sex, but "it was kind of plain and it had to go in this certain order, like the Puritan style, no oral sex," Holly says. "He didn't seem very into it, and I know I'm not an ugly girl." (I found Holly through a Yankee cousin of Charles's, one of several relatives who sided with Holly in the divorce. The cousin told me that Holly is indeed very pretty.)

"I was thinking something was wrong with this person, but I didn't know what," Holly says. Then she found a folder full of porn on his computer and confronted him. He didn't defend it as normal, as a Nerve.com guy might have, because porn was not OK with any of their spiritual guides: not the Buddha, not the angels, not Jesus, not the men with Indian-type names. He admitted he had a problem with porn and promised Holly he'd do counseling but never did.

A few days later, Holly found an unfamiliar medicine in the cabinet, looked it up online, and found out it was for herpes; Charles confessed he'd been engaged for seven years to someone who had the lifelong STD, but claimed he never had outbreaks. Then the crowning ick in a week full of them: he admitted he'd been arrested when he was in his twenties for peeping into the windows of female dormitories and masturbating. He asked Holly's forgiveness, saying, "I was young." She yelled back, "You were at the master's level!"

The fall after the wedding, Holly's grandfather died and Charles offered no comfort. He told Holly, "You'll get over it." She started going to her parents' house for longer and longer visits, and in February, told Charles she was unhappy. They agreed to "take a break." He never called her again. She only found out he'd started dating again accidentally when she went with her parents to pick up her things from the stable. She found his eHarmony profile printed out on the bookshelf.

So much for eHarmony's ability to weed out the bad apples. Acting on her divorce attorney's advice, Holly contacted eHarmony and tipped them off to Charles's still being married. "My lawyer didn't want a situation where another woman could file suit if it came out he was still married and looking. . . . I would be responsible for half of any debt due to us still being married. I did contact the site and they replied quickly. I was impressed with their response."

BACK ON THE HORSE

Holly moved in with her parents back in Georgia and got her old job back six months later. A year and a half after her return, she tried online dating again. She signed up on eHarmony (!!) because of "the extensive interview process and a good reputation" despite the fact that they'd accepted Charles.

"I definitely see the pros of online dating even with my bad experience," she concludes. "One really bad experience will not affect the good guys out there. But, boy, I am more careful. I watch for those red flags. I watch for control issues, sharing, being honest and open, and little things like having a cell phone. My ex never had one because he didn't want 'a nagging wife calling him constantly.' Those words came out of his mouth, in front of my mother!" Holly established a new policy of e-mailing for no longer than a few weeks before meeting. In person she looks for "listening skills, asking questions about me, what they say about their interests and dreams, how they treat other people in public (like the waiter). I trust action now, not words."

When we last spoke, though, she'd stopped online dating because "it got to be a second job. Plus I didn't find I was matched with the right guys at all by eHarmony. I do outdoor wilderness stuff, archery—not for hunting—and they'd match me up with these hunters in gold chains. I called eHarmony to complain and they said they match on core values, not interests. So I'd look at the core values part of these guys' profiles and it would be blank."

The experience with Charles and then eHarmony has made her value RL interactions more. "There's a local coffeehouse and I'll meet guys, and my girlfriends and I now introduce each other to our exes. I'm out and about more. I don't want to online-date. I don't want to be one of twenty girls a guy is talking to. And I don't like talking to them and thinking, 'Oh, I got to answer Brian too.' It's so much more special if a friend says, 'I think this guy is great; you should meet him.'"

You can meet a scoundrel offline, too, but Holly understandably fears a particular type of hopeful liar who feeds on the Internet. "I believed online dating and e-mailing was an honest way to met people. I was honest. Felt like I could discern when another was not being truthful. I was wrong. He talked the talk, but didn't walk the walk. Even in those first visits with his family and friends, he was acting out a part he wished to be in the world." Charles had perfect authority online, and it made him believe he could control everything in RL, too, from his money to his sexuality to his pliant young bride.

And though Holly should have insisted sooner on more walking the walk, she's not alone in being seduced by the words she wanted to hear. The Internet does enable the talkers of empty talk. They can build the ideal "country of two" out of nothing but words.

CHAPTER 9

Richard: Lying Is Fun!

ADULTERY ONLINE

Charles's was a deception much larger than most. More of the squirrelly Internet daters play shorter-term games with the truth—hiding, moving, sharing bits of it like acorns. Cock-picture-collector Trevor strategically hides one biographical nugget in particular. "I don't tell women on Craigslist I'm married right away because in America it scares a lot of them off. It keeps me from getting to have a flirty, persuasive conversation where I can explain it's not the marriage they think it is. . . . I tell them as soon as it's obvious there's going to be a dialogue. I eventually tell everything, I'm very open, and it gets them to share intimacies with me."

Trevor is sort of honest with his wife. They stopped sleeping together, he says, after their second kid was born ten years ago, but are staying together for the children with implicit permission to do what they want. "I think she has a lover, I've even teased her about it, but of course we don't tell each other." When I ask what makes it an open marriage and how they know, he snarls impatiently that they are both "European," with the scorn always directed at U.S. rubes for our vulgar, literal-minded obsession with "honesty" and "disclosure" and "spelling out details like do we fuck other people and lie about it." Trevor trills nostalgically, "My father died in the arms of his mistress of at least twenty years and my mother always knew, though it was never discussed. She hated the mistress. It's a way of life that works for people like me and my wife."

I'm wondering if his mother thought the way of life worked when Trevor's tone veers jaggedly. "My wife and I have somewhat separate social lives partly because she doesn't give a damn," he spits out with sudden force. In that curdled "give a damn," I glimpse a years-long slide through familiarity, indifference, hurt, anger, justification, cheating, confrontation, a grim truce, and increasing distance from everything. You could call Trevor a compartmentalizer, but he describes his niches—his loveless marriage, his work in television, his e-assignments—as too shallow to be actual compartments. He says sadly, "Some nights when my family's away, I feel lonely; I use the Internet as a substitute for going to a bar, or come home from the bar because it's time to stop being out, but I'm not sleepy yet. I'll see if I can hook a flirtatious or erotic conversation at two a.m."

Studies estimate between one-fifth and one-third of all online daters are married cheaters. I used to think the people who didn't post pictures in their profiles were homely, but in fact most of them are married. The preponderance of cheating creates several vast markets: a number of sites cater to suspicious cuckolds. There's Catchacheat.com, or Spytechweb.com and eBlaster.com, which sell electronic snooping products. For the cuckolders, there's DiscreetAdventures.com, Marriedsecrets.com, or Ashley madison.com (slogan: "When Monogamy Becomes Monotony"). The latter boasts 425,000 members—8.5 men for every 1.5 women—and advertises on TV.

The Internet has revolutionized adultery (cell phones have also added a crucial nonhome, nonwork line of communication). It's not just the access and the anonymity online: it's the new gradations on the slippery slope from marital dissatisfaction to extramarital action. "Seeing what's out there" is just a couple of mouse clicks, not that different from looking at porn, really. And if someone seems just too perfect not to write, well, a correspondence is still technically innocent, even if it turns confessional/romantic/sexual. It's not that different from a fantasy. Then all the obsession and projection and feeling-understood tricks of e-mail kick in, and the next thing you know, someone's writing their advice columnist about another marriage wrecked by the Internet.

Nonmonogamy needn't be dishonest; a surprising number of Web-geek online daters I met identified as polyamorous or "polycurious." Most complained it was a hard sell to prospective dates, but they felt committed to openness and freedom. But the poor polyamorists, who insist they aren't just "swingers," suffer from a persistent image problem. One fortyish restaurant manager admitted she wasn't quite satisfied with her don't-ask-don't-tell open marriage but couldn't find a free love gang to join. "Frankly, I do want something polyamorous," she said, "but that community is all guys with graying ponytails calling themselves Silverwolf and hitting on much younger women."

RICHARD: ISO A NEW MIRROR

Richard's dating life is instructive for anyone who's ever wondered, "What happened to that guy/gal? I thought we had fun." Maybe He's Just Not That Into You, but maybe You Just Dodged a Bullet. In the two years he's been living with Frances (he picked the pseudonym because "I've always wanted to date a Frances") Richard's had sex with seven women he met on Craigslist. "One person maybe once a week for two months, five of them once or twice, and another two I saw over a few-week period several times." When Frances is out of town, Richard brings the tricks to "his" place, which was Frances's place before he moved in. He explains, "The women I meet all seem to live on fifth-floor walkups and have two or more pets. Forget that. I like my home."

His response to my Craigslist ad for interviewees included this: "i am too self aware wrt online dating . . . i know how different each person is and how misleading all of this can become of what is real." I meet him on a corner in the East Village per his request; it is a secret assignation for him. He flicks away his cigarette as I arrive, looks me up and down, and steers us to barstools in a sleek lounge with pricey cocktails and no customers. He seems to be enjoying the newness of the situation, like a date but better: he gets to do all the talking. Curly-haired and a bit pudgy, Richard resembles a quieter, more passive (-aggressive) Al Franken.

Richard was married for eight years, and began online dating when he got divorced at age thirty-three. "I liked the idea of meeting someone outside the circle, interesting people who didn't intersect with your real life." He says he has always compartmentalized. "I like the idea of a girlfriend who does some of the same things, but I like it to be independent. Even when I was married, I did certain things on my own. . . . If I've stopped having sex with someone, I don't want to see them, I don't want to be friends."

He started out on Nerve.com after his divorce because a friend in the fashion business told him all her girlfriends were on there. After four months, he started posting on Craigslist, which is how he met Frances. They fell in love and moved in together two years ago, but he kept online dating. He explains,

---

Frances is great; I feel loved, I have fun, we have great sex, but I want a little more. That excitement of meeting someone new, I really enjoyed that when I split up with my ex-wife. It turned me on intellectually to meet someone I just clicked with. I didn't want to give that up.

I mostly don't feel guilty. I'd feel guilty if Frances

got hurt, but I don't care about these other people. I don't know how someone could get hurt after seeing someone for a week, I think it's weird. Ninety percent of the time I lie, I don't tell them I live with someone. Why? It's kind of fun. I don't lie anywhere else in my life, and it's neat to have this little world where I can lie. And I don't think most of them would go out with me if they knew.

He's certainly not the first married/domestically partnered man who, rather than set up a workshop or a den, carves his private space out of secrets.

Richard's in bars three or four nights a week, but prefers to contain his cruising online. Though he welcomes relatively random online encounters, he finds their real-life counterparts annoying. "If a woman at a bar asks me for a cigarette, I'm offended. I feel like she's just using being a woman to be all flirty and get a cigarette. . . . When I'm out I'm not looking to meet someone; I'm out to enjoy my time alone or see friends. I tend to go to the same bars and restaurants and I don't want anyone to know where they can find me, to be honest."

A financial analyst, Richard calls his ads his art, his creative outlet. "I went as far as I could within the boxes on Nerve. I got a lot of responses from Berlin," he says. He's particularly proud of his line "Ché is sexy; Peter Sellers is sexier." Before the interview, he sends me a bunch of his posts from Craigslist, plus a few from Frances and some recent paramours praising his wit and eloquence. Here's one of his:

No LONGER afraid of the wide BOULEVARDS or the dif. b/n NEED and WANT

I hope that you are fiercely strong and radically independent but suppose you believed that you didn't really exist and holding on to yourself as your body starts to shake, you imagine the following:

you catch the eye of an appealing someone and you think to

yourself as you stop, smiling, your back to the sun you think this is the one who will certify my existence . . . you stand there, smiling faintly, not moving, and the eyes of that man are upon you, and slowly, very slowly like honey dripping from a spoon into a cup of frozen tea, your physical self dissolves, and disappears like a slow fade, in front of his fascinated eyes and deep consciousness.

it could happen and i could be that certain someone!

i want: a drink with someone new tonight . . . it's wednesday

i need: someone smart

i dream of: a rough and tumble game of crazy eights

i = me = 36, tall enough and an ex said smart enough, 6ft, brn wavy hair and eyes and an exceptional taste in music

The ad asks for a fantasy he wills into life long enough to distract him. She also must be tough enough to disappear (or disintegrate, according to his creepy fantasy) quietly when she's banished three or twelve or 123 hours later. He explains that every Craigslist post, from both the single days and the current cheating regime, requests "strong and independent" because such women "tend to be more interesting and they're not my mother. I don't know if my mother's ever written a check in her life. My ex-wife is a little dependent; she didn't know how to drive. I want the opposite of that. Frances is strong . . . she has a support network outside of me." The support network is going to come in handy when she finds out and leaves his ass.

He loves when women show independence in a Craigslist fling: "One woman who was cool and interesting woke me up at four a.m. and said, 'I have a lot of work to do and you're snoring too much; you have to leave,' and I was like, 'Great, no awkward morning conversation. Fuck no, I don't want to get brunch!' "

Throughout the evening, Richard invites me to share his glee at rudeness, his and others', as well as his contempt for women's rather standard remarks and expectations. He admits he's gotten less forgiving since he's been cheating. "I was more open to someone I could have a connection with before. . . . Now, I'm wondering, 'How is this person going to entertain me, what can she do to make me want to see her again?' Because I'm going to go home to someone great I love. A lot of people will send an e-mail like, 'Hey, what's up, why haven't I heard from you?' They want me to say let's get together or to explain something and I don't want to do that. I don't know why they feel like there's some connection when you've just had some drinks and maybe kissed. Maybe it does warrant some response but I don't feel like doing that."

Richard makes me think of all the first dates that my friends and I have scrutinized like Ikea assembly instructions. If we just identify and label every scrap of the date and fit it into the ur-date framework, it will make sense, so we pore over every remark and gesture and disclosure. We aren't idiots. We know perfectly well there are loose screws like Richard out there. But something about returning again and again to the online date store of our choice, armed with our years of experience, lets us forget how little control we have and how little we know about this stranger. Everything up to the date is incredibly smooth and streamlined, but we still can't gauge character any quicker than before the tech or even the Industrial Revolution. All we've got is an illusion of control and efficiency because this date was so easy to procure.

My evening with Richard, though not a date, is a cautionary tale about expectations and deviations. I'm embarrassed to admit it, surrounded as I am here by Richard's self-hanging rope of disclosure, but I was somewhat charmed by him until I transcribed the interview. Since the same thing happened with Trevor, I start to worry I'm somehow both too picky and a distressingly easy mark. Thrown off balance by his honesty, I just plain missed Richard's cruelty the first time around, which throws the supposed reliability of F2F contact into question.

The "truth" of Richard, or anyway what a date ought to know about him, isn't in his body language or deep voice or flirty compliments—or his Dada-for-dummies Craigslist ads. It's in his actions, which are misrepresented to most of his victims. The greater bandwidth of in-person contact only distorted in this case. And Richard doesn't even possess the extraordinary beauty that lowers your I.Q. and raises his! It's enough to make you consider taping your dates.

Even more embarrassing: Richard's not putting on his usual performance for me. I'm taping the man behind the curtain. He tells me toward the end of the interview, "None of my friends know I do this. You're the only person in the world who knows this. You're removed from my world, I like the idea of helping you write the book, and I'm curious to hear your reactions." His confession has its intended effect of making me feel special in person, but hearing it again on tape at home, my response is "Well, duh. Of course you don't let your friends know what a prick you are."

His dates are bad-faith interviews—him full of pride at the creativity of his lies and contempt for the audience he's suckered. He says with a sigh that Craigslist dating "can be tiring. Sometimes I'd rather stay home and watch a movie with Frances but I have a date and have to go be clever."

E-dating's bounty of first dates brings out the voyeur in people much kinder (and singler) than Richard, and it's frightening how much fun he has observing the specimens. "Some traditionally less attractive women send pictures on Craigslist without being asked, maybe because they get rejected a lot and they're like, 'This is what I look like and if you can get past that, let's go out.'" (Trevor's also fascinated with the plight of the unbeautiful woman online.) Richard applauds himself for his openness: "I'll go out with some like that as long as they say something interesting. I met someone in June who was very ugly. Really ugly. Her mother would have said she was ugly.

I had two drinks and said I gotta get going. It wasn't awkward. I always tell people I have a plan later on, so I have an ending to the date."

Richard's self-analysis is generally a random pile of facts and self-serving perceptions he then bundles into some incongruous conclusion. "The first time I cheated on Frances, it was easy and I didn't have much guilt. And it got easier, like it was easier to drop a class after the first time. Looking back I think sex with Frances was better, but at first sex with the new person was very exciting. But that excitement wears off." Then without a pause, "I'm the good-boyfriend type, I'm just really nice, so that's why I get girls to go out with me."

He can't really think in the context of this conversation that he's nice or a good boyfriend, can he? But for someone lacking any unifying framework of values, beliefs, or ethics, perception is everything. He's utterly outer-directed. Richard says he's "the good-boyfriend type," not a good boyfriend. By "nice," he obviously doesn't mean kind or thoughtful or generous or honest, he means someone who can "do" nice for an evening, a "nice-guy type."

Many narcissists admit they're just throwing seductive bullshit out there to see what works. Nobody's really driving the car; nobody's coordinating actions or shaping a consistent set of responses across audiences. They tend to hate it when worlds collide and sure enough, Richard says, "I'm better one on one; I'm not good at mixing friends." Online dating is perfect for getting to know people outside any context.

He says he wants to have children and wouldn't keep cheating after he was a father because "I'll have more gray hair and I'd be the slimy old guy." But soon thereafter he's imagining marriage with a side of cheating, again as a picture, like his picture of himself as a "nice guy." "I think ahead and wonder what's worse: a forty-five-year-old single man dating thirty-year-old women or a forty-five-year-old married guy dating thirty-year-old women? I think I'd rather be the married guy. That doesn't look as pathetic."

Craigslist gives Richard individual audiences for his little prose poems, his e-flirtation, and then his impersonation of a single man. Unlike those who use the Internet to develop parts of themselves, he creates brief fictions, separate from himself, for short-term audiences. His Craigslist dates don't exist beyond their thumbs-up or thumbs-down on his appeal. Once she reflects back to him that he's seductive, not pathetic, he's done (he doesn't generally give his phone number out). Then, next time he needs to prove it all night, he writes a new ad.

He said he felt guilty once. "She had a five-year-old kid and I didn't know that when we had sex. When she told me, I felt bad this was a young single mother who felt afraid to tell me she had a kid. She seemed lonely; I guess it's hard to find a guy in Manhattan who will date someone with a five-year-old. I just hoped I didn't get her hopes up; that I didn't hurt her feelings when I didn't call her back." He trails off a little sadly, then brightens up as he remembers that she is after all just a reflection. "She noticed all my Craigslist ads, figured out they were all me. I thought she was really smart to figure that out."

BUSTING THE LIARS

It was depressingly inevitable that online dating sites would spawn *Consumer Reports*–style "review" sites. TrueDater.com, Opinity.com, and LemonDate.com ("Was your date a lemon or a plum?") let e-daters publicly debrief on dates, identified by dating site and profile name. TrueDater encourages, for example, "reporting that someone is 4 inches shorter than they claim or that they have gained 20 pounds since the picture they posted. We discourage you from entering reviews of the person themselves or their personality or telling stories about your date since these kinds of subjective judgments can be hurtful and may not be helpful to other people who are thinking about meeting this person."

Browsing through the TrueDater.com reviews is a cruel entertainment: lurid, fascinating, heartbreaking. It leaves me ready for the nunnery (and grateful nobody's reviewed me).

> Complete Liar
>
> By: anonymous
>
> He is an alcoholic and a woman beater. He is divorced not single, never been married. He lives at home with his mommy and daddy and has serious anger issues. I know first hand because I spent many years of my life with him and was very surprised to see him on yahoo with so many lies. Watch out for this one ladies . . . just fair warning.

> Liar and a cheat!
>
> By: phadrusisanass
>
> After 6 months I caught him cheating on me. He then told ME that I was "the best girlfriend he ever had" BUT I was "too fat" for him AND that he hadn't wanted to break it off because "You might loose weight and then I'll regret having broken up with you." This took a LOT of nerve because his BMI was WAY HIGHER than mine!!!! The reason I had gained some weight is from eating with him all the time. After we broke it off I lost all the weight and then some. Save yourself the trouble, date someone who has some class and isn't a shallow < . . . >.

> dentistador is a nasty talker
>
> By: 50218725
>
> Nasty talker, no intellect or values looking for Persian virgins only . . .

A Houston woman warned her TrueDater sisters that her Match.com date

> Said he was into art, but has not visited the art museum or any galleries. He has no manners—did not open the car door for me, walked ahead of me, slurped his coffee loudly, took cell phone calls at the restaurant. He has feminine traits that lead me to believe he goes both ways. Loves to bake—has every imagineable kitchen gadget. Shaves his legs, arms, and chest.

"Anonymous" laid quite the trap for "realgirlinvegas" and reported his results on TrueDater:

> While conducting research on match.com, I posted 7 fake profiles of men. Each profile represented different demographics. Realgirlinvegas sent emails and winks to the wealthyist profiles. She showed no interest in anyone making less then $100k. This one is a GOLD-DIGGER. Don't waste your time.

Had I dated Richard, my TrueDater ad might go a little something like this:

> Don't be a lab rat!
> "Dif btwn need and want" is creative in the worst way—a sportliar. And I don't just mean that he keeps harping on being 6 feet but looks more like 5'9" and isn't as clever as he thinks. He's cheating on his live-in girlfriend and laughs at the online dates he lies to for being stupid enough to think sex means anything. Stay away from this sociopath and his cruel experiments on human hearts.

THE PANOPTICON

Eighteenth-century English philosopher Jeremy Bentham came up with the panopticon—a prison in which the guards theoretically could always be watching the prisoners. Michel Foucault expanded the idea to cover more of society's disciplinary tactics—any instance where the fear of observation is used to control behavior. The entire Internet looks more and more like a panopticon as government and corporate interests are revealed to have basically unlimited access to our "private" data and our actions online. Online dating is a minipanopticon: the technology and sites like TrueDater encourage spying, which has come to seem the new American way of getting to know.

Every newcomer quickly learns about the horrible visibility within the cybermating preserve: you can immediately tell if your date's online now or if she last logged on two hours ago, within the last twenty-four hours, more than three weeks ago. Everyone's as monitorable as if they wore electronic ankle bands, and sometimes it's just too tempting to check up.

It's especially painful to find someone prowling right after a good date. You come home thinking, "That went pretty well," and get ready for bed, replaying all the new information of body and gestures and eye contact and conversation. You meet your eyes while you brush your teeth and add, "Didn't it?" Now you start turning up clues that he perhaps wasn't as enamored as you were and come to think of it, he wasn't that great himself, and there's plenty more where he came from, right there in your computer full of dream dates, which tonight wasn't quite. What was it he'd said about strong women under What I'm Looking For, again? It had seemed cute, but added to that thing he said about his mother at dinner, maybe it's a warning sign, hell, it's not even midnight, why did he want to leave the bar so quickly, well, that leaves time to check the date data against the profile and the e-mails; he's bookmarked, so it's a quick click.

And there it is: "Online now!" blinking like a tow truck. I've comforted many a girlfriend who came home and thus discovered the guy back on the prowl before he's even digested the dinner they shared by pointing out, "Maybe he was checking to see if you got online." And one male friend said that after a good date, sometimes he'd click into that woman's profile "to go back to the pot for more honey." But it doesn't strike me as the action of a happy dater to go right back to the catalog.

Nor is it private—most of the sites have added the feature See Who's Viewed Your Profile. Nerve, which has grown depressingly more and more like Match et al., adopted this recently; you can also see who's added you to their Hotlist. I gasped in shock when I saw the bachelors lined up under that heading, realizing my idle profile clicks were now visible too. I felt unpleasantly exposed, but some say the visible mutual-view volley is just like exchanging glances across the room at a party—a slight opening if you're feeling bold. Some daters I know take comfort in seeing who's viewed them, but it seems more like a rejection to me. They checked you out and decided not to write.

My friend Steven showed me how complicated checking up can get with the story of his yearlong relationship with Toni, a fellow computer geek he met on Nerve. After a few months of dating, exclusivity was implied but never promised, and both kept their Nerve ads up. Steven noticed that Toni went on to Nerve.com every day; he could tell when she got home from work by the "online within 2 hours" line underneath her picture. After months, he finally asked, "Hey, why do you still go on Nerve?" and she replied, "I only go on there to check up on you!" He said, "Well, I only go on to check up on you!" So after that exchange, they would wait a point-scoring amount of time, a week or more, to see if the other went back on, as he or she inevitably had.

Once they'd busted each other, they just accepted their mutual presence on the site and the games got more complicated. Steven explained to Toni one night over the phone that you could still see old profiles that had been taken down from inside your old messages. He heard her clicking on her keyboard and then exclaiming, "That little shit!" Steven figured out that Toni had clicked into the profile of an ex she called "evil" but still slept with sometimes and found out that he hadn't taken his profile down like he'd told her; he'd actually only blocked her from seeing him.

Steven tells me about later machinations that started right before Toni left for a weekend with "the evil guy." "Thursday night, after getting off the phone with her, I changed my headline. I wanted her to see it and know that I'm dating other people too," he says. Sure enough, Friday morning he logs on and she's changed her headline. Steven's fairly sure it's a response to him changing his ad and to not returning her second Thursday night call. She also changed What I'm Looking For to what he read as an oblique reference to her self-destructive tendencies—like dating evil.

Steven would put himself in "stealth mode" in instant message so he could see what Toni was doing without her knowing he was online (he would be revealed, of course, if he went onto Nerve, so he didn't). He partly watched because he worried about her compulsiveness around the computer. "She'd tell me she had to go home and go to bed and I'd time it—I'd wait forty-five minutes and there she'd be. Every night she'd be instant messaging till two or three and she gets up at seven a.m. for work. I know stalking her online is creepy, but it tells me something I need to know about her," Steven admits ruefully.

Steven has also creeped out a few online dates by Googling them. He's inadvertently revealed on the first date that he knows where they've worked or which bulletin boards they've posted on, and the less tech-savvy have felt spied upon. Googling doesn't bother everyone: Michele calls it "a way to get to know me" and with my weird name and sex-writing gig, I've come to expect it. I think it shows a commendable curiosity and initiative to Google one's date, particularly if their writing or other creations can be found online. Steven has been rejected for it, but he can't stop. "For a geek," he explains, "online dating is the ultimate hack. You want to see how much you can find out before the date."

I generally believe what people say. It's a tendency, but also a choice: I'd rather be occasionally suckered than live in fear and mistrust. It makes me feel good to extend the benefit of the doubt, and I do my best to live among people who deserve it. It may sound superstitious to connect these two, but I have been lucky online vis-à-vis liars. There was the Pittsburgh guy who told me he lived with his girlfriend and the forty-six-year-old who admitted to fifty-three, but mostly I've met men who look like their pictures, talk like what they wrote, and are basically honest.

Or seem basically honest, a correction online dating compels me to make. I haven't betrayed anyone or been betrayed, but suspicion nonetheless swirls through online dating, the dust we all breathe. The number of strangers you meet, the number of rejections that need softening (since you obviously want a boyfriend), the friends and dates raging about people who look nothing like their pictures or worse, the panopticon of Googling and checking and forwarding e-mails, and of course True.com's and the media's stirring up fears of the Internet predators— these do not create an atmosphere of trust.

PART FOUR
PLAYING THE NUMBERS

The opportunities for deception, self-creation, and spying aren't the only changes wrought by online dating. Another change springs directly from the increased access to the ones that we want: lots of dates. More dates than many of us have ever had before, dates selected by the criteria we most care about, dates we didn't have to leave home to get, a date for every night of the week, or as Rachel scheduled them, four on one efficient Saturday.

This bounty may be the most extreme of online dating's paradoxes. The increase in number of dates is at first glance an incontestable good. What could be a better solution to the problem of finding a mate? More dates make you better at dating and help you learn, as Michele did, to flirt and not to worry so much. By joining a dating site, we've acknowledged that the world is not delivering a mate and that we are ready to create our own luck: we get the bounce of proactivity. And most basic and important of all, more dates mean more chances to meet someone compatible.

But sometimes too much is too much, as Barry Schwartz describes in his 2004 book *The Paradox of Choice.* Schwartz cites years of studies proving that too much choice paralyzes people: one showed that people offered free jam were more likely to buy a jar when given six kinds to choose from than when they had to pick from twenty-four kinds. Heavy online daters have similar trouble choosing. Many ward off disappointment by finding flaws in the profile and in the person on the first date. As a sad-eyed Nerve date said to me once, "It seems like people use Nerve to cull a list, rather than connect with someone."

One is bound to approach a date differently when they're lined up like job interviews. After almost six years, I still haven't figured out how the heavy daters balance their hope with their insouciance. My date is someone I could hope to fall in love with, so how do I simultaneously nurture that and not care, night after night? The self-protection of "there are always more profiles" starts to insulate you from your own instincts and desires. "Only connect" should be all the online directive you need, but as the dates stretch out into ever-flatter waves of hope and disappointment, you can forget how that happens or what it even means.

CHAPTER 10

Abe: Grandpa in the Candy Store

The last U.S. census found seventy men for every one hundred women sixty-five and older. As a seventy-year-old widower, Abe has a huge statistical advantage and online dating sticks it right under his nose. Women on JDate are always writing Abe, who's six feet tall and has all his hair. This has not opened his heart to them.

"Women online are desperate," says Abe, who lives in Los Angeles. "Some of these women are on five sites, it's sad. Women from Florida and New Jersey say 'Let's meet,' but I don't see the point. They're geographically undesirable." Abe has a lot of things he won't compromise on, because he doesn't have to. "It's easier for me if she's Jewish. I'm too old to put up a Christmas tree."

Abe was married forty-two years to the love of his life, Ruth. After Ruth was diagnosed with cancer, they moved from New Jersey to Los Angeles for the gentler climate, and Abe retired from his career as a dentist to care for her. She died four years ago, and Abe found himself a widower in a strange new land of "flashy, showbiz-type women, some of them very aggressive."

Abe's been on JDate for the last couple of years on and off. He's a hot commodity—he quit online dating for a few months while he tried out a matchmaker, and 140 e-mails piled up in his inbox. He hasn't fallen for anyone on JDate (or through the matchmaker: "One they sent me was stupid and the other one doesn't drive"). He characterizes his JDates, twenty of whom he's met in person, as scheming, greedy, insufficiently family-friendly, or fast. This is partly an adjustment to post-sexual-revolution dating, a context in which he never saw Ruth. "My wife was sweet and refined," he says mournfully. But he's also grown fussy because there are always more women to go out with. Abe was raised to be a hunter, so all this prey advertising itself—or even hunting back—makes him suspicious.

Abe had been widowed for six months when his friends started to set him up. One of those relationships lasted a year and shaped his subsequent online dating. He doesn't have much good to say about Pam other than "she was hot stuff. The physical part of the relationship kept me in there." But outside of bed, wealthy, twice-married Pam was "too cold to other people, my granddaughters, my friends; she resented my time with my family." Abe shouts, "We'd visit her family and I never saw her pick up a baby! All she knew was spending eight hundred dollars on a sweater." Woody Allen–like, she married her stepson after her husband, twenty years older, died. "She had a kid with the father and then with the son," Abe says. "She was with the son for fifteen years. I met him. He's a jerk."

After Abe broke up with Pam, his divorced sister suggested he try JDate, which she'd been doing for a few years. He already used the computer for e-mailing and research, so the technology wasn't a problem. The mediation struck him as odd, though. "Computer dating seemed strange; in college you'd see a pretty girl and take her out."

His JDate profile harks back to when he was courting Ruth. His About Me blank says,

> Very young 70-year-old . . . devoted father and grandfather. For-
> merly active in Jewish philanthropic areas and temple life. I am a
> very traditional man, with East Coast schtick. Neatness is impor-
> tant. My life has been terrific and I want it to continue in this man-
> ner, with someone to share my future. I might add that I have
> always been considered a good dancer. Sports was a very big part
> of my early days and I was a very good athlete and popular guy.

His pictures include one of him on the golf course and one riding a horse. His ideal match is "a beautiful lady with a sweet
disposition," age fifty-eight to sixty-five, "who makes my pulse
race like a 20-year-old's."

He explains to me over the phone, "A lot of guys want
someone younger, but I don't." (Five to twelve years younger
isn't "younger"—JDate math.) "I don't have anything in common with someone fifty-five. I want someone who's in her sixties but good-looking. Maybe I'm shallow, but I want pretty.
I've always liked pretty girls. But not flashy. Out here there's a
lot of phoniness and I'm a small-town guy. I'm not looking for
a woman who's used to ultra-glamour. Most of the people out
here have been married twice. Not that you can blame them for
that," he adds in a voice that clearly does.

Abe is a friend of one of my friends' fathers, and his JDate
stories are the hit of their group's get-togethers. This is true of
many groups that include an e-dater and illustrates another
problem of the date glut. A good defense against caring too
much about any one date—and against giving someone a
chance after a faux pas—is "if it's bad enough, it will at least
make a good story."

Abe rattles off a few on the phone with a stand-up's timing.
"One looked really good in her picture. I liked that she was
from New York. Instead of meeting at a neutral place, she had
me come to her house. I get there and there's a note on the door
that says [he pitches his voice girlishly high], 'Abe, I'm in the
hot tub, come on in, make yourself a drink and I'll be down.'"

It sounds like the opening to a *Penthouse Forum* letter, but dating's a little different at seventy. Abe continues, "So I walk in and I'm calling and calling her name, thinking, 'God, now I'm in this house, what if this woman dies in the tub?'

"Another one, I got there and her teeth were so bad, I backed out of the driveway and did seven hundred dollars' worth of damage to my car. I'm a dentist, remember, teeth like that are very upsetting to me. One woman posted a picture that had to be twenty years old and I backed out as soon as I saw her. I said, 'I have to leave now, I have to go babysit.' She was lying about her age, so I didn't feel that bad. Another problem is health issues, I met someone very smart, professor at UCLA, very lovely, but she told me she'd had a mastectomy, and I couldn't deal with that, my wife died of breast cancer."

He complains so much about everyone, I finally ask him why he keeps doing it. "The access to people is terrific," Abe says, and he figures it should deliver what he wants. "You can't play golf and have sex forever. I need more. Not my big love, I've had that. Now I just want some companionship. My obligation to myself and my kids is to be happy." But his online dating is scarier and sleazier than the rest of his life and fits in awkwardly with his beloved family. He makes fun of the women who respond to his profile with his nine-year-old granddaughter. "She's very smart. She came over one night and changed my profile to I live in Beijing and I want an overweight smoker."

PLANET OF THE BABES

The last time Abe dated was the late 1950s. It was simpler: boy pursues girl with mostly economic lures, girl withholds sex till marriage—the exchange of sexual and domestic comfort for financial support. While he built his dental practice and Ruth raised their children, other women were getting degrees, careers, divorces, financial independence, the Pill, skimpier clothes, and generally more demanding. Dating in the twenty-first century is for Abe like stepping onto a new planet.

What seems to throw him off the most is the mixed blessing of women putting out. "I married a virgin!" he cries out. "I know that's not going to happen again, it's a different world. But if she's going to jump in bed with me, how many other guys has she done that with? I don't think the second or third date is the right date to have sex. I can tell by how they are that they've had a world of experience and it's a little scary. I'm not a prude, but these women think if they get a guy in the sack fast they can get him to marry them. But I'd stay more interested if they made me wait. The chase is fun, that's the thrill."

Online dating does rewrite the first moves of boy-chases-girl. Everybody can play all roles. Men and women post pictures and profiles; contact or are contacted; chase or dodge. Abe is approached more than he approaches, and in general, males actually are gazed upon more because women are likelier to hide their profiles and do the hunting. (This allows them to choose and to avoid the embarrassment of being seen online.) Anybody can initiate the exchange of real names and e-mail addresses, the move to the phone, the F2F meeting. The first few steps are refreshingly genderless—refreshing to me, that is, not to Abe.

That equality falls apart at the date. "Man pays" seems an odd holdover in a microcosm where the first date is an experiment. Many guys are understandably irritated at dropping what can be hundreds of dollars a week on women they'll never see again. Abe says, "Only one woman out of the twenty offered to split the bill, and I let her because I knew I wasn't going to see her again. Now if I was trying to romance her, I wouldn't be a cheapskate." People of all ages say something similar—men who don't pay the bill are cheap, and most women don't reach for their wallets.

I thought back in 2000 that online dating might move us forward from this played-out game. Cruising the profiles reminds you that in general, women have jobs, everyone likes sex, and everyone's searching for a mate with the same electronic tools. We move in reality further and further from our roles as ho and john, chattel and owner, damsel and protector. So why do we keep these creaky dating structures in place? Abe's not ready to abandon the old ways, but he sees room for adjustment. He says, "If the woman picks an expensive restaurant, she should pay half. I prefer a quick coffee date so it's not an issue."

He's not sure what he's buying anymore, and it makes him suspicious. The women who let Abe pay may be giving him the wrong idea. He says, "Some of these women are looking for a meal ticket and I don't want to support someone. I retired at sixty-three, worked all my life, I want my kids to get my money when I die." Yet it sounds like a lot of the flashy, twice-married fur-coat wearers have their own money and just want companionship and sex.

Take Abe's latest JDate, the first one he's had sex with out of the twenty he's met. "On our third date, we'd gone to a winery and she got upset about something and was pouting. Then we went back to her house and suddenly she got all flirty. And we went to bed. Yeah, it was fun, but she's show business, her son's in show business. And she talked about how her first two husbands had limos and bought her furs and diamonds, and when they tell you this, you know they're saying this is what they want. If I was with her, it'd just be for sex."

He seems to be placing her, classifying her as he talks. Her "giving it up" threw their power balance out of whack—he can't figure out what she wants from him in exchange for the sex. He flails around for a condemnation. "You have to become friends before you become lovers," Abe tells me and himself. "This woman and I weren't friends yet. I don't know if I'm going to see her again—why would I? She was a showgirl in New York, talks about guys buying her things, I told her that's not my style, that's not my life. So she may not want me. I want more brainpower anyway."

Most e-daters in their sixties and seventies do want a

long-term companion. According to my mother and her friends, the men want to remarry while the women balk at "waiting on some guy again." But the huge number of dates and the changes from the courtship rituals they grew up with make the genders suspicious of each other. They all played a certain, simpler game when they were young to attract their first mates. Some of the more passive men and aggressive women like the change, but some, like Abe, want the men to be the chasers and the women harder to catch.

And the online daters are searching among strangers for someone to fill these unfamiliar niches like sex partner/companion. Nobody comes recommended by friends or family; Abe has Judaism in common with his dates, but that doesn't seem to buy them much benefit of the doubt. Abe points out how unnatural and tiring the stranger-dating is: "It's hard to go out with a couple people at the same time—you have to remember everyone's details, are they widowed, divorced, names of children and grandchildren."

There's a greater game-to-relationship ratio among older online daters, and the game isn't clear to Abe. "Right now, I have four women out there to have dates with, all smart and successful," he says vigorously toward the end of our conversation, as if psyching himself up. "The whole thing is an adventure. I'm up for meeting these four women. If they're good, I have to get them before someone else does. I know I'm a better catch than most of these guys. They may be wealthier, but they're not going to be nicer than me. I look good for my age, I'm a nice guy. I'm very confident, if there's a great woman, I know I'm going to win."

LITTLE LIES STAND IN

"The best thing about online dating?" Abe says. "The access. The worst thing is people lie. They're all fifty-seven when they're really sixty-two. They'll say 'I ski' and maybe they went skiing once. They'll tell me their friends told them to lie. One tells me she's fifty-seven and she has a son, forty-four. What's that? She told me, 'We'll go to a casual restaurant,' and it was this fancy place. My sister online-dates too. Some guy told her he went to Yale; she calls them up and they never heard of him."

Truth in advertising is a new criterion specific to online dating, a new way to be disappointed in someone you barely know. "S/he lied about weight/height/age!" usually stands in for greater disappointment. Deeper frustrations run like a fault line under the superficial complaints about lies of vanity. Because there's a pressure to want what you said you wanted, people seize on misleading profiles to explain their lack of "chemistry." Abe accuses his JDates of being gold-diggers or superficial or somehow unwholesome when they're guilty only of not being Ruth.

Online dating has made Abe fussier, and he's not alone. Everyone who online-dates, especially in a big city, needs to cull the herd somehow. I won't write or reply to anyone who has any race preference checked, who falls outside of his own requested age range (though I'm usually too well steeped to be his cup of tea either), whose What I'm Looking For is a list of physical characteristics, who identifies as a Christian, who's graphically sexual (unless he's very funny about it), who writes in clichés, who brags, and so on. I can spend two hours going through profiles and only write to one person. People I know and like in RL have probably committed all my "deal-breakers" at some point, but this system normalizes discrimination.

CHAPTER 11

Hans: The Magic Key

Dissatisfaction and suspicion, thankfully, are not the only fallout of too many dates. For some who know what they want, including Bergen County's Rachel, it's simply a matter of patience. Even if it takes forty-four stranger-dates, these types will look till they find. Abe is more suspicious after twenty dates, but the same number of dates led Hans to his now-wife. The previous nineteen did nothing to dampen his unqualified ardor for online dating, which he calls the perfect solution to every dating problem he'd ever known.

Hans is a union leader who sends out Happy May Day e-mails to all the "comrades" on his e-list. If anyone doesn't love the marketplace, it's him, but he sees online dating more as power to the people, equal access for all. He loves e-dating so much, it's honored in his home. For Valentine's Day his then-fiancée Emily gave him their Nerve.com profiles facing each other in a hinged picture frame, and they've displayed it in their living room.

Over a year and a half and twenty or so women, Hans says he only had one vaguely bad experience, the same one almost all the fellows recount. It seems every man who's ever e-dated has a story about meeting someone heavier than indicated by her picture and self-description. The men telling the story almost all say something like, "I didn't mind her size, it's that she lied," and a weirdly high percentage of the stories end with the woman drinking too much and throwing herself at the guy. (A friend I told about the anecdote's recurrence conjectured it was the same alcoholic endomorph out with a new man every night.) Hans's version wasn't terribly traumatic. The tipsy woman lunged at him; Hans dodged and said, "No, really. No," and ran down the subway steps.

He describes online dating as a breakthrough on par with penicillin or the telegraph. "I finally had a way to deal with something I cared about a lot; I wanted to find a relationship. Not as in I'm almost forty and then something bad happens, but more like I want to share my life with someone and I'm tired of having experiences without a partner. I do interesting things and life is fun and I want to share that with someone."

I fell toward the end of Hans's online run. In March 2003, I answered his Nerve.com ad. I loved how he filled in Religion: "is opium, but I respect tradition, custom, ritual." His Why You Should Get to Know Me included "I like doing hard things" and "I have a good shrink." He was Looking For "someone who cares about politics, art, changing the world through big and small acts of passion."

A funny, smart mensch—the trifecta! And when I walked into the bar he'd picked, he was, as claimed, "tall, dark, and handsome." The date was long but didn't feel it. He was responsive, nice, smart, animated, easy to talk to. We discovered we both had relatives who'd fought for Hitler and agreed that we liked to think we would not have done the same in their place. ("You're against Nazis? Ohmigod, me too!") We knew people in common. He'd dated a beautiful acquaintance of mine, and I sheepishly admit that raised his value in my eyes ("Really? You dumped *her*?").

It's hard to square the attractive, smart, articulate guy with all the pre-online-dating striking out Hans describes.

I'd met women through friends, but your friends only have so many single friends. I've never met anyone in a bar; just because you both happen to be in the same bar, what does that tell you about someone? I would sometimes try to pick up women at cultural events, after a movie, say, "What did you think of the film?" Because there's some connection, we both chose to go to this movie. But that never worked. I tried talking to women on the subway and then saying, "Here's my card." That has never worked, ever. In years.

It's such a hard thing; for me, it feels like there's a world out there of people I'd love to meet and there's no way we're ever going to connect. I've always had this feeling, traveling around, living in Europe in my twenties, I'd think, "Wow, there's a beautiful woman and I'm never going to know anything about her." And the Internet evaporated that frustration—now I could meet them!

I'm still not sure why I lost interest in Hans, one of the best guys I met online. I sensed a possible irony gap the night I dragged him to the insane Joan Crawford Western *Johnny Guitar,* which is camper than a row of tents. His comment afterward was distressingly literal: "She was a strong woman" or something. I tried to keep my interest alive—I mean, who cares if a man doesn't share all my fag hag sensibilities, he is after all a hetero—but my heart sank. He said a date or two later, "You don't seem that psyched about this," and I didn't argue.

I remember while interviewing him how I'd liked his enthusiasm, especially impressive in a socialist living here in the laissez-faire capital. We'd run into each other about a year after our dates, and I told him I was writing about online dating. He introduced me to his fiancée, Emily, and told me they met on Nerve. We met for an interview at an Indian restaurant in the East Village twenty-eight days before his wedding. After he requisitely bitched about wedding plans, which as a good feminist man he was helping organize, he told me his love story, with Emily and with online dating.

PROBLEM SOLVED

Hans's longest relationship had been three years. Soon after it ended in March of 2001, a friend from Pittsburgh told him about Nerve.com and how the New York women were the best. Hans never checked out any other sites "because I didn't know there were any others, and I liked it. It was a little edgy, not so serious.

"So I put up a profile, and it was fun to think about how to write about myself in a way that was playful but says something real and makes me seem special but not too weird." Hans likens online dating to revenge of the nerds (in the nontech sense). "In grade school I was not a good athlete and I always envied the kids who were good at sports and they had this mode of communication that they could do. And I'm a good writer and I like to write and online dating is like my sports. Now I imagine those poor people who can't write; maybe they have a way of communicating with each other." We conjecture about how you'd spell an interested grunt or bicep-flex.

A mensch wouldn't be a mensch if he didn't agonize about his advantages. "Because I like writing and because I do it well, I can sell myself well. I became wary of tricking people into this picture of me. I'm sure everyone has ways of talking about their lives to make them seem incredibly interesting and exotic and sexy and smart and successful. Part of me feels, 'Why don't you let people find that out on their own?' If I'm those things, I shouldn't be the one telling them."

After second-guessing his own self-inflation, he cuts other people slack for theirs. He's as fair as anyone I've met about this process.

I think it's a medium that lets us present ourselves in a way that is (a) who we think we are and how we'd like to be seen and (b) lets us be seen as such. Now if you'd seen me today in my suit and tie and umbrella walking down the street, you'd have said, "Who's this straight corporate jerk and what's he doing in my East Village?" [false assumptions across the board, BTW]. And it turns out there's actually more of a story here. It gives us a context, a forum to see each other more readily, which is great.

Hans assumes people's self-assessments will reveal something true about themselves. He believes in people's good intentions, and the white lies he did come across didn't anger or alienate him. He doesn't think there's anything inherently better about meeting in real life. The only offline dating he did during the year and a half was to reunite with old girlfriends. "Why do real-world dating when there's a better option out there?" he asks, mostly not kidding. He checked Nerve.com every day or two when he was single.

He never needed a break and he never felt addicted. "Maybe there's a higher level of intensity or volume [in online than in offline dating], but I don't think it changes our emotional constitution. If I'm a person who has a problem with intimacy and I use sex as a way to avoid that, it doesn't matter if I'm doing that in a bar or online. Some people are readily addicted to tobacco, some people are addicted to online dating." He says he didn't feel any difference in relations with people he met online.

Hans is one of those rare creatures who likes dating. "Dating was always fun. The energy of it, the frisson, the spark, the encounter is so mysterious, not even just sexual, there's something about meeting a person and, how do you negotiate that? How do you figure that out? How do you talk to someone? It's the dance you do."

He swears he never worried about whether the woman would like him or not. "Nope, I don't have that one. I have other anxieties but not that one. I figure she will like me and if she doesn't, that's OK. I know I can at least make a fun evening. I have more the anxiety of the unknown, of not meeting someone. So my anxiety was completely dissolved by the Internet. I no longer felt the longing and the loss of the thing I don't know."

Hans managed to enjoy himself without a break through nineteen online assignations that didn't work out, that ended with him rejecting or being rejected. He debates that characterization. "What do you mean, 'rejected'? What are you expecting? To have sex? Get married? Have babies? Each time, I had a great drink, a great dinner, eventually maybe fun sex, some vacations together with the ones that went further. I saw a few women for a few months, long enough to go away together."

He enjoyed meeting "sweet women, beautiful women, fascinating women," including a top architect, a performance artist who blows things up, and the daughter of a writer he admires. This may be the groom-to-be talking, but Hans's one regret is that he didn't check Play along with Dating and Serious Relationship.

I think it should have been more sexual for me, I should have been more focused on sex; I could have gotten laid more. But I didn't think of dating as about getting laid. I thought of it as meeting people, getting a new friend, getting a girlfriend, someone who I'd eventually have sex with. . . . I wish my comfort level didn't need to be so high to have sex with someone. I couldn't believe people would have sex on the first date; women would later say, "What took you so long?" but in my mind that's what sleazy guys do, they hit early and they hit hard. But now I realize that it's not just sleazy people doing that.

He doesn't regret his nonsleazy policy about subsequent dates. "If I had dinner with someone one night, that's not a relationship, but at the point of having sex, then it kind of is. Then I'd stop seeing other people." (When I am Queen, this will be standard protocol—assume an ongoing sexual relationship is exclusive unless otherwise specified.) Hans says the women younger than him, in their midthirties, were more likely to hop in bed and less likely to think it meant something. "With the women my age and older, it felt more like we were on the same page, we were waiting to see what happened, if we had relationship potential."

I ask Hans if keeping his expectations low helped him enjoy himself and hang in there. "Low expectations? Ha! Every time I saw a profile I liked, I thought, 'We're going to get married and have babies.' Or the first time I went to someone's apartment and thought, 'Oh my god, she has such great taste and such a cool life and we're going to get married.' And then it doesn't go there. It doesn't go there. I definitely projected. I was thinking, 'This is a good one.' But another part of me was saying, 'Well, it has only been three weeks, it's not so surprising we didn't connect.'"

What kept lifting him up each time he got knocked down was the enormous supply side—the same vast resource that made Abe and others suspicious and second-guessing. "It would only take a few days to find another profile that seemed interesting and exciting and I'd meet them and they'd be really cool too. That's what I was talking about before about the longing and the lost connections and the emptiness at the end of it all, it was like, no, there's more. This isn't the end."

The endless supply helped Hans do a little work on himself. (He started therapy for the first time just before he began online dating and didn't stop until he and Emily were engaged.)

My problem's always been staying; I usually leave the relationship early. So I was trying to learn to be more flexible. I was trying to experiment, be less critical, narrow-minded, picky. Give it a try. Go with this relationship. Even if you think you know this isn't going to work, try to have fun, go on some dates, have a little sex, relax, be more casual. It felt like I had nothing to lose. I used to think that the right thing to do is that unless you're a hundred percent sure this relationship has serious potential, you have to get out, because it's not honest. But as I started to learn and think and experience more and had women explain it to me, I realized, "You don't have to know everything right now. Just chill and experience this."

I used to think, I'm not happy enough so I should bail. She's already at this point going to get hurt and it's only going to get worse. It's dishonest and she's going to get hurt.

A lot of people adjust to high-volume Internet dating by toughening up, expecting less, curbing their enthusiasm. Hans has a different spin.

I don't think it was a toughening. It was more of a softening, an opening. It wasn't so much "I'm going to risk hurting her in a way that I wouldn't before." It was "I'm going to risk being open to her." There was something about the medium that made me feel so much more relaxed and at ease; I felt like more open, more like I could be a better self than a narrow, nervous, neurotic self. I felt like I had a tool to solve a problem I never knew how to solve before.

The problem was always how to get to know someone, to pursue intimacy, to meet people in an intimate way. It doesn't work giving them a business card on the subway, it doesn't work leaving a little note with the tip for the waitress. It was always a project out there, and every time I had to figure it out new, and there was something burdensome about it. And after a long-term relationship that ended badly, I was especially despairing. And then the Internet came along and it was like a window to open and it's all fresh air. It really was like a liberation.

He's hitting his stride, and I'm entranced by what he's saying, partly because I want to be convinced; I want the Internet to liberate me too. He's digging me digging his words, and for a moment, it's like a good date. For all his confidence and happiness and good looks and beautiful fiancée, he's still a little amazed he can wow women. He still thinks of himself as the nerdy benchwarmer. He rolls on:

Besides the fact that I met really amazing people, a very high percentage of the people I met either knew someone I knew, had worked somewhere I'd worked— there was almost always some kind of six degrees. That's unusual for me because I don't come from anywhere, I've lived in New York for six years, Pittsburgh for four, Germany for ten. There's no way anyone should know me or I should know anyone. It was so heartening, it was like, "This isn't a coincidence, I didn't just meet you because you're hot, though that's nice. There's actually something going on here that makes sense, something in the medium makes sense, you're someone I should have met." It facilitates meeting people who were in my world anyway.

Several other Nerve.com users describe a similar six-degree overlap across the site and RL.

EUREKA

Of all the encouraging things about Hans's story, my favorite is that he didn't lose his enthusiasm about the people and the possibilities. He was as open to Lucky Number 20 as 1 through 19.

It's the spring of 2003 and it's late and I'm still at work. I didn't have high-speed Internet at home, so I had to do my Nerve dating late at the office. I've been through ten pages or so. It's all the same people, as you know, but often enough someone new turns up; hope springs eternal. I'd go through a search every other day and once photos became de rigueur, it'd be easy, you could just breeze through—"Seen that photo, seen that photo." Something made me click on one more page and there was a photograph of a woman who looked really cute. Her headline was "glossolalia," which was totally cool.

So anyway, I skimmed the profile and I'm like, "Oh my god, I'm going to die, this is just too good." She was German-Jewish and a practicing Buddhist. Her last great book read was Sebald's *Rings of Saturn,* which I'd just finished. She was a history professor. She said she was looking for someone who didn't have a rigid definition of gender roles. I didn't know exactly what she meant, but it resonated somehow.

I thought, I can't let this one get away, even though it was really late and I had to get out of the office. So I wrote a quick note; normally I would have been more thoughtful. We started e-mailing, turned out she had lived in Berlin the same time I had, she speaks German, she's tall, cute. We're both Leos, turns out we were born like ten days apart, both about to turn forty.

So we set up a date. I'd always get nervous, but she seemed especially great.

He then calmed himself, as many of us do, by tallying up the cons. She lived in Manhattan, he was in Brooklyn. He'd sent his brother three profiles of his three upcoming dates and asked for an opinion: his brother picked someone else. But the only true obstacle lay between them like a dragon at the cave's mouth, a beast that could reduce Hans to weeping and gasping. "The one bad thing in her profile," he says, "is she wrote how much she loves her dog. I'm so allergic I've had to go to the hospital. If there's a seeing-eye dog on the subway I have to move to the other end of the car."

Hans then hastens to point out the silver lining. "It had always been a screen I used, in real life and online. I know it could never go anywhere, so that was kind of a relief. I'd see this beautiful or fascinating woman with a dog and I'd know I didn't have to worry about her. You do need a screen on the Internet; there's so many people, you can't get excited about everyone. So even if they were interesting, sexy, beautiful, if they had a dog, I just didn't go there." It's a quite reasonable form of culling.

But something about Emily spurred Hans on, and he answered his first dog-owner ad ever. She got to the restaurant first,

---

and I walk in and she's cute. We had a great time, talked about the whole German thing, the Nazi thing; her family was upper-middle-class German Jews, and they all got out. So it got a little heavy. So at the end of the dinner, she said, "I have to go home and walk my dog." And I heard myself saying, "Can I walk your dog with you?" And I don't know where that came from. It's not just that I'm deathly allergic; I don't like dogs, I'm not interested, I don't care. So I waited downstairs while she went up and got the dog. We walked him.

I asked if he kissed her good night and he says, "Oh no. I mean, the European cheek kissing, but no making out."

He went home with the future unfolding in his head. He says one clue that this could be it was that "in a way it was almost less fun, because it felt so real. This isn't just fun, OK, now you're getting down to work. The work of a relationship. Mind you this was all in my head, the date itself was fun and playful. The seriousness was in my head and had no objective reality to it."

For the next date, Emily invited him over to her apartment, which she was preparing to sublet. "And I was like, what the fuck am I going to do? The lady has invited me over. So I went to the pharmacy the day of the date to buy all this Benadryl to dope myself up, and I'm in line and I see this sign for Claritin, which had just gone OTC that week, and I knew it was an allergy drug, so I bought Claritin and took some and went over to her apartment and sat all evening there and I was fine. And this has been a huge part of my life since I was five years old, so I took it as a sign."

As someone who's had longer relationships with pets than men, I'm fascinated by this cross-species *Sophie's Choice*. As they moved into couplehood, Hans and Emily adjusted the best they could. "It wasn't ideal. If we slept at her apartment, I'd wake up in pretty bad shape even with the Claritin, and I'd have to leave first thing in the morning." Emily had owned the dog less than a year, but it was still "huge and intense and hard for both of us" when she gave the dog away, a few months after she and Hans got involved.

She also explained the gender roles thing: her previous relationship, of twelve years, was with a woman. Instead of being worried she might cross back to lesbianism, Hans felt a kinship. "I've only had sex with men twice, when I was twenty, but I feel like I'm bi. Can you be bi and not do anything about it? It's an aspect of our intimacy that my sort-of bisexuality isn't weird to her, and she's not weird to me; we share this way of being in the world that's different."

They got married in September 2004. As they planned the wedding they went into couples counseling, partly because Hans had been so helped by solo therapy before. "After my three-year relationship ended," he said,

one of my longest, I started seeing a therapist for the first time and it was because "this is bigger than me, I want to be in a relationship and here I am again, maybe therapy can help me figure it out." I'd been very skeptical about therapy but it was a great experience, right up there with Internet dating. I didn't find surprises, a smoking gun. Finally, like Internet dating, I felt like I had a tool to solve a problem I didn't know how to solve. Not answers, but a tool. The therapist gave me a way to think about and analyze things I hadn't been able to figure out before, the same way online dating didn't give me a partner, it gave me a way to find a partner.

A tool to find a partner: the most basic truth about online dating. Despite all the side effects—suspicion, deception, salesmanship, disappointment, deadening of feeling, loss of faith in one's instincts and fellow man—it remains the best cure we have for unwanted singleness. What are Hans, Rachel, Michele and Benton, and all the other succeeders doing differently from the still-at-it? They all share a Who I Am and a What I Want that's clear, yet flexible. They stayed enthusiastic about the technology even when it delivered disappointment; they didn't generalize out from bad dates into sweeping critiques of whole genders. They came to online dating the way E. B. White said you must come to New York: prepared to be lucky.

PART FIVE
SEX AND LOVE

With no particular place to go, an instant attraction in RL can lead anywhere. If you "get out of here" with somebody you meet at a party, the possibilities range from creeping home before dawn to marriage. RL lust has always been unwieldy like that, no matter how cultures try to manage its flow with arranged marriage or prostitution or the Rules.

Online dating does some of that organizing and clarifying and pulls apart the overlapping hunts for sex and love. When you meet online, you've channeled the possibilities into specific streams. Checking Relationship instead of Play signals intent. The careful exchange of biography and shared interests online determines girl/boyfriendability, and it tends to lead to more of the same type of conversation on the date. It is more old-fashioned because a date signals more intent than hanging out or a hook-up, and the process acts as brakes on sexual impulses. If a computer date has boyfriend potential, I and most women I know generally don't have sex with him that night. (And yes, how unfair to the nice guys that the unsuitables get so much more impulse sex.)

Online dating has made each goal—Mr./Ms. Right or

Mr./Ms. Right Now—easier to target. More and more sites have added options like "Intimate Encounters" or "Short-Term Relationship" to their menus of human consumption, and plenty of sites cater only to the sex-seeker. Those are actually doing better business now overall than the relationship sites. Adult-FriendFinder, the most popular sex-oriented site, draws more than ten million unique visitors a month, according to Nielsen/NetRatings.

The FriendFinder empire mixes vanilla sites like German-FriendFinder, SeniorFriendFinder, and GayFriendFinder with the raunchier ALT.com, OutPersonals.com, and AdultFriendFinder. Andrew Conru, the CEO of FriendFinder, recently explained in an interview how AdultFriendFinder was born several years ago from the lust-love split. "When we started FriendFinder, we found a lot of guys were posting profiles that were more risqué than we wanted on the site," recalls Conru. "We started out deleting them, but then we recognized the opportunity and started AdultFriendFinder." Further niche-ing the niche, Adult-FriendFinder even added a PG-13 version, Passion.com, whose logo is a photo of boobs in a bra—second base—rather than AdultFF's long bare legs.

CHAPTER 12

Liz: Queen of the Ocean

Liz falls into the most peddled demographic on the Internet: she's pretty, young, Asian, and seeking sexual encounters. But she's not exploiting her advantages for luxuries. She won't let a guy from Craigslist or any of her "adult" sites so much as buy her a beer, and woe to him wanting China-doll malleability. Liz is online, a lot, to pick fights with male fantasists, casting herself as a more evolved cyber-Lothario. She's bisexual, maybe even pansexual, but mostly she fucks with the hetero power dynamic.

Liz moved from Hong Kong to Houston when she was ten, the oldest, biggest daughter of Buddhist/Christians-turned-Southern-Baptists who wanted her to be a lawyer. She's come a long way to her current cosmology, which she explains at our long, looping lunch interview. Stabbing her fork at the air in front of my face, she speaks softly but emphatically, with a fairly strong accent. "Sex connects everyone. A celebration. No matter how you and I are different, there's this one thing we can share."

Because it's harder to find boyfriends than sex partners online—"more amazing"—she won't use the computer for the former search. "I never look for a relationship online, because I don't think it's natural, not like looking for sex." She's been dialing up quickies online since she was seventeen, starting out on her father's AOL account. She estimates she's had about forty online-based sex-only assignations over the eleven to thirteen years since then. (Her age varies from site to site, and she answers my direct question with a deadpan "Twelve.")

Liz's promiscuity is part of a longing to transcend not just power relations but all hierarchies and boundaries. Surfing the Web is like sex, she says. "It connects me to the whole world. It's infinite. It's the same reason I love the ocean. I feel like once I put my hand in the ocean, I'm connected to everyone else."

Bringing free love from the commune into the cubicle is the vision of many Webtopian polyamorists. What foils them is generally the tenacious needs for control, protection, predictability, and exclusivity, tendencies Liz fights politically and personally and not always coherently. Her thirst for egoless immersion runs a bit counter to her bossy ads on various sites. She wishes humans didn't crave control, but since they do, she'll hold that whip, thank you.

Liz forbids men to talk about their jobs or to pay on dates. She warns that their pictures better be hot and they in good shape—and "don't try to make it about more than sex." Her e-demands bark like irritable dogs at the gate of Liz, but occasionally a man sneaks in for a while. She recently ended a relationship of eleven months that developed unexpectedly from an AdultFriendFinder hook-up. She broke it off because it ceased to be "flat" and "open"; she got attached and didn't like what it did to her.

JUST SEX, PLEASE

FriendFinder

AdultFriendFinder calls itself "the world's largest sex and swinger personals site," with over seventeen million members from Algeria to Zimbabwe, Albania to Yugoslavia, Alabama to

Wyoming. Its tone is breezy, unfazed, an efficient system of gears and pulleys orchestrating hook-ups and masturbation. Besides the standard anonymous communication channels, there are "hot erotic stories," with encouragement to "Pull down your pants and pull up a chair!" AdultFF also has a slew of chatrooms, including, on one recent night (the number in parentheses is members in the room):

European Couples Couch (0)
> Swing and swap talk all over the continent.

Polyamory Room (16)
> Consensual, responsible non-monogamy. You CAN love more than one person at the same time!

Dirty Thirty (9)
> The Dirty Thirty is our exclusive club for those with a bit more experience . . .

Mature (Over 50) Chatroom (22)
> Where seasoned lovers meet.

Gender eXchange Room (15)
> The Gender eXchange Room provides a forum for transsexuals, transvestites, the transgendered, or anyone who's interested in alternative gender labels.

Ebony Room (27)
> Brown, black, or just full of soul, this is the room for you!

Basement (18)
> The Basement is reserved for our B & D members—you WANT to go to the basement, you MUST go to the basement, you WILL go to the basement . . . If you're looking for quick, kinky sex, please use another room!

The Club House (1)
> The Club House is reserved for our gold and silver members—people serious about a good time!

I assume the Club House is for schmancy, "quality" people and that the lone gold-digger or silver fox in there feels silly. Maybe he or she should go take a nap on the European couch.

But a little vulgar snobbery is hardly enough to overshadow the friendliness of this vast rumpus room. The tone of the site is a pleasant surprise, free of online porn's harsh hawking of "dirty teen sluts choking on monster cocks." It may be blandly corporate, but the possibility of participation, it seems, calls forth the better angels of lust.

Edoggers

Edoggers is more freewheeling, a little raggedy next to the fairly slick AdultFriendFinder. The name comes from "dogger," which is British slang for voyeur, from the real-life practice of exhibitionists having sex in public, say a park, for voyeurs to watch. If the bobbies come round to break it up, everyone knows to say, "I was just out walking my dog, Officer," hence doggers. (How the exhibitionists get away with this is less clear: "You see, sir, I was bending down to scoop Rex's business when, it's the damnedest thing, my pants flew off and suddenly I was astride this naked person!")

Profiles feature pictures and a short list of particulars. Then comes the *American Idol* script-flip: Profile Statistics, where the pictures are graded. You see how many times a member has been viewed and voted on and his or her score. Five hollow stars sit beneath every picture, filled in to reflect average reviews of the pictures.

Submitting to this grading system makes the Edoggers seem timid and approval-seeking, lacking the boldness I like in a pervert. Before I saw the site, I imagined the subtext of the nude photos as "Let's get it on!" but the ranking system mews pathetically, "Am I pretty enough? Will you give me a good grade?" At least people are nice; most pictures sit atop at least four filled stars. I joined Edoggers to look around, but didn't post any pictures. I've gotten one message in two years, an invitation to play from "Lisa," whose picture indicates she is cleavage in a bustier.

PICTURES OF LIZ

The pictures, which dominate Edogger profiles, are a mix of full-body nudes or portraits in fetish gear, arty shots of body parts, and regular Match.com-type head shots. Liz has all but the last on her profile. Several of her art shots are lovely, her black silhouette against blue sky and white clouds; her in shadowy profile exhaling a pink puff of pot smoke. In the top left, "first" slot is Liz with huge red lipsticked mouth scowling, short black dress, sturdy stockinged legs crossed, and a whip across her lap. She's sitting between the stirrups of a gynecologist's chair. The two nudes are near the bottom: one displays her from mouth to waist, and to its right is a full-body naked picture of Liz taking a picture of herself taking a picture of herself, camera at her shoulder, full-hipped, crotch unshaved.

Just below her seven photos is a terse bulleted list of Age ("28"); Gender ("duh"); Location ("Baltimore and New York"); and Seeking, where Liz checked every box: Woman, Man, Man & Woman, Woman & Woman, Man & Man, Group, Transsexual, Transvestite. No favorite books or movies, no little essays. That's it for self-expression, so Liz made an admirable land grab by listing every sexual configuration there's a box for. (She says the only category above she hasn't had sex with is Transvestite.) Under Profile Statistics, we learn Liz has been viewed 5,054 times and voted on 129. She was scored an average of 4.41 out of 5, and the profile was recently changed.

I found Liz through a Friendster and saw her profiles before we met. When I remark on the rating system in Edoggers at our lunch interview, she rolls her eyes. It's easy to get her indignant. "I got this message from a total loser who wanted to talk about his great job and how long he could last in bed," she rages. "He said, 'You can tell that I like you from how good a rating I gave you,' and I'm like, 'Fuck you, I'm supposed to be honored that you gave me a five? Or a four?' I try not to focus so much on the ratings now, I look at who added me as friends and if I think they're attractive, I'll say, 'You're attractive, do you want to get together?' "

REWRITING THE RULES

Liz also takes the upper hand with the text of her Edoggers profile:

> i am looking for steamy sex, and to all the male out there . . . (because only men do this, women are way cooler about it): i am not interested in hearing about your job, and how successful or not you are. PLEASE PLEASE PLEASE Dont fucking tell me about your stupid job, it turns me off like nothing else.

Almost all her ads forbid men to brag about their work. Chapter 1's Lila, who is half Japanese, also complained about men puffing up their money-and-status feathers around her.

For our lunch, which stretched to almost four hours, Liz came to Manhattan, where she stays about a third of the time. Home base is Baltimore, where she produces left-wing radio news stories, plays piano with some avant-garde musicians, and does "social justice stuff " like running a community center. She's prettier, thinner, and younger-looking in person than her pictures, more girlish, with long black hair she flirts through. Any Transvestite, Man & Man, Woman, etc., arriving for a date would be pleased at what s/t/he/y saw.

Liz earns the "X yet X's opposite" profile cliché as fully as anyone I've met. Easy but impossible, utopian but fascist, every man's dream and a capricious nightmare, Liz is in some ways as all-encompassing as the rest of us claim to be. (In other ways, her online life has stayed remarkably constricted over the eleven to thirteen years.) She's shy and deferential most of the time, but she'll suddenly start denouncing and dismissing, waggling her head like Rosie Perez. She's smart but tilts her statements up at the end into questions? Which undercuts their, like, impact? Her carelessness in writing corresponds to a tangent-darting spaciness in person. At one point during lunch, she apologizes, "I'm having trouble focusing because I'm a little. . . ." After a long pause, I suggest, "Stoned?" She laughs. "Well, that too, but I was thinking of this emotional thing that happened this morning."

Stoned, scattered, and self-serving, yes, but Liz self-examines like a good ecstatic should. It's not always easy to lay an intellectual basis for hedonism, and she has intriguing theories about how online hook-ups become her. "I could go anywhere in Hong Kong, jump on the subway when I was eight and go meet my father for lunch in the city. Being in Houston isolated me and changed my understanding of freedom? and power? and my ability to navigate them? I started online chatting in high school."

There was plenty to restrict her freedom and power in her doubly pious home. What Liz found online was "a situation that was familiar but I was in another point. I had the control. My parents controlled me, I controlled the online situation. My desire to become very flat and open drove me, that's what I longed for. By flat I mean nonhierarchical, more equal terms."

She gravitated to the twenties and thirties AOL chatrooms because "Seventeen-year-olds are mean. Adults are civil to each other even if they don't like each other. I tried to be an aggressive personality online, with a more confident, assured voice and tone. It was leveling. Because they cannot judge you for what they don't know. When I say something, it's given equal consideration. In real life, in school, you're just a learner, your opinions don't count." She promoted herself up the ladder from Chinese high school girl in the chatrooms.

More specifically, a Chinese girl who's 5'8" and was (or

considered herself) overweight. "My parents made me feel too big, too tall, too fat, and that nobody was going to love me for myself. I put myself out there to say, 'OK, what do you think?' " She began with just flirting, then had a cybersex session that bored her. She didn't intend to meet anyone. But one night in the summer she was seventeen, she met a twenty-four-year-old guy in a chatroom and they switched to e-mail. She told him she was twenty. He drove over at three a.m. while her parents slept and took her to his house, where they had sex.

Liz recounts, "Afterwards, I asked him, 'Well, what are we?' and he said 'We're lovers.' I said, 'Are you my boyfriend? Are you going to come back and want to hear my emotional problems?' These things were very attached in my head. He drove me home right after sex and never contacted me again. I may have had initial rejection feelings because it's a trained response, but I don't remember being upset. I never told anyone about it until now."

Once she'd diagnosed the "trained response," she always kept that realm a little remote. Sex and the computer and "casual" have stayed linked. The distance and contextlessness that dismay many of us are Liz's favorite aspect of online dating. She socializes IRL with various groups of musicians, activists, radio people, and do-gooders who sound awfully fun, but she's more excited by meeting someone completely separate from those worlds. She says it's "magic" to connect with a stranger's body.

PLUMBING THE UGLINESS

Liz also uses online dating to study what's hidden beneath sex, luring a cross-section of horny males with different profiles. In college, she found Matchmaker.com and scanned in a photo for the first time. "This would be 1998, 1999. I liked making the profile, it made me think about me as opposed to having to present myself; it was almost like an exercise. I never told anyone. I think there was a sense of shame that I couldn't meet someone in person."

After these typical responses, this pretty college girl did a strange thing. She set up a fake ad with someone else's picture. "I had two Matchmaker ads, one subdued that was the actual me. The other was sizzling, I was looking for Play and I put a picture of another woman on there who's not me. She was wearing a bathing suit, she was hot, she was also Asian. That ad said, 'I just want sex.'"

Liz's strange role-play was more dark-side exploration than free-love romp. "It gave me a look at all the sexual ugliness of men. I wanted to know what happened if I put up a hot woman who says 'I just want sex.' I never met anyone through this sexy, crazy, hot ad." But why is men's sex-wanting ugly? What about her sex-wanting? What about the connecting ocean? Liz explains, "because I'm assuming that they don't want to know me. The responses to the subdued ad were very different, men were much more civilized; and the others were much more raw."

She says forlornly of the fake profile, "I remember thinking the hot play ad is so much more fun than the real me." She's been riffing on the fake ad ever since, moving her e- and meat-selves closer to that hot girl. Soon after our interview, she e-mailed me a Craigslist ad she'd just posted.

who's around tonight

so, i am in the mood for sex with someone who is comfortable with his or her body. who has sex regularly, so i am not the first women in awhile. because sex otherwise is usually pretty fucking lame.

no need to impressive me with your job or anything yucky, just tell me about u. please send more than one pic if its a pic thats hard to tell what you look like. sexy pics are great.

no pics no reply, dont even BOTHER to check if i am real. i am over that. have a sense of adventure.

The last bit confuses me: Is she "over" being real? Is she after a fuck so pure that it doesn't even involve human beings? She explains in an e-mail:

i get A TON of emails saying "ahum, i know you asked for a pic, but i dont know if you are for real. email me back then i will email you my pic" now meanwhile my ad explicit say "i wont read emails without a picture attached." These people are not realizing the truth to the number game, which is in my favor, as someone who also happens to like to have sex with heterosexual male.

    as you know, there seems to be more men out hunting for sex than girls. well at least explicitly. so as a women i can choose from about 30 emails. while if a hetero-male put out the same post, he would prolly get NOTHING. :)

Liz says her insistence that men leave their money out of this is not based on any rancid sugar-daddy experience. She waves her fist and scolds. "If you go online you play on equal terms, not like [she adopts a whiny girly-girl voice] 'I want a dinner.' Fuck that dinner, girl! You can pay for your own dinner. You work hard. Nobody needs to take care of you! Maybe I'm reconstructing the heterosexual dynamic so I'm the one in control, the man." It's not a full role-swap, however: she insists on going dutch, not on picking up the whole bill.

FLAT, BUT ABOVE

Liz doesn't just make herself the man; she also makes the guy her bitch. "My Craigslist ads usually say, 'This is the role you're going to play if you want to play with me,'" she says. Liz has dabbled in BD/SM as, not surprisingly, a dominant—for fun, not money. On Nerve.com, Liz relaxes the role requirements a bit. Her ad is still way more sexual and aggressive than most Nerve ads, and she's checked everything except Serious Relationship

(Dating, Play, Friendship). But compared with her "shut-up-and-put-out" ads on the other sites, Liz dots her i's with hearts on Nerve, simply by listing a few interests outside of bed. (She's twenty-eight on Edoggers and thirty on Nerve.)

Liz studied music in college and still plays, but connecting with her on that level is a minefield. Someone responding to a composer she mentioned in her Nerve profile "doesn't tell you anything, because people will just Google or Amazon.com your reference and pretend they've heard of it! Like if someone says, 'Oh, Shostakovich, oh, I like his fifth symphony that he wrote in Leningrad,' I'm like, shut up, motherfucker, you don't even know, first of all if you know I'm a pianist, you would talk about a piano piece he wrote. Don't bullshit me about music, it's too important; it's like talking about my mother."

The Shostakovich Google was a new move to me: Googling your date, sure, but her interests? It seems pathetic in the same way Herb Vest looking up what color jacket his target demographic will respond to is pathetic. So much work to not be yourself! To Google Shostakovich rather than ask a question to start a conversation seems not just unnecessary but a mistake. People like talking about their passions.

GRASPING AT DRAWERS

Liz met Rafe on AdultFriendFinder. He got a second date because he said something smart about music and was cute and good in bed. They started out promisingly "flat" and "open," but after a few months, Liz became the dreaded cling-on. "I would leave clothes in his space, I have two drawers in his dresser now," she confesses at lunch. "I tried to mark my territory, and that's so not me! That's not who I want to be." Online she's the heartless hunter, but too long with one man IRL and she gets all girly and needy. "I want to be more open, that's what I think it means to love him, to not have control, to let him have space. He will love me and ask me to leave my stuff if he wants me to." To control her need to control, she jumped back in the Internet-sex ocean to spread and "flatten" her desire. Rafe wanted monogamy, she says, but had agreed to an open relationship.

Liz finally tells me what upset her right before our lunch: she found out that morning that Rafe had slept with another woman. She's infuriated that jealousy has roughed up her "flat" equanimity. "I hate when things get entangled, complicated, take too much processing. I want to love him like I love my friends, with no possessing." Liz and Rafe split soon after our lunch and she e-mailed me her postmortem two months after that. "He is just actually very much an exclusive kind of guy, but he was trying to keep it open because he knows that it would be the only way to be with me, since i am polyamorous. there are other things too but i feel that it was the biggest difference which we cant really work out. its like dating someone who breathes another type of air than you do."

Relationships are suffocating and autonomy is lonely— what's a girl to do? Liz's answer is to keep moving. With her head waggling and her index finger back-and-forthing like a windshield wiper, she insists,

> I do not mind life happening to me and I will change accordingly. I work in this hip-hop bar on the weekends. I don't believe in a hip-hop Top 40 scene, but I put on a short skirt to fit into this role. I like to put on a fake accent in the airport sometimes. I'm conscious of all these parts of me and I can be any of the things I am any of the time. I don't want to have kids now, for example, but I know that could change. It doesn't mean I'm going through a phase, it means anything is possible.

Online dating is perfect for those who don't want to limit themselves by choosing—endless possibility is always right there in your computer.

Liz's description of her online evolution echoes that of forty-two-year-old Michele of the multiple Web sites and pseudonyms. I flash on Liz happier, saner, easier, in thirty or eleven or thirteen years.

Being online, you can become this other character. That's wearing off for me. I was trying to be someone who I think I'm more of now. I'm creating my identity; I'm filling it in. If I hadn't done that, I'd probably be working as a programmer or a lawyer like my parents wanted. I wouldn't have gone to music school. There was no place for me to go, there was never anyone asking, "What do you want?" I had to figure out another way to be to get to a place I like.

She calls that place "Nonattachment. But at the same time this willingness to connect."

Horrified by her own possessiveness with Rafe, Liz went back to the Internet for more sex partners, but she can't escape the casual sex conundrum: if it's bad sex, the gamble didn't pay off. And if it's good, you want more. You want more of the good sex, you want more of the person, you want to be more to him or her, you want the two of you to be more than users of each other's bodies. You may want a drawer or two.

The Internet has helped Liz rewrite her work life from business to art, but it's not served her romantic life especially well. As she seems to have figured out back in college, just-sex ads tend to draw men who don't want to know her. Yet she's stayed in that arena for eleven (or thirteen) years, trying to become "flat." While Lila, Michele, Hans, and others have made themselves more online, Liz uses the Internet to be less for more people—as if enough strangers rolling over and under her can squeeze out all her possessiveness and need.

CHAPTER 13

Clive: Girly Pix and Live Nude Women

Like many a freelancer, Clive had his erotic life rewired by the Internet. He spends the day at home e-mailing, researching, writing, blogging, and reading blogs. For the last few years, he's also been cruising, for hours a day, Nerve, Match, Friendster, Yahoo.com, and Rightstuffdating.com, a site for Ivy League graduates. But the background to everything else is always Internet porn. If the computer's on, at least one porn window is open.

Clive first discovered I-porn in the mid-1990s and has been consuming more and more ever since. He was caught downloading it at two different office jobs and still didn't stop. When he first mentioned this most glamorous vice—everyone on Nerve especially brags about how porn-positive and insatiable they are—it was with blasé wit. As we went deeper into the day-to-day reality of his compulsion, his bravado slid into mordant despair.

For as long as five or six hours at a stretch, Clive will switch back and forth like a DJ between the romantic and sexual sites. He first described this montage in an e-mail several years ago:

I've got five pages of recently updated 29- to 39-year-old women within five miles of my zip code loading up on one browser, and the latest scans and clips of shaved and silicone-enhanced blondes doing ungodly things to inhumanly large cocks on the other. Back and forth I go. . . . Both activities provide endless numbers of possible mates. Both have as much to do with fantasy as reality. Both online dating and Internet porn are not nearly like the real thing, but close enough if you've got nothing better to do and are unshaven in your PJs. Both are free, to a point, but can get expensive fast. Both can also take huge chunks of time out of your life.

Clive and I are old friends who've mostly lived in different cities. I didn't know the extent of his image consumption until I interviewed him for this book. I was surprised because he's handsome and flirtatious, has many women friends, and dates a lot—nothing like the misogynist mouth-breather I've imagined (unfairly, no doubt) as the ur-porn addict. Soon after we met, he moved to Denver to join Julie, a college girlfriend he'd reunited with; he called her the love of his life. Their relationship fell apart, for reasons I never understood, and soon thereafter, he started e-dating. We've been swapping profile links, e-mails from prospective suitors, and flame war stories ever since.

Clive's forty-one and a little bit Nerve, a little bit Match .com—a health care writer and consultant, smart, fashion-conscious, not artsy. (His Nerve profile says, "I don't like museums but don't mind if you do.") He loved the initial rush of possibility and the self-exploration of profile making. He also found online dating softened the real world, which he describes in the addict's parlance of craving-relief, anxiety-comfort. "It takes the edge off of feeling like you're the last single person you know; all of a sudden, there are pages of them in front of you, and walking down the street you start to think that everyone might be single rather than coupled up."

From that typical first yippee at the abundance and the access, he soured rather quickly, after several months, forty to fifty people contacted, and about ten dates. Very early on, he complained about "the lack of momentum, humanity, or context. Meeting someone for the first time from an online service is a double blind date. There's no friend in common to talk about, no context or flow, no surrounding dinner party conversation."

Clive's first online date was in 2002.

I found her profile on Nerve and liked the combination of sass and sincerity. We both turned out to be writers and like obscure foods. And when the time came for the next thing, she wisely suggested we meet for a drink at a dive in her neighborhood instead of more e-flirting. She looked good and was fun to talk to. I didn't mess things up in any obvious way. A week or so later, we went out for a second drink, which also seemed to go pretty well.

But in the end there was no momentum. No work or social context, no chance meeting at the coffee shop two days later. And so we moved into friendship mode, talking about work things and seeing each other once in a while in group settings. That's fine. I'm glad to have her as a friend and I'm not saying we were star-crossed lovers kept apart only by the Internet. But at the same time I felt like even if we did have a connection, there was really nothing to carry us forward. I told her later I thought we might have liked each other better if we'd met at a party, and she agreed (though of course she could have been being polite).

"She looked good . . . I didn't mess up" sounds like he may have emotionally disengaged to get through the audition, only to look back and realize (or decide), "Hey, I liked her." And loneliness and lust are usually enough to push attracted, compatible strangers into each other's lives: why would he need more context or momentum than "I like you and we both live here"? Clive seems weirdly passive and mistrustful of his instincts—but then again those instincts have rooted him to his computer chair for the last ten years.

Whatever the reasons, he kept being disappointed online. "The feeling of freshness from meeting someone new lasts just a minute before you want to know how she might fit in your life." Clive's an extreme case, but this impatience and restlessness characterize profile surfing in general. So many profiles— surely you'll find that effortless fit if you just keep looking.

ADDICTION

Almost every online dater I talked to described feeling "addicted" and "burned out" at some point as well as "exhilarated" and "empowered." Even nonobsessives constantly check their e-mail and troll the sites, and set up more dates than they could possibly focus on. Some keep their heads and manage to stop shopping when they find the, or a, match. Others find it harder to stop. Clive says disparagingly, "Trying as many people as you can, casting a wider net, that's how men rationalize getting turned down or rejected a lot. The more times you pull the lever the better your chances." A girlfriend of mine who's a heavy e-dater also has referred to "pulling the lever over and over like some burnt-out shell in Vegas." Both she and Clive soothe romantic disappointment by setting up more dates right away.

Both worry that their brains could get stuck in hunt mode. "What if you miss your perfect match just because you can't stop?" Clive wonders. He also thinks the frantic e-dating may be too rickety a foundation. "How the relationship starts is important somehow to its health and success," says Clive. "Relationships need a clean path. The temptation is too great to go on too many dates. When I'm trolling online I'm not focusing on one person. There's the cycle of getting excited to meet someone, pondering it, and you don't have time to reset before the next date." I have the same need for more space between people, both to reset and to imbue our date with some specialness.

Online dating has worked for Clive: he's met several women whom he's dated for a few months. But it drugs him in depressingly familiar ways. He e-mailed,

My online dating was hard to regulate or sequence—the faucet was either full on or full off—and i basically turned off during my day to day real world life over time. little by little, it was like why bother to try and make eye contact with the hottie in the coffee shop if you don't even know if she's single or straight and there are a hundred definitely straight, definitely single online profiles to look at online.

I felt less on when I was online dating when I was out in the world. The safety and access of online dating reduced my curiosity and openness to the world when I was out on the street. that was the sick part i really didn't like—when online dating starts to mess with your head like porn does and the virtual becomes more important or more appealing than the real.

The flipping back and forth between the bachelorettes on Match et al. and the "hot dirty sluts" is bound to affect his view of the former. (I'd be more convinced that porn was totally benign and groovy if its teasers weren't so universally hostile. Wouldn't "pretty young naked people having sex" convey the content just fine?) Clive isn't sexist or objectifying when he talks (to me) about the women he's e-mailing: instead he tars online dating itself with the porn brush. He calls both "dehumanizing, more about quantity than quality."

The comparison only works with unsuccessful online dating. If it works, it's like shopping—you find what you want and then you get to stop. Internet porn, meanwhile, is meant to keep you clicking. The craving as Clive describes it is bottomless, as with cocaine or potato chips or slot machines, designed not to satisfy, but to stimulate more craving. Porn isolates consumers who will, if they develop a habit like Clives's, keep clicking and clicking to fill the holes that the habit's drilled into their psyches. "Porn along with masturbation has separated sexual release from being with someone," Clive writes. "People like me don't need a partner, and sometimes prefer not having one. We've got a whole different thing going on that, at times at least, seems like a viable surrogate for the real thing." Clive's constant pursuit of more fantasy fodder may keep him from alighting for very long on any of the real women behind the dating profiles.

He tries to keep the two online worlds apart by breaking the "rule" of limiting first F2F dates to a coffee or beer. For a first date, he proposes an activity—"exploring a neighborhood, Scrabble, playing bocce or horseshoes in the park." It's a great idea: everyone could stand to inject more real life into the airless chamber of the audition date. Clive *needs* the wholesome activity, though, to turn pictures into people.

He's talked to shrinks about it and even joined Sex Addicts Anonymous but concluded that "I couldn't imagine not having [porn] around. With the interent, porn has gone from a sexual release to a habit, a comfort like a pint of ice cream—different in form but just as unhealthy, and just as divorced from real need. i use porn when i'm stressed, or angry, or confused, or need to go to sleep, or to escape—much more frequently than i would if i just used it when i was horny. i'm surfing porn in between writing sentences here."

I've battled with an addiction or two, so I know the cycles of renunciation, backsliding, hollow satiety, self-hatred, and back to renunciation—cycles that come around reliably as winter. But though tobacco, for instance, was killing me more than streaming video could, and I hated myself for not stopping, none of my vices was woven so deep into my relations with the opposite sex. Online dating has blurred into Clive's porn addiction, messing up his What I Want.

Especially during the last ten years, porn has increasingly skewed my sense of women's bodies. In older *Playboys* the women were exceptionally fit or

whatever, but basically natural. It was idealized reality. These days, women in porn aren't just thin with big tits, they're thin with really big tits and no hair. There's no reality there. The fact that the women are now much younger than i am only makes the whole thing stranger, and makes it harder to think of women my own age—real women—as attractive. Women my age seem to have aged shockingly, suddenly, and I'm not sure why. Maybe it's because men fall apart sooner: you've had more time to get used to us being fat and bald.

TWO-WAY STREET

On the dating sites, the bachelorettes look at him too, and this is a huge difference from porn. It appeases Clive's sense of fairness. Let his attributes and presentation be judged for a change: let him walk a mile in another human's fuck-me stilettos. He says that posting his pictures and profiles felt empathic after years of porn-gazing.

For all the objectifying he does, Clive's feminine side is quite developed. He gossips and analyzes and self-deprecates with such flow you forget you're talking to a man. He studies social groups warily and tactically, attuned to who's in or out, up or down, in a way I associate with teen-girl cliques. He carefully parses testimonials on Friendster. His Nerve ad ends with a feminine mix of self-promotion and insecurity: "i've got great eyelashes and an amazing apartment. i'm a good listener, a decent cook, and a great (or at least not horrible) kisser."

He's vain about his looks and tweaks his pictures and his age on his profiles. He frets about the fifty or so pounds he's gained in the last ten years, which his 6'4" frame accommodates pretty well. He was a head-turner then; he's still handsome in a bulkier way. Clive's male and female sides meet in his twin addictions to sex and food, which work together to keep him even more isolated at the computer as he expands physically.

Sometimes, Clive sounds like the fortyish women I interviewed who found themselves and their beloveds online. He's using online dating to ask for what he wants, which is also a declaration of self-acceptance. Like his middle-aged sisters, he's now "more aware of my preferences and more likely to say them. i'm a complicated, sensitive boy. i need time alone. i like to talk about work. i tend to stay up late. i had those preferences before, and just hid them until i couldn't. so i'm not sure it's so much that i've changed but that i'm more clear about who i am. but maybe that makes me less flexible." He says he's trying to find someone "solid and reliable" and to resist what he's been drawn to in the past, someone "sparkly."

This connects with Who I Am too. Clive fears that he's too passive, too seductive, and too much of a pleaser, and he's trying to be more discriminating in his online dating. "There's a difference between being picked and picking and too often I let someone pick me. Dating and flirting with more than one person at a time is inherently compromising, it turns the flirty stuff on high and the reality/sincerity goes lower." He also hasn't been happy dating women in their twenties. "It's too unbalanced, I know too much more." So he's trying to use online dating to reprogram himself to more "appropriate" desires. He raised his desired age range to extend a little above his own, on my advice. He'll send me profiles, asking, "what do you think?" and "pretty good for forty-three, right?"

He's smart and therapized and tech-savvy enough to succeed like his women peers, but how are Denver's thirty- to forty-three-year-olds gonna compete with all the siliconed genies just waiting to be summoned from his computer? Clive knows the Internet has distorted What He Wants, but he can't look away; there's too much happening. He e-mails me in early 2006 about the state of the art. "There's always more porn, and there are always more profiles—younger, older, in another town, in the town you went to college at. Then there are the sites that combine porn and profiles—no, not AdultFriendFinder but MySpace."

MySpace

I'd joined MySpace.com recently too, just before the wave of news stories about pedophiles infesting it. By 2006, the social networking site was suddenly sixty million members strong and a vital cog in the star-maker machinery, as useful as radio or TV for promoting bands. For example, Bright Eyes, the *nom de song* of indie rock dreamboat Conor Oberst, had 32,335 friends when I checked, many of whom post MP3s of their own sensitive songs. Record sellers have always promoted their artists as potential boyfriends (Beatles' wives were kept secret), but MySpace takes the illusion further than ever before, by folding the stars into the kids' e-club.

You must be over fourteen to post a page on MySpace, but younger kids sneak on. I would have loved this technology in junior high. Teenagers collage glittery graphics, camera-phone pictures, pop songs, and the same cretinous bons mots that we used to broadcast via black T-shirts you buy on the boardwalk. One sixteen-year-old girl's page greets visitors with a garish cartoon of a naked girl straddling a boy in big jeans and a jersey, with pink cursive lecturing that "Life is like a dick. If it's hard, fuck it." The testimonials from friends and the mail read like notes passed in class or yearbook signings, but they're visible to—and part of—the adult world. My newest MySpace message, for example, is from eighteen-year-old Kevin: "Your very sexy and u can hit me up if you want." I guess this no longer means borrowing money.

According to the cautionary news stories, the pedophiles, of which I am not one, read *Seventeen* magazine and watch MTV to find out what the kids like. Then they disguise themselves and speak the kids' language to seduce them online. Just like the record company execs cruising for sales hooks and the next big teen thing. Everybody's preying on the same herd of lambs, who of course love the attention.

Clive's not a pedophile either, but barely legal girls do pull him off his path to RL love. "I'll start out looking for someone my age and in my neighborhood and end up looking at coeds in san diego with gaudy personalized backgrounds and stupid rap playing. And on all these new sites, there are amateur nude pictures shot by boyfriends or the girls themselves that then become porn for the rest of us and blur the line between surfing for porn and for a date. They get closer and closer." And Clive gets further and further from the possibility that a woman will ever leap off the screen into his home.

HOW DO YOU GET TO CARNEGIE HALL?

Clive has never posted a just-sex ad. "I'm more into clothes-on couch-wrestling than full-on sex for a one-night thing," he says, which is much likelier to happen some drunken night out. (Though it certainly could be arranged, down to the exact wrestling outfits, on Craigslist.) Clive worries that casual sex takes him from his long-term mating goals—not as much as porn does, but some. "My take on the Miss Right / Miss Right Now thing is that right now is fun and tempting but doesn't get you anywhere closer to right. doing the right now thing is like playing gigs at the corner bar and telling yourself you're practicing for carnegie hall. the skills are different, maybe even antithetical. the one is not going to get you to the other, and theoretically could distract you from where you're trying to go. sounds prudish, and i haven't followed it, but that's my take."

I've pondered this one for years but never for too many months in a row. I like the symphony *and* bar bands. A one-night stand almost always puts a spring in my step, but sometimes it does intensify the longing for a partner enough that I wonder if it's worth that short-term bounce. My best shrink ever suggested I was devaluing myself with adventuring and to wait for a deeper connection. I diagnosed that advice as prefeminist and bourgeois—"Would you tell a male client that?" I demanded. But around that time my friend Dana, who'd stopped having sex for a year, met the love of her life. I told a fellow slut I was considering Dana's tactic and she accused me of "magical thinking." She added cruelly, "Do you think you cause rain by not bringing your umbrella?"

Single people who are sexually active all ponder this bar band–Carnegie Hall dilemma at some point, and online dating does bring it into sharper relief by signaling clearly which it's gonna be. My friend Jim—forty, gay, wonderful—is still waiting for a relationship that lasts more than a few months. He advocates the sex sacrifice—like Clive and me, in the abstract—for slightly different reasons. He e-mails,

I don't think casual sex is bad in and of itself. It's like junk food. You keep eating it and it makes you feel full temporarily, but it isn't fulfilling, or enriching. Eventually the rush is gone and you feel empty all over again.

One-night stands, or even repeat encounters with a fuck buddy, can give me the temporary sensation of intimacy, and when I'm able to string enough of them together in a row, the periods of profound loneliness become shorter. Thus lowering my motivation to do the hard work of seeking out what I truly desire: a stable long-term relationship. It makes me feel just lovable or desirable enough to put off the search for another day; to not work too hard to fix the faults that might be impeding me (in my case my weight); to not put all of my energy into finding the thing I supposedly want more than anything.

He also doesn't put his energy into going where the boys are; he doesn't drink or like bars. Because of the Internet, Jim can arrange enough sexual encounters to maintain his lovableness minimums.

Christopher, the Chelsea boyfriend seeker who's found only hook-ups, looked skeptical when I asked if holding out for sex with a real boyfriend might help him get his man. "I don't know," he says, swirling his wine. "I guess [promiscuity] might make you jaded. At the same time, being this insane celibate

person on a mission could be harder than being a crazy slut."
His boyfriend hunting approximates mine and most of my single friends'. As Christopher puts it, "I'm looking for something serious but if you're a hot little hottie, I'm willing to go where that takes us."

He says there's no gay equivalent of women's wait-a-date-or-three strategy to get a man to stick around. "There's no stigma about being a ho. You're just one guy in New York, stigma can't stick to you; I never run into people I've slept with. There is no stigma unless a guy's some filthy disease-hole or something. It's a mark of respect. Think of straight guys, they're all bragging about their conquests, what makes you think gay guys are different? I'll be telling my stories and my friends will be laughing and high-fiving me."

He doesn't think men derail love by sleeping together too early. "If I'm liking this guy and am attracted to him, I am so going to bed with him. . . . I don't fear the transformation from lay into like life would be impossible. I could go from fooling around with the guy to integrating him into the whole scheme," he says. He admits this is theoretical; it has never happened or come close online. In advertising for online dates, now means now.

CHAPTER 14

Beth and Vivian: Pigs in Love

Once you've posted for sex online, can you make room for more? Where do you find the momentum to break out of that box? Heterosexuals in particular seem to have trouble breaching the boundaries between dirty, nasty sex with a hot slut and respectful, friendly courtship. It's even harder online, after you've written out the dirty words and the intent to use. Not surprisingly, the online couple I found that moved most smoothly from lust to love did so outside the fences of heterosexuality.

ALIENS ON PLANETOUT

Beth and Vivian both felt like aliens among the earnest, PC, low-libido, second-date-proposing dyke population of the San Francisco Bay Area. They'd both been advertising on PlanetOut for a while when they met, their ads growing steadily more sexual. Or as they put it, more true. As Beth explains in her dusky growl of a voice, "Vivian and I connected on the level that we're both pigs. I was attracted to her ad because it was really irreverent and cocky. It said, 'If you think other women don't talk to you because you're too beautiful, then I'm your girl.' And 'I like to objectify women' and 'I like to do this and that and this to women.' I read it and was like, 'Yes.' "

Beth is lanky, confident, stacked, skeptical. She makes everything sound a little dirty, with that conspiratorial machismo that's so much more attractive in a woman. ("Hot" isn't even that annoying when she and Vivian overuse it.) She says out of the side of her mouth, "I always wanted to be reincarnated as a gay man. I can go to the park, get a blow job, and be done, right? With the Internet, I was able to date more like a gay man and get laid and not get emotionally involved and it was fun." Vivian talks just as much trash as Beth and just as affectionately. Their sex swagger is refreshingly separate from its usual drinking buddies: the inability/disinclination to couple or to parent; an addiction to conquests; misogyny.

Vivian is plump and pink-cheeked as a Renoir, with blue eyes and thick black hair—a butch often misclassified as femme because of her soft looks. Beth misclassifies her differently, declaring, "I've often had relationships with beautiful Jewish girls with curly hair with warm families," as she runs her fingers through Vivian's curls. Vivian leans her head back into Beth's stomach and says, "But I'm Italian, honey." Beth shrugs. "Same thing."

We're in Beth's Victorian rowhouse on an iffy edge of the gentrifying Mission neighborhood in San Francisco; Vivian lives across the Golden Gate Bridge in Marin County. Vivian and I start the interview in Beth's backyard while Beth settles her eight-year-old daughter Leah in front of a *Pee-wee's Playhouse* tape. Under a tree bearing softball-sized lemons, Vivian and I use California's sort-of-legal medical marijuana to treat our shared condition of thinking it'd be fun to get high. Over the course of the day, Vivian stays on top of all our oral needs, preparing drinks and snacks as well as the interview pipe.

Both women came onto PlanetOut as mothers of young

daughters. Both children were conceived with a gay friend's sperm in collaboration with a woman each had expected to be with forever. I figure this line of coincidences must be rare even in the Bay Area, but they don't make much of it. They gush instead about each other's lips and cleavage, wit, irreverence, and a sexual compatibility so unprecedented that Vivian just figured out at age thirty-eight that she's a top.

They like their relationship fun; there's enough serious in their lives. Leah was born brain-damaged and requires expensive care and close supervision. Though Leah's other mom is still involved, Beth has no support from parents or siblings. She's a public health researcher studying HIV-positive drug users; Vivian's a freelance graphic designer. Neither exactly drips with disposable income in this, one of the country's most expensive cities.

Vivian's for-life relationship broke up while she was still pregnant, and she moved in with her mother to have the baby. For four years afterward, she says, "It didn't occur to me to date. I was in love with my daughter. Then a friend of mine dragged me out to a couple of gay bars and I met someone who kind of woke me up sexually by jumping on me in the parking lot outside the bar. I was like, 'Wow, I'd forgotten how fun this was,' then, 'OK, I want to date now,' but I didn't know what to do."

She went onto PlanetOut in 1999, when it was still free. The site welcomes all queers but focuses on lesbians, while brother company Gay.com caters muscularly and shirtlessly to men. Gay.com has about three million members to PlanetOut's half a million. Over the three years Vivian used PlanetOut, she met about thirty women and had sex with about ten. Several of those she saw for months. Most of the dates were the standard bad ones: someone fifty pounds heavier than advertised, another who used someone else's picture, and someone "as dumb as a box of rocks. I thought English was her second language, and that was cool because I was on my Latina kick. But she was just illiterate."

Her two main complaints about the women she met, however, were clinginess and misrepresentation. "I started out looking for a girlfriend and then got so disgusted with how dishonest people were. When my ad said, 'single mom, looking for love of life,' a more lesbian kind of ad, what I ended up getting was people who painted their lives in ways that turned out not to be true." Beth chimes in, "The people on the site tended to take themselves so seriously, almost as if they're trying to write their biography. This is who I am and this is what's deep about me." Vivian interrupts excitedly, "Women describing how they want to be perceived, not how they are! Saying they had their shit together when they really didn't. I got jaded."

Vivian had an epiphany a year or so in. "I realized, 'Shit, I could just go for sex,' and that's when my ad started morphing. I took out 'hiking partner' and 'relationship' and 'daughter,' till I had just checked 'sex' and said I wanted to date someone beautiful, period." Seventy-year-old Abe was the only other interviewee who took Vivan's strong tack away from relationship toward sex with hot babes, and for similar reasons. Both Vivian and Abe complained that women misrepresented, and it made them both more callous. I've heard other online daters allude to that underlying threat: if you lie, I feel more free to use you.

Not that Vivian—or Beth—ever vengeance-fucked or feigned serious intent. They were transparent and honest about their pigginess, and paid for it with very low ad responses. Vivian e-mails, "It was very fun for me to 'play the field,' which just is not done in the Lesbian community. You cannot really pick up a girl in a bar. At least I was never able to." Beth says, "You know that joke about a second date for lesbians is renting a U-Haul? Well, it's true!"

To be a dyke who plays the field is to hurt and disappoint. (Slutty men hurt and disappoint straight women, but we're more braced for it.) Hurting/disappointing others tends to make nonsociopaths feel bad; feeling bad leads to lashing out at the one who prompted the guilt. Anyone who's ever been picked on, yelled at, and criticized for a few weeks or months by a lover preparing to dump her knows this less than adorable side of human nature. Beth and Vivian, obviously nice people, seem too angry at their cuddly sisters. Mocking the "typical lesbian ad," they sneer "soulmate" or "spiritual connection" with the same disdain they'd pronounce "child molester" or "Bush administration."

The mate-seeking ads stirred up more than guilt; they dragged both abandoned women back to serious relationshipville, site of carnage they were both fleeing. Online daters need to somehow lower the stakes to not get overwhelmed. Edoggers Trevor and Liz cut down risk by focusing on sex, not relationship. Twenty-seven-year-old Alice strives for lightness of ad. Beth and Vivian did both. They ran with the pigs.

HEALING HEARTBREAK AS A HO

Beth was with Leah's "other mom" for eleven years. For about a year after that breakup, Beth was miserable,

---

and then I started getting really horny, though I still had the broken heart. I was about thirty-eight and I was clear I wasn't ready for a commitment, didn't want to put my heart back on the line, but I wanted to have fun. There was a part of me that had been frustrated in those eleven years of monogamy. So I thought, "Now I can do whatever the hell I want."

PlanetOut was great for me. I really liked how easy it was to communicate that part of me that was looking for a good time. My ad said, "I want to date, I want to have sex, I want to have fun, I'm not interested in a commitment or in being monogamous." My headline was "L is for Libidinous."

Vivian asks, "And you got what, about four hits on that ad?" Vivian says she always dated people who answered her ad; Beth had more luck answering ads. Neither ever posted pictures. Between-relationship limbo agreed with Beth.

I was scared to fall in love again anyway, and I met all these women I wouldn't have met otherwise. Some were really fun and interesting, some were really hot. I'm a lefty progressive do-gooder and I dated a woman with a Porsche. It was fun to ride around in the Porsche! And it was fun to go out on a Saturday night and have a couple drinks and flirt and do that little dance of are we going to go home together or not. It was really liberating. . . . I had done all that in my twenties but it's much better when you're almost forty, you know who you are. I didn't take it to heart if someone wasn't into me, and I felt comfortable saying, "Look, you're a nice person but this isn't working for me." The Internet gave me a platform to put out there what I was looking for, made it OK to be this unusual thing of a lesbian not looking for a relationship.

She also managed to have a "just-sex" relationship with a woman they both call "the hottie" for a year and a half, including a nine-month overlap with Vivian.

Vivian also achieved impressive levels of fuck-buddyism. When she tells me she dated a couple before she met Beth, I assume she means a few women. But no, she means a couple: "I met Chloe online and dated her for a while and then she told me she had a girlfriend, Jen, but that Jen had given her permission because Jen was the only woman Chloe had ever been with and Jen wanted her to have more experience. Then I met Jen and slept with *her*, and we had this triangle going on. I slept with them both separately and then we had a couple three-ways.

Everybody knew everything; it was really fun, but then it disintegrated for them because Jen got jealous."

GET REAL

Beth and particularly Vivian insist they are the only two honest people in cyberspace. Vivian says, "I've gone back a few times and looked at mine and Beth's e-mails and we were both so honest . . . there wasn't one thing that either one of us said that wasn't a hundred percent true and that's what truly amazes me. Everything you read, it's us. Neither of us were putting on any airs." Beth loved Vivian's headline "So Normal, So Wild," which she felt encapsulated her own mix of fiscal/maternal responsibility and sexual friskiness. Each followed her typical online protocol: Beth liked writing women, while Vivian (the top!) preferred to be written.

They claim "real" a lot, but admit they're very different online and off. Vivian says PlanetOut "gave me an advantage, because I'm awkward on first meeting and more who I really am on e-mail." Beth, who's kind but straightforward and blunt, surprises me with,

---

It was liberating not to worry so much. When I'm talking with a person, I can see their reactions and like anyone, I want people to like me. I'm a woman, I've been trained to please others. Conversation is more about noticing and responding to cues. That happens in the Internet, the cueing, but it's more in blocks. I get this message from Vivian and I write this message back. I didn't feel any desire or need to be disingenuous. Take me or leave me.

Yet another woman who found online dating a respite from pleaserhood and the path to a new integrity.

But the odd thing about their claims to "real" is that the "hundred percent honest e-mails" were fiction! "One thing I learned from the hottie," says Beth,

---

was doing pornographic e-mail back and forth, flirting on e-mail, cybersex or whatever you call it. So when I saw Vivian's ad and she was so out there and sassy, I wrote back to her, "a hottie responds" and with very little preamble I started this story of us meeting in a café. We continued it all week in e-mails that might start out, "hey, how you doing, I'm busy at work," but then launch into the next installment. By the second or third e-mail, we're talking in the café and then "I grab your hand and pull it inside my shirt." We did this back and forth thing all week because she was on vacation out of town, and it just got steamier and steamier, and it was so much fun.

Vivian says, "She'd done this online sex thing before, I hadn't. I hadn't met anyone as sassy or slutty as her online. I was sitting at my computer with my mouth open. I bit, she put the hook out and I bit, it was very easy to respond to that." When asked if she masturbated while reading or writing, Vivian says, "I was in a hotel room in Hawaii with my mom and my kid, so no."

Beth says she didn't jill off either, despite the e-mails being mostly sex talk. "We gave broad sketches of our everyday lives, that I lived in San Francisco and she in Marin and we each of us had a kid. I don't think we even knew what kind of work each other did. There was never the small talk from when you first meet; we were interacting on this other plane. We described each other, she sent a picture, I didn't have one, so I told her I had long legs and a pleasing cleavage, and she claims that is true."

Their bravado faltered a little before the date, as it tends to when cybersex or phone sex has come first. "We were both really nervous," Beth says. "I was much bolder on the Internet. We seemed sexually compatible, but you don't know for sure." Vivian, who is not just the marijuana but also the TV connoisseuse of the pair, says, "I e-mailed her, 'You're not going to show up weighing 400 pounds carrying your own salami, are you?'" I ask Beth if she got the allusion to the old *SCTV* skit starring John Candy as Pavarotti. "No, but I still wanted to show up carrying a salami."

Vivian was more ready for a girlfriend, tired of dating and of spicing up Jen and Chloe's relationship. Beth says,

> For Vivian, our date was more of a trial thing. For me it was, hey, if she looks decent and seems like a nice person, I want to go for it. I was maybe not expecting but certainly hoping we would turn around and go home together.
>
> And then I saw her and thought, "Yum. Cute." She's got the kind of body I like, I'm crazy for curly hair, a little bit more butch than me, and I was like, "Yeah!" It was a little embarrassing after all the e-mails, but at that point I had done a lot of Internet dating and sexual flirtation, and I was self-conscious but not unbearably so. We scaled back and finally had that normal small-talk conversation about our lives and kids and our work.

Vivian, laughing, describes first-date Beth as "demure." The two Beths merged in the parking lot, she explains. "The person I was e-mailing with—I ran into her right outside the restaurant after dinner." Beth elaborates, "I slammed one on her. . . . I love initiating the first kiss, that was my favorite thing about dating. There's always all this nervousness and I love lighting that spark. The minute we walked out of the restaurant I jumped on her. I'd been dying to kiss her for ten days." She then, with some coaxing, got Vivian back to her place for sex.

Beth e-mails, "We didn't 'act out' the fantasy we'd created

over e-mail, but the dynamic and tenor of the sex was very much in keeping with our mutually created 'fiction.' Our story did express our true sexual natures, and we're lucky they're so complementary." It's impossible to separate out hindsight, but I've never heard anyone describe the integration of e-self and meatself as being so seamless.

Vivian's characterization of meeting the e-mail Beth when they kissed is an anomaly in online dating. Most shoppers measure the human being against the fantasy date in their heads: Vivian and Beth cocreated one they'd like—and then liked it. The Internet truth in this case was true, albeit retroactively. The steamy e-mails came true.

Vivian defers to Beth as she explains how she, Vivian, is a top. When Vivian says she prefers giving orgasms to receiving them, Beth sighs, "I have the best job in the world." Vivian continues, "She's amazed that I don't need to be 'done.' I can totally focus on her for hours, and then she'll feel guilty if she's tired and wants to go to sleep, but that's fine, it turns me on more to get her off. Even after all this time, that flabbergasts her." I ask if what makes it top behavior is controlling the orgasms.

Vivian says,

Top for me in that context means you're the instigator, the one doing the pleasuring. I'm like that with everyone, I'm the one who's all hands, all lips, all over you, and she just loves it. I didn't know that part of myself, but that was something I discovered when Beth and I met, that I'd been going out with the wrong girls all this time. I'd been going out with girls who were topping me, which was OK, I like being topped but it's not who I am only. My ex was a top and I was with her for six years, we were totally mismatched in the sack. She totally controlled that part of our relationship and I let her, I didn't know myself well enough, I didn't know what I wanted.

Beth and Vivian started sexually defining themselves in their first e-mails, Vivian in particular editing in the new sexual information women tend to absorb in their thirties.

At first their schedules of work and kids and Beth's graduate school allowed them to date only once a month or so. Vivian's triangle collapsed, and then Beth broke it off with the hottie, nine months after she met Vivian. Vivian says, "She would come home after being with hottie and I was having a hard time. I guess that's the woman part of us." After about nine months, they met each other's daughters. "Kids get attached to people, so once we got attached, we thought about the kids," Beth says. "It's a huge gap to separate out this central part of your life, your kid, from the rest of it. Once it's a serious committed relationship, of course they have to meet your kid. . . . We want that. We were both cautious, but we both want it."

Beth doesn't get mushy (as opposed to lusty-appreciative) till I've been there for hours. She says, "I didn't fall easily. But it gets to be more fun all the time. Our lifestyles are compatible, we have the same priorities, our kids come first. Vivian is a really smart, sensible, down-to-earth, wonderful, warm person and I think most of those things except maybe warm apply to me as well. We both just really clicked. We're different, but we're very compatible." Vivian says, "I feel like I've found the one. We're so compatible in so many ways I can't imagine anyone else even coming close."

So where are the "pigs"? Their term is misleading, but it's not a bad animal spirit for them. Beth and Vivian are like the tomboy cousins of San Francisco's tantric hippie goddesses in their patchouli and clit rings. Instead of "yoni-worshipping," they say "pig," but they are erotic idealists. Beth squints into the sunset and says, "It's hard to describe the feeling I get sometimes when I see an attractive woman . . . the pleasure, the lust, and the beauty in that moment. But I know Vivian understands because she feels the same thing . . . it's a bond between us."

Pigs, maybe, but not cads. Neither of them disparaged any sex partner in all our hours together; they parted amicably from their longtime fuck buddies; their domesticity is both comfy and sexually charged; and their relationship remains open. They haven't actually had sex with anyone else since nine months after they got together. But the door stays open, as Beth puts it, "to honor the pig part."

There's much swagger and pose in sexual self-descriptions online, including Beth's and Vivian's. But their PlanetOut profiles also had integrity. They ran a different sort of risk than straight women advertising their lust: neither Beth nor Vivian complained as Liz did that their dates "didn't want to know me." They just didn't get many responses. Their story is a powerful refutation to the twenty-first-century push by eHarmony, True, Match, et al., to appeal to as many "customers" as possible with a generically appealing ad. Love came to Beth and Vivian when they told the unpopular truth.

THE LIMITS OF WRITING

In some ways, sex is like any other personal aspect shared online—an opportunity for obfuscation or for growth. Online dating is a chance to write the sexual self you've aspired to safely and invisibly and a chance to find someone who shares your kink or fantasy and maybe bring it to RL fruition. The more specific the kink, the more sense it makes to introduce the script in writing. This is especially true of dominant-submissive relationships: "Tell me what's going to happen" is central to those encounters. And many transgendered people say online was the perfect place to try on the new gender before wearing it in public.

I suspect I speak for other nonkinky people here, but just in case, I'll say "I," not "we": I come to sex more in a spirit of exploration. I know what I like done to me, and, sure, I'm trying to communicate that, but at the same time I'm learning what he likes and getting more excited when I guess right. And right guesses lead to more pleasure giving, permission implicitly asked and granted, risk rewarded with more openness and more personalizing of the standard moves. That feedback loop builds feelings of trust and connection, which allows more communication, and two people find themselves creating something they couldn't have scripted because they didn't know this other person yet. Great sex feels both familiar and unique.

That loop, for me, can't start in writing. Much more than boyfriend criteria like wit and shared interests and intelligence, sexual compatibility can only be read in the flesh. Most primal is physical attraction—the one thing you cannot know online. Then the reading of glances, body language, talking and listening, eye contact, laughter, and the beginning of risk—flirting. It's not that I'm above premeditated casual sex: I've definitely gone out hoping for it and dressed for it and made it happen. But to begin in writing with "I'm horny, how about you?" such as on Craigslist, seems impossible because I won't know till I meet him. I can't imagine beginning a sexual encounter with an audition date. I need to feel more than "you'll do" to step into that space with someone.

Except for Beth and Vivian, the online sex adventurers I spoke with didn't shake me from my disinclination to use the Internet for hook-ups. Liz, Trevor, and Richard use the technology to hide, to not risk, and to not know the other person. They structure their F2F assignations like pornographic, virtual-reality sessions employing actual bodies.

PART SIX
THE ROMANCE WRITERS

Romance has a lot in common with sexual kinkiness. It too is a shortcut across individuality, a path of footprints to guide you across the treacherous terrain of intimacy. There's less need for negotiations when new couples can defer to "this is what the guy does" or "here's how the girl responds" or "this is what happens on the third date." Love stories are popular because nobody's sure they're doing it right, and we long for guidance.

Online dating seduces a lot of romantics who like to write. They make up their narratives as they go, same as the self-creators, but follow a more familiar script. That narrative may come from art, media, cultural norms; it springs less from Who I Am or What I Want than from Here's What Love's Supposed to Look Like. Like all writers, the romantics like control and assume their collaborators are on the same page, no matter how glaring the evidence to the contrary. The e-daters in this section built elaborate futures with their invisible partners. They wrote themselves as comrades building their own house and an ethical life; as slaves to life-changing, soul-melding sexual passion; as a damsel and her Renaissance Faire swain.

And then they met.

CHAPTER 15

Ellen: Straw-Bale Castles in the Air

Ellen is the best- and the worst-suited e-dater I interviewed. The pluses: She's geographically isolated and willing to relocate. She wants a life partner. She's fifty and feels beyond romantic folderol. She doesn't need cute. What matters to her can be accurately listed: interests, goals, and beliefs. She's a good writer. She tracked down the sites where her kindred spirits cluster, including Secularsingles.com.

On that site she met Douglas, a fellow atheist who cared about the same things Ellen did. The two shared eight months of daily e-mails and good-night phone calls in the dark before she finally flew from Vermont to Nevada to consummate their relationship. During those eight months, Douglas, fifty-six, divorced his third wife, with Ellen providing a little papers-signing pressure by withholding digital photographs of herself. Back in Vermont, a week after she returned, Ellen debriefed me on her trip to his bachelor pad in the desert.

Four years ago, Ellen bought her first home, in Barre, Vermont, after years of waiting for a man to set up house with. I picked her up for our interview there, and saw evidence of both her creative talent and her tendency not to finish. Her professional-looking photographs, some framed, some not, line one wall of a living room with just a couch. A table in an otherwise empty (dining?) room is full of nearly completed copper clocks she's made, and her huge metal sculptures sprout from her unmowed lawn. She met her last live-in boyfriend when she sold him a forklift three years earlier. Less than twenty-four hours after he moved out, she posted a profile on Secular singles.com, "for atheists, agnostics and other freethinkers."

I signed up on Secularsingles.com to check out Ellen's profile, and check in on my godless bachelors. There were four freethinking New York gentlemen thirty-nine to forty-five, and my favorite by far was "Christkiller," whose headline is "My penis is bigger than God's." What's not to like? Alas, he's a little *too* freethinking: he's "in an open marriage, as my wife and I are living in the 21st century." Intellectually that makes sense to me: lifelong monogamy seems far from an ideal system. But as much as I'd like to find my Benton, I don't think I could handle his and Michele's don't ask, don't tell policy, at least not in the first, trust-forming stages.

Ellen had realized that a true believer in no god was a nonnegotiable criterion before the forklift guy, during a short affair with Jake, whom she met five years ago on GreenSingles.com, for environmentalists. Her voice rises in anger as she describes the trouble with Jake. "His father was a minister of the Unitarian church, so Jake goes to church even though he's not a believer, for the com-*mu*-nity," she says, sneering the last word. "He will stand up and intone all this stuff he doesn't believe just to have someone to have coffee with! We had a huge fight about it." He never tried to make her go to church with him, but that's not Ellen's point. "I don't want a partner who's a hypocrite! You can do that if you want, but you can't be in my life."

One might think that being middle-aged, living in a town "with six bachelors," as Ellen puts it, and having zero tolerance for any spiritual squishiness would narrow the field enough. But Ellen's requirements are even more specific. "I'm only interested in men who are atheist, very liberal, and want to build a straw-bale house," she declares, my only interviewee to insist on something I'd never heard of. (It's an environmentally sustainable form of architecture popular in Vermont, apparently able to withstand both New England winters and wolves blowing it down.)

Because she knows what she wants and how rare it is, Ellen takes full advantage of the Web's dissolution of geographic limits, as do many older, rural people, especially those bound by particular beliefs. "When you live in a place like this and there aren't a lot of people to meet, casting the net worldwide is attractive. Why wouldn't you?" She adds a bit ruefully, "I don't doubt that there's some element of safety to online dating; I can travel without traveling. Plus it's not like having to bop into a bar and be appealing on that level."

Ellen isn't much of a preener, but Vermont tends to mistrust adornment anyway. For our outing to one of Barre's three bars, she wore no makeup and a big untucked flannel shirt over jeans and workboots. She fit right in. She has long graying hair, a pleasant round face, and an easy walk. She says she weighs 170 pounds, which to my eye makes her remarkably dense. She also looks younger than fifty, especially when she smiles, which isn't that often.

She says she's "unabashedly husband hunting," and the search can sound a little grim.

I'm not interested in dating. I don't do gregarious, er, gratuitous dating. I never have. I'm not interested in going out to have fun. I want a husband, I want a family, I want a partnership. . . . The person I want to be with wants that as much as I want it. Somewhere out there in that haystack, there has to be a male version of me. I know just from reading the personals there are serious types and nonserious types and I happen to be a serious one.

I ask Ellen if she worries that the straw-bale criterion might eliminate some otherwise decent bachelors. She answers, with one of the rare smiles, "Now how could a guy be compatible if he doesn't want a straw-bale house? That's a value system. I'm willing to debate straw bale versus, say, adobe, but alternative building has to be part of it." Like many middle-aged e-daters, she sees her evolving choosiness as coming into her own. She'd placed a personal ad in a magazine back in the late 1980s, and "I was getting responses from golf-playing Republicans. I thought, this is silly, why not say what I want. There's no better forum for doing that than online dating."

But Ellen's best argument for insisting on what she wants is Douglas. A smart, articulate, passionately godless lefty interested in sustainable architecture did indeed answer her ad. Not only did he share her worldview and values, as Ellen wrote in an account of the visit, he was "for eight months in e-mails and on the phone, the most calming, understanding, and supportive man I'd ever met" [sic].

When Ellen first put up her ad in December 2003, she used a five-year-old picture, partly because she weighed more than two hundred pounds at the time. Douglas first wrote her December 16—she knows because she printed and saved all one thousand pages of e-mails—and they first spoke on Christmas Day. Over the next eight months, he pressured her for more pictures, and she pressured him to finalize his divorce, with the pictures both bait and reward for legal steps taken. Meanwhile she joined a gym and dropped thirty pounds in anticipation of their meeting.

AFFAIR OF WORDS

Douglas started referring to Ellen as his girlfriend in the spring and though she didn't use the b-word, she did marvel at the growing connection and how alike they were. "I felt like we were eighty percent alike and only twenty percent different. The twenty percent was mostly cultural; I'm from an East Coast intellectual family, and he grew up in the South and in the West and only went to junior college, though he wished he'd gone to more. But there were many many more commonalities, including speech, turns of phrase. Sometimes it was like talking to myself."

They ended every day with a good-night phone call.

He kept begging me for pictures, saying "I'm a guy, I need the visual." I needed a digital camera anyway for my art—I'm trying to build up a portfolio—so I sent him some. He really liked this one of me and my dog and he put it up as a screen saver. He told me he was looking at my picture whenever we talked. I didn't look at his picture; I didn't want to build up some false expectation or relate his appearance to that experience on the phone. I didn't want to have fantasies about him.

She laughs. "Well, obviously, I was having fantasies, but I didn't want to get into the physical business, I didn't want to go there." There was no phone sex, but much emotional revelation.

Ellen has depression debilitating enough to be a full-time job: she lives on sixteen-thousand-dollar-a-year government disability payments. She refers frequently to "my doctor," a psychotherapist, and to childhood horrors that have shaped her brain and her life. Sharing these with Douglas was the first strong connector. During the holidays, Ellen says, she finally confronted the brother who molested her as a child and Douglas helped talk her through that. He continued to support her through more difficult visits with family members and then in July, the death of her dog. As she dug the grave in the woods, she talked to Douglas through her cell phone's headset and he cried along with her.

Ellen tends to diagnose everyone, or else she is, as she claims, "a magnet for mental illness." The forklift guy was "ADHD," the Unitarian minister's son was not just a hypocrite but a "hoarder, sort of like an anorexic about possessions." She dated one man with children, whose ex-wife "had Munchausen by proxy. My doctor and I joke I should get a PhD in psychology, I've already done the coursework."

It's harder to diagnose over e-mail and the phone, but she didn't have to guess with Douglas. He told her he was bipolar and that he'd tried to kill himself not long before, when his latest wife left. "He'd been hiding from himself and everyone else, but he was just coming back," Ellen explains. "He views mental illness as a character flaw, which is a big problem because that means he will never get treatment. His GP finally gave him this cocktail of drugs that helped a little, but he won't go to a shrink. He made me a promise before I left that he'd go to a shrink."

Call me crazy, but I'd worry more about bipolar disorder and a suicide attempt than, say, going to the Unitarian church or building with bricks. Ellen, however, relished the chance to sympathize and comfort. She had also tried to kill herself ten years earlier over a love affair gone wrong and knew the right things to say to Douglas. She even saw his struggles as a source of strength. "One of the biggest regrets of my life is that nobody has ever needed me," she says, "and if someone needed me, I think that would overcome my depression at that moment. It would give me a reason for being."

In a formulation that reminds me of Michele's toleration of an open relationship because of all Benton's other compatibilities, Ellen also reminds me impatiently of her wish list. "I was willing to be with someone bipolar, because I don't have a lot of options. If you find any over-fifty straw-bale-house-building atheist liberals, please send them my way!"

ALONE IN THE DESERT

In August, Douglas offered to fax Ellen his final divorce papers but she replied that she believed him and not to bother. The next day, as agreed, she booked a flight to Reno, using frequent flier miles she'd been saving for fourteen years. She originally suggested a three-day visit and Douglas talked her up to eight. They'd discussed the possibility of not being attracted to each other but Ellen said in that case she'd just take her Western trip on her own. She admits now that was unrealistic, that there was nothing casual about the trip. "Douglas and my doctor had become my entire support system. I didn't want him as a friend, I wanted him as a life partner."

No pressure or anything. I ask how she felt when she first laid eyes on him at the airport, and Ellen tells me instead about an earlier phone call where "he'd been so charming discussing all the ways we'd meet each other. I told my doctor I thought he might do something silly, we'd talked about holding up signs or pictures of each other."

Pressed to describe her impression, she mumbles, "I don't know, he was OK. He wasn't five-eleven, he was five-eight." (I've heard this and experienced it so many times, I've decided 5'8" *is* 5'11" in Internet-inches, an alternate scale like dog years.) Ellen continues, "He was OK. The four pictures he'd sent didn't look like each other and he didn't look like any of them. He was OK-looking enough. What do you want? I mean, come on, unless you're Robert Redford, there are only so many permutations of fifty-six."

Throughout our interview in the Barre bar, she returns wistfully to the golden age BN, Before Nevada. She wants to hang on to the Douglas of phone and e-mail. Ellen's account of the week is two-pronged: in addition to our taped chat in the bar is the sharp two-and-a-half-page wrap-up she wrote on the plane home, called "Dancing on the Edge of Reality." The title is drawn from a self-description of Douglas that she concludes she should have heeded. The essay opens:

No, it wasn't I doing the precarious tap dance. It was the guy I met on the Internet (and then in person)—a 56-year-old herpetic, pot-bellied, thrice-divorced, dyslexic, seriously caffeine-addicted, lactose-intolerant, bipolar phone repair guy who happened to be the best writer I'd ever met. Of course he'd never written anything for real—no self-respecting underachiever could justify taking himself seriously enough to actually do anything which might approach their true capability. The irony is that he rejected me because I happen to look my age— attractive but fifty—even as he put some of his teeth into a mug on the edge of the bathroom sink.

It wasn't a good week. And when I met Ellen, she was still struggling to make a narrative out of it, to assign blame and responsibility through a haze of rage and disappointment. When she answers my specific questions about what happened in the desert, it's not even clear that Douglas did reject her. This is partly because his awfulness makes a better story—she certainly didn't need to throw in "lactose-intolerant" to convince me that Douglas is a dud. And it's also because she makes no allowances for the mysterious chemistry or click. She liked him better on the phone than in person, so therefore he must have been lying or trying to trick her—or been dissatisfied with her appearance.

My distrust of her version also stems from her refusal or inability to describe her responses to him. "We had an awkward four-hour drive from the airport. He didn't seem like the e-mail guy, but I accepted that it was awkward. After all that build-up I knew there was no way it was going to all come out at once. I'd said, 'Let's give ourselves a break, let's give it a few days.'"

Her description of the first night sounds excruciating, almost as if she dissociated. Although his affect was strangely flat ("maybe it was the bipolar drugs") and they hadn't connected, they went to bed and had sex. "I didn't really have a problem sleeping with him." Ellen shrugs.

As I said to my doctor, it would almost be disingenuous not to. Here I'd spent eight months talking to this guy, and I know he looks fine, that's not the issue, so it would be weird to suddenly put up this wall. So it [sex] was all right. It wasn't until the next day I realized that this person was presenting in a whole different way.

But he did stupid stuff in bed. He said, "Best sex I've had in a year." I said to him, "You don't just say that, you need to personalize things with women."

(Her directive is as unintentionally hilarious as those ads for perfume that's supposed to smell different on every woman.) "Later he said, 'I love making love to a beautiful woman,' and again that was sort of generic and those were my first two clues that either he doesn't get it or there's something wrong."

There were less subtle clues. Douglas's house was covered with grime and dog hair.

He had three chairs that were in the house when he bought it, two of which were designated as dog chairs, so I had to sit in a fur-covered dog chair. There was dark paneling and orange trim, and he'd been living there almost a year. He bought it for thirty-five K, in a small town in the middle of nowhere. Anyone else would have painted over the paneling, or at least the trim. He hadn't even put on clean sheets, so we did that together when we got home; it was a hotel mattress that had the months printed on it, so you knew when to flip the mattress.

I said, "This is how a twenty-four-year-old would live," and he defended it by saying, "This is the first

house I've owned by myself and it's my safe place."
And this is a man who makes fifty thousand dollars a
year! I make sixteen thousand dollars and my house is
twenty times better than his, not because I have
money but because I have wherewithal or self-esteem
or whatever. I know where to get free paint.

The plane essay, going over this part, gives me my only
glimpse of Douglas's wit—a rather antisocial joke, but funny
nonetheless. Ellen writes, "his recently visiting brother had advised that he should add some charm to his bachelor pad before
hosting a non-family member; Douglas's response was that
perhaps he could nail some teddy bears to the wall."

Why didn't Ellen just up and leave? It seems like a combination of her emotional investment in Douglas, some familiarity
with poverty and squalor, and an inability to process such a gigantic disappointment. I remember feeling the latter confusion
on a smaller scale with Nick—the struggle to reconcile the two
Nicks was so overwhelming that the judging, assessing "I" was
temporarily disabled. Ellen's still reconciling. "In writing and
on the phone, he made me laugh," she says. "He didn't make
me laugh the whole time I was there, it was like he was gone.
He didn't even try. After the second day, I was thinking, 'This
isn't what I signed up for,' but also thinking maybe I'm wrong
or that I should hang in there."

When we talked Ellen was still grappling with assigning responsibility for the week and for her other relationships. What
does self-sufficiency or wholeness mean in the context of intimacy? Ellen had spent so many months writing and explaining
her needs and capabilities and expectations, she expected him
to understand her. On the second day,

I told him that "It seems as though the eighty percent
I thought we had in common and the twenty percent
we didn't is now flipped." I thought I was telling him

that I wasn't feeling this, you're not matching up to what I thought I knew. But he said, "No, you're like what I thought I knew and I'm getting to know you better every day and everything's hunky dory." He comes to tell me later in the week that that's not true, that he wasn't feeling it from the minute he saw me get off the plane.

So I was pissed that he was lying to me, because had I known we *both* weren't feeling it, I would have rented a car and had a nice little trip around the West. . . . He decided that we would have a nice casual week together and keep each other company— without checking to see if that was OK with me. And by doing that and not letting me know that there was no chemistry, he took away the decision from me by taking away my option to take my trip.

That he too may have been hoping the phone and letter relationship would somehow assert itself over the course of the week did not occur to her.

The failure of their partnership took a poignantly literal form. "A few weeks earlier, we'd talked about writing a play about this whole thing, and my computer looked like it might die, so I'd printed out all thousand pages of our correspondence and brought them with me. When I left—he doesn't know this yet—I put them in his woodstove; when he goes to first light his stove in September or October, he's going to find them."

She says of the play they planned to write, "It's an interesting example of how on the phone we could work each other up to a level of engagement and fun, and our imagination starts flying and we're applying our respective brains to this thing and then it vaporizes. And I said to him, 'It's so unbelievable that this stuff is so fragile that it can just evaporate.'"

Ellen then lights into previous boyfriends for failing to deliver on discussed collaborations. "What I'd like to do sometime is have that stuff solidify into something real. I may joke around, but part of why I broke up with the previous boyfriend [forklift guy] was we'd talk about doing stuff and making stuff and I'd be serious and it would turn out he'd be joking. They were bright, funny things we could have done and he was just kidding around. I wanted to be taken seriously. He was another under-achiever." This is also her bitterest accusation of Douglas.

As Ellen rails against underachieving boyfriends who won't collaborate amid her own half-finished projects, Gloria Steinem's remark about women "becoming the men we wanted to marry" springs to mind. But Ellen's mad at the feminists too. "I think of myself as a casualty of the women's-lib movement," she says, waving her beer.

When I came of age, it was very black-and-white in the women's movement. Up to this point, we were slaves and after this point we were fine on our own. We were there and now we're here. [Postfeminist] society as-sumed I wanted to go get some job because I was smart. I didn't admit this to myself for years, but be-cause of my skill set, I think I would have been happy staying at home raising kids. I'm very creative, I cook, I sew, I've always wanted to make Halloween costumes.

I've always wanted a husband and kids, that whole thing. But coming back from this trip, I have a new sense. I used to do stuff on my own like buy a house almost out of defiance. Now I don't have that defi-ance, I'm just going to live. And the next guy is going to court me. I'm not going to put myself through this shit where I'm so accommodating.

Ellen's crystallizing everything I fear about online dating—millions of disappointed people declaring their refusal to ever extend themselves emotionally again even as they throw themselves into more dates. Two days after she got back

from Nevada, Ellen signed up on Match.com, Atheistsingles
.com, Alternativesingles.com, NewEnglandmatchmaker.com,
Yahoopersonals.com, Loveinwar.com, Freethinkersmatch.com,
and Atheist.com and re-signed on at GreenSingles.com. She
also took the test for eHarmony, but they rejected her, as they
do 15 to 20 percent of applicants, for seeming depressed or not
ready.

When I ask Ellen if all her signing up was therapeutic, dis-
tracting, enjoyable, she snarls, "No! I don't like any of it. I de-
test setting up profiles; why would anyone like it? Look, I know
I'm not over Douglas yet, but I'm not going to let this get me
down." She adds that

> my doctor's theory is I was in love with Douglas.
> Douglas asked if we could remain friends and I said,
> "I don't know what that looks like. What, you're go-
> ing to call me and tell me about a straw-bale house
> you're building with someone else? I don't think so."
> He was looking for a way to stay connected, but I
> feared that we would sink back into what we had
> known and now I would know that it was totally un-
> real. I told him, "I don't trust you with my feelings,
> I don't trust you with anything."

Ellen's an example not just of idealizing e-mails, but also of online disappointment shutting someone down. Partly because
she has so few real-life people to balance out her online corre-
spondences, a "no-chemistry" disappointment blew up into "a
betrayal. I was completely sincere, a thousand percent sincere.
And I can't believe he was, because how can you go from being
funny and bright and engaging to being totally flat? Where did
it all go?" Being perfect online and in print didn't buy Douglas
any benefit of the doubt. It only made Ellen angrier at the "pot-
bellied, herpetic . . . phone repair guy" for not being the star of
the thousand-page play in the woodstove.

CHAPTER 16

Valerie: Get Me Rewrite!

The most common reason I've heard for signing up on a dating site is "to get over a heartbreak." Dumpers and dumpees alike go online to distract, to replace, to get it right this time, for revenge, but most of all to be in control. They're so eager to correct the old mistakes they forget that their dates consider themselves stars of their own dramas, not supporting players. The most controlling among them either roll over weaker players or crash into fellow preconceivers of the next relationship like drivers blinded by their headlights' reflection in the oncoming windshield. Valerie's done both.

Valerie started using Nerve, heavily, a few months after it ended with Jeremy, "the guy I thought was the love of my life." For him, she'd left a thirteen-year marriage that was steady, safe, and loving but erotically flatlining. Valerie had her great sexual awakening at age forty, during her affair with Jeremy, and interpreted the sensation and drama as lifelong love. The Jeremy affair thrashed across continents, through the offices of lawyers and psychiatrists, before finally collapsing, four years after they met.

Valerie hadn't dated in seventeen years, and Nerve.com

seemed the best place to let her blooming libido out to play. Her Nerve profile listed her as seeking only "Dating" rather than "Serious Relationship." Because she was raw from her breakup, she wasn't pursuing love, but rather "a sexual relationship I could control."

Mixed messages tripped over each other in her profile. The birth of her daughter, now eleven, is her "Most Humbling Moment," but her ideal man will "like, no, love sex," and her "best or worst lie ever told" is "No, I'm not sleeping with anyone else." (It is bafflingly common to tout adultery experience when answering this question.) Once e-mailing, Valerie quickly demanded things like "I couldn't be with someone who wasn't good at long-term intimacy: Were you married at least 10 years?" The sexy come-ons combined with the relationship demands unnerved a few noncommittal e-bachelors.

Valerie's a petite, sexy New Yorker who runs a small record label. She talks fast and intently, massive currents of dark hair vibrating around her face. Yoga keeps her in babelicious trim but she's about as mellow as a tornado. She rolls her eyes a lot, laughs loudly, and refuses to go too long without sex.

Our first interview was at a jazz bar in the Village. She had printed out all the e-mails from her first few months of online dating, and we shuffled though the phonebook-thick disaster log as we talked. Nerve.com was supposed to take her mind off her broken heart, but instead men reneged, disappeared, blurred fantasy and reality, and pled emotional wounds either real or faked. Valerie concludes from the last few bruising months, "Men lie, and online makes it a lot easier for them." Going through the record of Valerie's experiences, it seems men's dishonesty is part of the problem. But so was her refusal to believe what they said when it differed from her agenda—to find a relationship as safe as her marriage and as sexually unbound as her affair.

JEREMY HAUNTS

When Valerie first met her lover Jeremy, she recalls, "He talked about his divorce, I talked about the problems in my marriage, and we fucked our brains out for three days," adding plaintively, "People should be able to do both." That three-day idyll five years ago began Valerie's awakening from sexual hibernation. After six months that expanded the boundaries of sex as both knew it, they began to act out fantasies. Jeremy was six years younger, yet seemed more traveled. She laughs about their S&M games. "I thought he had experience, he thought I had experience. We realized we'd found the person we could try everything we've ever thought of together. Being with him changed me. So going onto Nerve was my first entry into the world as this new sexual person."

Jeremy's why Valerie pursued younger men online, even those who specifically requested women in their twenties and thirties. She is clearly not over Jeremy, but when I suggest alluding in her ad to the fact that she's still a bit of a mess, she snaps, "I'm not a mess, I can't afford to be a mess, I've got a daughter to raise and a business to run. Besides, nobody's going to want to date a mess." It reminded me of the most common Internet truths—you *are* the age, weight, and height you can pass for. If you can get away with looking like you're holding it together, then you must not be shattered.

Another part of Jeremy's legacy is "he taught me how to write sex and I got very good at it," she says. Thus she perked up at fifty-one-year-old Paul's first note in her inbox, which said in part: "you seem appealing—smart, fun, sexy and i love your mouth—and truly love sex and lingerie on you of course."

Valerie says, "I think a lot of people think they're sexually adventurous, but most people are boring. Paul came off so direct, so open." But sex talk turned out to be a curtain he hid behind, leading to a bleakly comic back-and-forth in which Valerie insisted on keeping her sexuality a part of her whole heartbroken self, while Paul pulled away from all life details back to, well, he probably has a keystroke macro for the phrase "my cock." Below is a sampling of their nearly-hundred-page correspondence comprising dozens of e-mails a day.

After he'd sent several e-mails reiterating his interest in her mouth, Valerie wrote him back at 10:02 on a Friday morning:

Paul, would you like to talk on the phone? My server keeps going down. Let me know and I could call you.
Valerie
P.S. my mouth is still here.

Paul, 10:04:

it is a difficult day phone wise
i can try later
Send the #
mean time
tell me a few things
there is much that could be done with your mouth
and i suspect you know just what to do . . .

Valerie, 12:01:

Listen, I need to say this now. I like to play around as much as the next person. And I can write sexy emails to you all day that will have both of us so turned on that it wouldn't matter if we ever met . . . the reason I'm not interested in a serious relationship is because I just got out of one. But I need to have an emotional connection to a man. . . . I'm so playful, at ease with my body, open, that men mistake me for being like them. I'm not. . . . As for the other stuff, trust me. I'm not into S&M—I tried it and found I don't need it. But I love stockings

and garterbelts/lacy bras/high heels. I love my body and I love turning a man on
with it. I'll do anything with my mouth you want and you'll love it.
But everything else I've said I want to know what you think. . . .

Paul ignored the last request and kept on for several e-mails
about her stockings and her servicing him and finally was bad-
gered into this a few days later:

. . . at the moment i am mainly seeking sexual fun (which does not preclude
food or movies, etc.) . . .
i do like stockings; i don't need S&M but i do like to be in control and you
seem to like to take direction
and i suspect you are good at doing the things i like and more
so . . . we can enjoy each other fully even if for only a short time
do you have another photo by the way

Valerie refused to send another photo and bristled at "short
time," but after a few rounds of short "what do you wanna
do," "I don't know, what do YOU wanna do?" e-mails in which
Paul avoided giving his phone number, he wondered

if you are vocal
if you cum easily and often
if you like kneeling in front of me and sucking me until I cum all over you
and what pleases you

and so on in a pornographic vein that Valerie later calls "boring"
but at the time tried to top. She answered:

I like a man who can stay hard for me, starting slow, let me start, kissing,
real kissing just that for a long time. I like to lie on top of you, put you in and
use you until I cum with your hands on my ass, maybe one finger all the way
up, talking to me about my body, my tits, my cunt, my ass, my mouth, all of
it, you have to really mean it. . . . I like you to let me do whatever I

want/things rough but not too rough/pulling my hair/biting my lip/just short of pain/I like it standing up.

At 2:34 she added:

I think it took me until my early 40s to know what I really wanted and it happened because I fell in love with someone who gave me permission. Listen to the words, gave me permission. It seems to be different with women now where they expect it like men. It can't work like that for me because I mostly need a man who will be the sexual aggressor. Even when I'm in control we both know he's in control. I don't think this is a fantasy. It's physical.

Paul, 2:37:

yes
i am in control
And i know you like that
my confidence, my power, my sexuality
that turns you on

Valerie, 2:53 (after a flurry of quick dirty e-mails):

I have to take my daughter to the dentist . . . here's my number. If for some reason I don't get it leave me a message with a number and I'll call you back. Unless you don't want me to cuz you really are married.

He didn't call and wrote back the next day with an excuse. He started sex-typing again and Valerie came back with a wonderfully detailed scenario beginning with the removal of her gray cashmere sweater and pushing up her skirt. It culminates,

you pick me up in yr arms take me upstairs to the couch on my stomach and take me from behind . . . and when you cum you scream and then collapse on top of me yr hands around my waist again. We stay that way for a while. I get up with yr cum dripping out of me, straighten my skirt go down the stairs, put on my coat and scarf go up and kiss you (yr half asleep), then go, the coat covering the cum dripping down my thighs, stockings, everything all sticky, wet. I feel so good.

4:27, Valerie:

say something.

4:29, Paul:

yes
just like that
no drink
but not today
soon

4:33, Paul:

my cock is hard as a rock right now

4:34, Valerie:

That's good

4:35, Paul:

be honest
you want to walk in and get fucked
and then disappear
don't you

4:37, Valerie:

Yes, but I want to come back. If it's any good that is, and I think it would be. Still can't completely tell cuz you're controlling the information I get. We haven't met. Don't know what will happen when we do. Maybe we won't want one another for real. Be honest. How can you know?

4:38, Paul:

i am who i say
And you know i want to fuck you
not drink
and you will come over
and fuck me
and leave

4:40, Valerie:

And you don't want to play around with me and have me ask you questions about your work or ask me anything about myself. Is that how you want it?

4:41, Paul:

those things are fine if we are out having a drink
otherwise
they are in the way of the intensity of the fucking

4:43, Valerie:

I'm sorry, those things meaning who we are in the real world? Don't you think we can forget about them in the fucking? Don't you think you can pretend with me? I can pretend with you.

Over the next few days it went on like this, till Paul wrote,

what do you want to do that is "more than that"
how about to start you come over and get fucked

Valerie answered six minutes later,

First I want to look at you. And I want you to look at me. Really look. I want to be wanted and I need to want. It's essential. The eyes open are important. I like to fuck with my eyes open because I like to watch. If I'm not really turned on by someone I can't keep my eyes open. I want to disappear. So with you I would want to appear. Most important moment for me, before anything happens.

Reading this tender admission, I want to time-travel back, hack into their systems, and keep Paul from answering something about his stupid cock. I'm also realizing that another rookie tendency Valerie has is tenacity, which may be why she's a veteran of actual relationships—unlike so many online flakes. She kept up this correspondence for another week or so, because it seemed more like sex with Jeremy than anything since Jeremy. The memory kept her from noticing that Paul wriggled away from any F2F plans, until she finally had to face it and they had this final exchange over the course of a Monday morning. Paul started:

you seem very needy
i just want to fuck you
you seem to want more

Valerie:

Listen, this isn't going to work. I'm not who you think I am. I'm not interested in an online relationship or a phone relationship. You tell me you want to meet me, we have this volley online, then you disappear for 10 days. I don't want more of what you're interested in.

Paul:

i want something real
but you seem to want something more than just sex
that is all I want

Valerie:

So why are you writing me back if you think I want something more than sex?

Paul:

did you meet anyone yet
i want you to just come over

Valerie:

Yeah, right, just like the last time. I don't trust you.

Valerie was bewildered and frustrated but says,

With Paul I have to take equal responsibility because I thought it was something it wasn't. I've been involved with men like this but they weren't crazy—men who primarily wanted a sexual relationship and came on very strong and aggressively without any of the civilities. I had one relationship like that, it started out just sex, but we ended up falling in love, we started talking, we went to the ballet and the opera. I realized when Paul disappeared that he wasn't that.

She's not the first woman to be baffled by the phenomenon of men who would rather masturbate at the computer than have sex with a real woman. For obvious reasons these fantasists online-date, mixing in with the regular people, though Valerie's tale of Paul was the first time I'd ever heard of someone pretending for so long he might meet rather than just admitting he wanted only a cybersex partner.

Perhaps she stayed interested so long because "Paul just kept control over it, not giving me his phone number, calling me and wanting to have phone sex with me, controlling the dialogue." The whole episode was an astonishing power struggle, each pushing the other to be what he or she needed, and reading the other's continued presence as hope for eventual victory.

They were writing past each other. Paul's generic scenes of ever-ready cocks and cum-soaked slaves seemed porn-based, but they resonated with Valerie because her last love had included explicit sex writing. She was, in the early adolescence of her online life, confusing sex and love—and present with past. Her script was the Jeremy story: the elaborate e-mail with the gray cashmere sweater and dripping thighs was a retelling of a scene from their life together. "I'd call Jeremy up, say, 'I'm coming over to fuck you,' show up in thigh-highs and a coat, fuck him, then go home and change and go back to work, then we'd have dinner together and never discuss it," she says, shivering a little at the memory.

"But on Nerve, it's not true; when this guy writes, 'me, Paul, wants to do this with you, Valerie,' he doesn't know me," she adds sadly. Those who've never been e–swept up might say, well duh. But the fast back-and-forth of sexual e-mails can be so visceral it almost feels like sex: the slight delay of even quick responses like teasing, the description of the effect the other's typings has perhaps more verbally explicit than they would be in person.

The definition of online "knowing" someone is in constant flux, because secrets are confessed but not necessarily "heard." Without the real-time opportunity to ask, "So what do you think of that?" or read a facial expression, we have no idea what's sunk in, much less if we've been understood. And we're left pondering a conundrum that feels Sphinx-worthy—that "he didn't even know me" can be true of someone to whom we've confessed things we've never told anyone else and with whom we've had a form of sex.

WRITING PAST EACH OTHER

After the Paul debacle, Valerie's shrink weighed in. "Did he say he thought you needed to take a break and learn how to be alone?" I ask pointedly. "No," she answers, "he thinks I should try Match.com because Nerve has too many perverts." I was impressed with his practicality—were Freud practicing today, would he know the distinctions among the various services? (He'd probably be trolling them for analysands and case studies.) But things were no smoother out in the cybersuburbs of Match. First came a passionate two-week affair ending in Valerie's being abruptly dumped. (A surprising number of us have had this happen with affairs begun online: two weeks is a common duration.)

Then came a bully named Ari whose first contact struck a chord with Valerie because she'd been mulling over her relationship with Jeremy. Her Match.com profile included this:

> I've been married for over 12 years, recently out of a 4+ year relationship with a man who I thought was the love of my life.

Ari quoted that line back and then went on:

> **Don't you think that the problem was not that HE was not the love of your life, but YOUR idea that such a concept as "the love of my life" does even exist? If you ever consider to have another man "in" your life, we might be able to negotiate.**
>
> **Ari**

I say if a man insults the most vulnerable part of your profile, then offers you a chance to "negotiate" if you change your bad thinking, he can go fuck himself. Add the stupid quote marks around "in," and he can fuck himself twice. But Valerie wrote back. "You caught me on a bad day which may be a good thing. I said 'i thought he was the love of my life.' If I still thought I could find the love of my life do you think I'd be doing this? No, I don't believe in it anymore because, in fact, though the relationship had a lot ultimately it was two people projecting fantasies. And the whole house of cards came down."

I recognized what Valerie was doing, though I do it with guys I know a little better: aggressively discuss relationship, pushing and accusing and challenging and defending until it feels like relationship itself. Single people, or feisty ones anyway, miss processing as much as they miss the sex and the backrubs and getting a ride to the airport. And so the Web overflows with intimate arguments between strangers. Coming out of two big breakups, squabbling felt like intimacy to Valerie. Squabbling and sexy flirting. We *can* write some of the love life we're not having.

She kept e-mailing Ari, who contradicted her or seemed to deliberately misunderstand her at every turn. To her friendly gushing, "european men are so romantic! you don't think we're too strong willed—both of us, even already? do you even like american women (I guess so since you live here)? tell me more," Ari answered, in full, "What is an 'American Woman'? As for the rest of your questions, I will respond appropriately when the time is right."

Valerie overexplained and e-placated Ari, then arranged to meet him for Sunday brunch. When he got to the restaurant he was much older-looking than his picture, but she resolved to give him a chance. Talk turned to e-dating and he told her a story about meeting a woman and being disappointed in her looks, but having sex with her anyway, to perhaps create some attraction. But, he concluded, "There was nothing there," then added in a quieter voice, "Just like there's nothing here."

Valerie was shocked still, like she'd been slapped in the face. After a few silent minutes, Ari got up, paid the bill, and left. She stayed at the table, collecting herself. As she told me the story, she marveled, "I did better with the guys who disappeared than with this. Why did he have to do that?" Ari turned out to be not just nasty and rude but also living a whopper of a lie. When I went to look at his profile three weeks after his date with Valerie, he'd morphed from forty-five to fifty-nine—same pictures, same profile. From prematurely to appropriately crotchety, just like that!

Perhaps the reason Valerie entertained this creep so long is that he challenged her on "love of my life." She got to process her current revision of the Jeremy affair as "two people projecting fantasies" and "a house of cards." She liked talking about her husband with Jeremy; perhaps she could discuss Jeremy with Ari. Valerie, thinking of herself as "this new sexual person," kept running into fellow controllers like Paul and Ari and mistaking them for partners, coconspirators.

She was also victim to a few old-fashioned seducers, including a sexy, ardent pursuer to whom she at first said "No" as an experiment in self-protection. This fellow begged her to let him sleep over in her Upper West Side apartment, pleading that it was too late for him to drive back to Westchester; he promised he'd leave her alone. Of course he wanted to have sex with her, he purred, but he respected her boundaries, so could he please just stay over? She relented. As soon as her apartment door shut, he jumped her bones, assuring her he really dug her and this was the start of something great. She had the sex she too wanted to have and then went to work all aglow and hopeful. It took her two days to realize she was never going to hear from him again.

She says, shaking her head,

I thought that by e-dating I was going to meet all the fabulous people coming from the same place as me: divorced, had had time to reflect on their relationships, the second time around they were going to be more open. What's the sense of playing your cards so close to the vest? And it's been the complete opposite, people are either scared or overstimulated or both and not willing to take risks. People seem to go online when they're raw from divorce because they think they'll be protected because they don't really know the person. . . . I just miss the realness of Jeremy so much that the encounters feel impersonal, and I don't feel affected by them.

Feeling this alienated depressed me, but Valerie's more anchored by her past relationships. She does not worry that she'll get in the habit of defending herself against men.

"Nothing that goes on in e-dating is going to make me cynical," she declares. "I think most people are very frightened. I have concrete experience of love—it's the hardest thing in the world, even with a child, but that's why it matters." Valerie is usually working or practicing yoga or caring for her daughter, and most of her friends are married. Without the Web, she wouldn't have dates. With it, she has disastrous dates. But she's tough enough to learn, albeit slowly, from the knocks.

In our first interview, she describes the difference between love and like. "That love feeling has nothing to do with liking them, the love feeling of 'he gets me more than anyone else does.'" She says that last in an awestruck tone, then her voice gets dismissive: "Liking is being able to see them as separate from you, first of all, you are interested in how they think, who they are, what they do, how they see the world, the way they treat you; their thoughts, ideas, and opinions intrigue you." This all sounds pretty ideal, but Valerie concludes surprisingly, "Liking someone is a million notches down from loving someone." In other words, them getting you is way better than you getting them.

After a year and a half of seeking a mirror for her "new sexual self," Valerie's vision is starting to take in others. She'd told Paul she needed him to "see her" in order to "appear"—a lovely metaphor for intimacy but a tall order from a guy who won't even give you his phone number. More recently she told me her new tack "is to just listen. I already know how I feel. I'll listen to what they want, and invariably they'll let me know where they are." Valerie had already found what she wanted offline and she wanted it back. Online she's fitting other people's wants into the picture and realizing that the next love may be unlike any that came before.

THE WRITERS, THE SCRIPT

Valerie's distinction between liking and loving articulates my worst fears about *vive-la-différence* boy-girl romance—that it's selfish, blind, narcissistic. Limiting for women, who must stay mysterious and vague. Monetarily costly, emotionally stifling, and scary for men who can't admit, for example, that they don't know from Shostakovich. I'm afraid of how many Valerie speaks for when she describes her ideal online date. "We meet and we talk and spend hours together and he's a grown-up and tells me that he really likes me and can we have dinner on Thursday and he calls the next day and says he had a great time. And I don't have to do anything. He calls. And I want him to pay. I reach and he says, 'No.' Not 'You can pay next time'; just 'No.' If they want their masculinity back, they can have it, but they have to do stuff."

Valerie's dream date is my nightmare—men jumping through hoops for a masculinity treat, while I jump through my hoops—suppressing opinions, feigning unavailability, limping on high heels—for my free dinner. Demanding that the other fulfill generic fantasies seems a terrible way to start a close relationship, with resentment already building. Every time someone does or doesn't pay or drive or call or fuck in order to be a real man or a seductive woman, they're bound to resent their partner and the whole heterosexuality game more. Boy-girl romance is also a formidable weapon of the fear-of-ending-up-alone industry, bullying us into buying diamond rings, heart-shaped candy boxes, and aisles worth of beauty aids.

But roles have their roles. Romance at best does get people unstuck when they don't know how to move closer. A familiar template is especially good for novice online daters, even more so if they follow an Internet-friendly one like courtly love.

CHAPTER 17

Talia and Santiago: I Love You, Let's Meet

They met in a writers' chatroom four years before their first F2F. Talia refers to herself as "primarily a romance writer," but she describes a luxuriant passivity before the muse. "Everything I write turns into poetry or romance, occasionally spilling into erotica." She's always thought of herself as a character she's writing, and the Internet let her spread herself across several. (She picked the pseudonyms Talia and Santiago.)

Talia moved among three distinct identities over the years. She first entered the room in 1998 as "tosca"—the name honored her late father, an opera buff. Then she splintered into "sweetdesire" to explore cybersex. Her third incarnation was "teatime," the disguise she was wearing when she and Santiago fell in love.

In the chatroom, Santiago's screen name was "blackliripipe"—a liripipe is a medieval hat. A Renaissance Faire buff, Santiago says his "preferred genre" is fantasy, and like Talia he is also a poet. Santiago didn't know he'd been corresponding with one person, just that he liked all three versions of Talia he wrote to over the four years. "It doesn't matter how she changes her garb, we kept running into each other in the room and we kept hitting it off," he says with his big, beatific grin.

I first met them at a trivia night that a friend hosts in a bar in Manhattan. I'd noticed the bulky guy in the green velvet cape and toe-curled shoes before. He was hard to miss. But in the few months since I'd last attended, Santiago, or "the Elf," as he was known among the trivia crowd, had joined up with my team. On this night in December 2004, Santiago came into the bar pushing a woman in a wheelchair, whom he happily introduced as his girlfriend.

Though obviously a sweet guy, Santiago takes a little getting used to in person: his eyes, behind thick plastic glasses, dart away from eye contact, usually upward. His laugh is a loud bark at the ceiling, both unsettling and infectious. Talia is more socially adept, friendlier and less shy than Santiago, with a thick New York accent. She was born with spina bifida and has never walked. From the waist up, she is normally proportioned, a little on the zaftig side. Her tiny, nonfunctioning legs stretch straight out in front of her on the wheelchair. On that trivia night, in response to Santiago's request she come "in garb," she wore a blue damask cloak he'd given her. They nuzzled and petted each other continuously, and about an hour after the games began, it became clear why he'd requested her finery.

While Round 2 was being scored, the DJ put on Simon and Garfunkel's "Dangling Conversation," as previously arranged. Santiago pulled a small box from beneath his cloak and opened it. He slid the ring onto Talia's finger and she stretched up out of her wheelchair to kiss him. They had just gotten engaged. Stunned at such a momentous event on trivia night, the team raised our glasses to the betrothed and readied our scorepad for Round 3. They told me after our second-place finish that they'd met online. The three of us arranged to meet later at a Queens restaurant near her apartment, where they told me their twist-filled story.

Santiago was only looking for friendly chat when he first approached her, because tosca was listed as "taken" in her AOL profile. Tosca *was* taken: Talia had been essentially married, though without benefit of clergy, for nine years. But by 2002, the relationship was dying, and Talia was ready for the training-wheels version of cheating—cybersex. She birthed a new avatar to lure a chatroom crush, not Santiago but a flirty chatroom regular screen-named Lone Ranger. Lone Ranger was "safe" because he lived in Texas and was twenty years older. "He was a very good friend and my writing mentor and he wasn't paying any attention to Talia the good girl. So I wanted to see if I could interest him in sweetdesire," Talia says dramatically. She succeeded, and Lone Ranger and sweetdesire finally spent a night typing caresses and licks, throbs and thrusts.

It was a deception stranger than any in Shakespeare. Sex made of words with a friend she'd never met clad in a deliberately faulty disguise. "I gave him a different real name; I gave him the name Gigi. He was so dense he didn't get it—his nickname for me was GoodGirl. And I'm scared he's going to find out, because we were just starting to talk on the phone"—in the innocent, tosca guise.

In December 2003, Talia ended her marriage, but she and her ex continued to share an apartment, and a chaste bed, because neither could afford to move out of their government-subsidized handicap-accessible building. Talia can devote herself to her writing in part because she receives a small but livable income of disability payments.

After the in-house split, Talia let her cyberlove breathe a little more. "Lone Ranger and I went through several phases, friendship at first, and that led to an area where we could not define what we were to each other. He was divorced, I had ended my relationship. I kept being the person he would go to when his heart got broken. He knew I was in love with him but he kept coming to me for comfort."

Talia is more comfortable than most in such pleasurably painful murk: it's where the romance writer lives and heaves. But the fantasy slammed shut when someone else from the writers' group, someone Lone Ranger had hankered after for years, started planning a flesh-and-blood visit to Texas. Talia's disappointment propelled her into another e-mail correspondence, with Santiago.

From: Teatime [Talia]
Subject: Thank you
Date: 3/25 9:58 PM

Blackliripipe [Santiago],

I just wanted to thank you for a most enjoyable evening. . . .

I too write, and as it happens some is even poetry. I agree it often can and does speak volumes.

If I don't find you on when I get back, have a pleasant evening.

Teatime

From: Blackliripipe
Subject: Re: Thank you
Date: 3/30 10:19 PM

Thank you Teatime, it was a pleasure to [e-]chat with you the other evening (work can be such a bummer)! Anyway a little ditty.

Time isn't what is there
Even if taken on a dare.
It is not a doubt that
eyes cast wide, but the hat.
Always the hat hides treats
that are well and strong sweets.
There is more, but another
letter will unlock sure
questions and enlighten
and create a good win.
And a good spot of Tea as well. :)

From: Teatime
Subject: Re: Thank you
Date: 3/31 11:06 PM
    Blackliripipe,
    How you do make this modest teapot shine. Sorry to have missed you
this evening. Your poem has a flair I've not seen before. <Head tilted, ever so
slightly> I do so enjoy the glimpse beneath the hat. I do so look forward to
more glimpses.

They continued on for a few more weeks, him writing poems, her wondering if they might be meant for her. His last one was the steamiest and included the lines:

English Tea with a flair for Wow.
It makes me scream for more, right now.

She wrote back, shortening his handle to

Ripple:
so apropos, for you have surely sent ripples through my mind and beyond.
What an unexpected pleasure this has been.
    It would seem we have so much in common, so many things beyond
what might have at first been obvious. Though I have tried to temper my feel-
ings, censor my thoughts. . . . It all gives so much hope.

THE FIRST REVEAL

They spoke on the phone for the first time a few weeks after this correspondence had begun. Both of them refer to this as a huge leap, as momentous as the F2F date is for most couples. Though they'd shared some biographical information in IM and e-mail, both considered their online selves fantasies in some sense. They both say the phone "makes it real." Santiago calls that first conversation "the first step of figuring out, is this OK or not? Are they compatible? Is this going to turn into something else?"

His use of the third person for his real self is only one of the fascinating blips in Santiago's spoken communications. The bold love poet "screaming for more" is in person tentative and awkward. He speaks like a smart, big-hearted preadolescent first trying on sarcasm, his scorn wobbly as a fawn. Santiago's thirty-two and has lived all but a year of his life with his parents and siblings; his youngest brother is now thirteen. Talia is his first girlfriend as an adult. This all makes more sense when they tell me, months later, that he has Asperger's syndrome, a mild form of autism.

We meet in a huge restaurant, the only three people there not watching the Super Bowl on the dozens of TVs. Santiago ignores all the screens as he explains how he got online in 1999, at his job, and how a huge part of his social life has been online ever since. "I went looking for a chatroom because I wanted to find people who were intelligent and could be interesting, because in the mundane life—well, there just weren't a lot of interesting people in it! The writers' chatroom became my favorite place to go. A lot more intelligent adults in the room than I came across out in the world." He wasn't looking for a girlfriend, "but when bonds start developing, and then eventually things start to click and then, well, I had several false starts happen that way. Due to circumstances beyond anyone's control, those things didn't pan out."

Presumably those "clicks" were women's receptions of poems like the ones to Talia, which Santiago says he doesn't perceive as romantic, sexual, or flirtatious. But he also says, "My logical self and my emotional self are almost never in the same place," acknowledging he could have been in the dark about his own yearning lines.

He was also in the dark about whom he'd been typing to. He did know that tosca was Talia, but not that his passionate correspondent teatime corresponded to either. Before the phone call, he typed, "What may I call you, m'lady?" and she typed back, "I am Lady Talia." Santiago re-creates his double take: "I said, 'Wait a minute! Are they one and the same?' "

He was stung by the omission, "but she was very apologetic about leading me down a road that just wasn't the case. I wasn't sure what to do about it. She said, 'I could understand if you wanted to run at this point,' but I chose not to run. We'd built enough as teatime and blackliripipe." It's another case of the lie and confession leading to trust, but there was still more to reveal. When she told him she'd broken off her real-life relationship, he suggested they move to the phone.

What he "knew" about the person behind the chat, e-mails, and IMs spread across four years and three screen names is rather vague—little more than that Talia appeared to be a good cybercitizen in all her guises. This orderliness is important to Santiago, who likes how well regulated chatrooms are. If only bullies and rude people could get thrown out of real life like they are from the chatroom! "Tosca hosted, I knew that. I'd noticed that Talia was a steady person, she was solid, she had her head on straight. There have been flakes in that room, never mind the people who show up just to cause problems. I also knew from our previous [e-mail] conversations that she was a few years older than me, that she was OK to talk to, that we could figure out what we are, where we are, compatibility level, et cetera." He never once speaks of curiosity about what she looked like.

When I ask what constitutes compatibility for him, he says, "Personality type," then starts to stammer. "I find that I'm a bit of a, I'm not exactly, there's certain types of personalities that don't work for me, ah, highly aggressive people." Suddenly he speaks faster and with a derision that seems to act as ballast for him whenever he flounders. "It kind of helps if they've got a wit on them, because if they don't, I'm going to lose them." Talia chimes in adoringly, "He's got a wicked wit."

Talia was terrified about the phone call not just because it "made it real," but because she had to tell her sexually inexperienced suitor that her former spouse and current roommate was a woman. Talia says she agreed to the call partly because "I was afraid he would never call me if I typed that I was bisexual. He needed to hear the sincerity in my voice when I told him these things. I was terrified but I had to tell him."

Her voice cracks; she's near tears in the restaurant as she rushes on:

> I was scared of so many things. He lived close by; this could be real. With Lone Ranger in Texas it was never going to be real. Once Santiago told me he lived near the Metropolitan Museum of Art, one of my fantasies was we'd run into each other at the Met and have coffee and then go have hot sex and then never see each other again. I could only fantasize him as an affair, nothing real. I only knew, "I cannot hurt this man; I will not hurt this man." Better to block him than to drag him into something that wouldn't work because I was so afraid. I was ready for the fantasy of Lone Ranger but not the reality of Santiago.

Santiago sees her getting worked up, scoots his chair closer, and takes her hand; she leans into his arm, gazes up at him.

SELVES WITHOUT BODIES

Santiago says he didn't know about the spina bifida when they first spoke on April 9. Talia corrects him, indulgently, "The picture I sent you was in a wheelchair! Hel-lo." She swings her attention to me and adopts her "can we tawk?" wised-up New Yorker persona. "I'd sent him a picture earlier after lying about not having one. I'd sent him my first scanned picture ever like

three years ago, as tosca, and I was hoping he'd remember."
Santiago says evenly, "And I flat did not remember that." Talia
sent him a few more pictures, group shots with friends and
family, after her confession. "I wanted to make sure he knew
what he was getting into. It took about three or four shots till
he figured out which one in group photos was me."

Talia sent me a few short pieces of her writing, including
one called "Do I Like My Body." She gives a nod to the func-
tionality of her "upper half," then:

Now the lower portion . . . Do I like how it moves?
What moves? I have to drag it kicking and screaming,
by the cuff of a pant leg or the top of a sock. My feet
have been called sweet, cute, and tiny. That's nice, but
the truth is they just sort of lay there or worse flopping
to and fro, now if you find that cute, so be it. As for
me, I am tired of Chinese slippers and isotoner boots.
. . . Do I like how it works? I like when it works.
. . . Do I like what it feels like? I like what it feels
like when it's in the capable hands of a skillful lover. I
love when it's stroked and caressed and I feel alive.

Do I like what it says about me? Well, do any of us
like what our bodies say about us, when we fail to live
up to impossible ideals? Who among us is Winona
Ryder, Lara Flynn Boyle and who among us could live
that way for long?

Do I like what it says about you? What does my
body say about you? What do you see when you look
at me?

But for the most part, Talia, who's forty-two, doesn't talk much
about her disability. She identifies more with less physical aspects
of her being. "The first two things I know about myself when
I wake up in the morning is that I'm Jewish and that I love

Santiago," she declares. When I express surprise that this is her first thought every day—does Philip *Roth* even wake to his own Jewishness?—Talia snaps, "Why not? What else?" When she's re-gnashing her agonies from before meeting Santiago, it's the age gap, her full figure, their different religions she cites as fears, never her disability. This is not atypical—many early Web enthusiasts had physical disabilities that they left out of their online identities.

Talia had lived with her ex Kate, who has epilepsy, for several years before their relationship turned sexual. Talia joined the writers' chatroom in 1998, where she adopted different personas, she says melodramatically,

---

because Talia wasn't good enough. Because I was a writer and I could. Because my forte was romance. I played with different types of seductress, changing font and vocabulary. If I'm playing a role, I will write the way that person speaks, like she went to college or has a professional job. I'm a good chameleon. The chameleon is good for the beginning of relationships, because you can find out that person's needs and fill them, so that they'll like you and they'll stay. What I want and who I am gets lost.

When she began falling for Lone Ranger, she says, "My feelings for him were as real as my feelings for [her first love, a disabled girl she saw throughout and after high school]. In a way we got closer than people who sleep together, more intimate, because when you sleep with people, it can just be on that level."

Above all else, it's just so damn *literary* to create a character who takes over and experiences your emotional life. To feel the "realest" love since childhood for someone she'd never met who was interacting with "sweetdesire" was a choice. A choice like the religious make to love God, but also a choice like fiction writers make. Novelists describe characters leading them to their plot; Talia created sweetdesire as a "feeler" for romance and sex, "to see if it made me more curious about being with a man offline."

Once she was written into existence, sweetdesire needed someone to feel for. Without a lover, she was like a soldier without an enemy, though what Talia wanted was more like a video game of combat than an actual battlefield. And that's what Lone Ranger was, the virtual practice boyfriend that prepared her for the next level, Santiago. "Lone Ranger made me feel safe after we took it offline, onto the phone too." As with Santiago, Talia confessed all on the phone "because it was driving him crazy and I saw he was hurting." Lone Ranger was angry and said he felt manipulated but eventually forgave Talia; they are still friends.

The love stirrings were new, but sweetdesire was no virgin when she seduced Lone Ranger. Kate had shut down sexually, and Talia, not getting any at home, had thrown herself a few years earlier into that sex wave that breaks upon so many women in their mid- and late thirties. Except that it was all cybersex. She describes her sentimental education in the "romance rooms." With "the bad ones," she wouldn't masturbate, just halfheartedly type them off. "I'd check my e-mail, pay my bills, once in a while click back to the chat and type 'oh yeah.'"

Her lukewarm attitude is still hotter than most: she's the only remotely enthusiastic cybersexer among the women I interviewed. (Since Benton's an enthusiast, Michele tried, but found it "stupid"; Valerie and Beth were both good at it, but wanted to get to the real sex.) Talia says, "There were good ones, repeaters you'd go back to. . . . What makes someone good is listening, just like offline, finding out what you like. One guy asked, 'What are the words that work for you?' and he told me his. That was really good for me, because some words turn me off."

Kate, who shared both computer and bed with Talia, figured out Talia was satisfying herself elsewhere. "I was online more and asking for sex less, and finally I just told her she didn't have to worry about pleasing me, but not to worry because I wasn't having an affair with a real person, they don't know my real name." Talia and Santiago's correspondence was already careening forward in spring 2004; once they'd talked on the phone and Santiago had accepted Talia's confession, they gave themselves over to no-brakes infatuation. For another two weeks, they had three-hour phone calls and long IM sessions whenever they could get to their respective computers.

Talia was still afraid this might be the best part. She was ten years older; she'd never had an able-bodied lover; she wasn't even sure she could be physically attracted to a man IRL. Santiago asked her out to lunch for Easter Sunday, and Talia, knowing he was Puerto Rican, blurted out, "We can't on Easter; you're Catholic." Santiago replied that no, he wasn't Catholic, so she "had to scramble for why I couldn't do that. I was stalling."

She finally agreed to meet him for dinner the Wednesday after Easter. She wasn't alone in predate nervousness. Tuesday Santiago practiced the entire date, taking the two-hour subway ride to the appointed corner, then walking to and eating by himself at one of the two restaurants they were considering. He decided it wasn't good enough and that they'd go to the other one. The next night, he brought a rose and a gift and waited on the corner for Talia while she made herself late changing clothes.

She met him several blocks from her house, Talia explains, "because it still was an online date, even though I trusted him. Plus my building is for the elderly, and if it was a nice night people would be sitting outside and they would talk." Santiago jumps in and grabs the narrative. "So I'm at the corner, rose in my hand. I was hyper. Nerves were kicking in. Was I pacing somewhat? Yes. And she comes around the corner. Fortunately she'd given me a picture of herself, or otherwise I would have been worried. In a group of IMs before the date she'd explained spina bifida, that she'd had it her whole life, but it was still a shock. It took me about six or seven dates to get used to the wheelchair."

"He's adapted so well," Talia says, grabbing his hand. "He was warning me that he doesn't adapt to new things but that all went out the window. On the first date we walked side by side, sometimes holding hands, and whenever I'd stop, he'd stop. He didn't know he didn't have to. The second date I let him push the chair a bit, which was tricky because I didn't want to be a burden."

On that first date, Santiago kissed her hand and gave her the rose and at dinner presented her with a gift uniquely perfect for the two of them. It was a journal for them to share—she would keep it for a week and write her thoughts, then he would take it for a week. They kept it going for four months. Santiago explains his thinking, which Talia immediately got. "We both write, we both needed to share in a manner that would be OK for us." When I ask if writing in the journal was easier than saying things face to face, they answer in unison, "Yes." Talia adds, "We can't always get to a computer either. IM was the first place he told me he loved me, about a month after the first F2F meeting."

Their first kiss was on the third date, him sitting at the edge of a bench on "their corner." Talia sighs. "I did not want to leave from that kiss. French kissing a man always felt unnatural and weird to me before. Men's tongues always felt like sandpaper. But after kissing Santiago, I went up the street humming 'I Could Have Danced All Night.'" They slept together soon afterward.

Their courtship has been constricted by their living arrangements. Santiago's parents don't want them sleeping together at their house, so they stay once or twice a week at Talia's one-bedroom apartment, which means Kate has to sleep on the couch in the living room.

So they're doing what frustrated lovers have done for

centuries: getting married. I asked Talia why Santiago popped the question at trivia night and she says fondly, "We love Santiago, but Santiago doesn't have much dating experience. He at first wanted to ask me at a huge engagement party, and I realized he didn't know a lot of things. I sent him links to the Web sites Lovingyou.com and Romance.com. They give you ideas where to propose—picnics, park bench, restaurant, romantic dinner at home—but no, he went for trivia night."

"KNOWING" IN WRITING

Santiago admits that in the writing phase, "I was struggling with what I was feeling, wondering what was really going on here. Logically I was thinking, 'I don't know her! She could be anything!' Poetry was the best way to figure out if she was real and responsive, sort of a test. If she understood the imagery in the poems, we'd be OK." At that point, all she needed to be real was to be a close reader.

At the diner, we're discussing speech versus writing, and I point out that Plato declared back-and-forth, dynamic speech superior to written pieces "that always give one unvarying answer." Talia answers quickly, "Yeah, well, Plato didn't have IM."

According to almost everyone I spoke with, IM is the most intoxicating form of online lovemaking. Every wired love affair has its breathless IM marathons, thoughts spilling out faster than fingers can type, messages overlapping, the other person blocking out everything else on the computer, the room, the day, till you look up and it's eleven p.m. and you're still in the office. *L'amour* IM gets so *fou* so fast because it's a crush made manifest onscreen. The message box thrusts itself in front of whatever you're working on as insistently as the reveries of infatuation—and the thoughts actually travel to the other mind.

Talia and Santiago agree that they didn't need F2F interaction to know each other better, just more writing. Talia says she'd fallen in love by the time they met. "The essence of who Santiago was came through the writing and when he'd explain why he used certain words. The level of trust he was showing in the IMs let me trust him. Santiago's taught me more about trust than anyone."

She's been online long enough to know that the Web is rife with deception, but she insists her trust was based on reason. "I'd IMed with so many other people I could tell. Santiago had been a presence in the room so long, and he didn't play games, he didn't flirt, he didn't try to cyber, he didn't try to get information from me. Other people tried to get sweetdesire's phone number, they'd tell me to call a cell phone and insisted my number would never show up on it. No. I know better. I'm a native New Yorker. But there's no reason to be suspicious. He's guileless. He's wissywig." (She explains in a later e-mail, "wysiwyg = What you see is what you get. It simply means he does not put on Aires.")

Trusting Santiago to be his words, Talia was hoping for the same generosity. She put her faith in the right man. She's older and more experienced and in many ways has led them forward, but he generously shifts the foundation of their relationship, right in front of me. I ask him in what medium he feels most himself, and Santiago declares, "Face to face." Talia does a double take. "Whoa, I need to recover for a minute! He's always said online before." He says, "I know," smiles at her, and charges manfully into what look like clichés on the page but are clearly fresh discoveries.

"With Talia, all the rules changed. Because she knows when I'm trying to hide things. She knows when I'm not doing well. The hard thing is risk taking and admitting you have feelings. Even now I'm very risk-averse, she'll tell you. But what I'm finding is that sharing it is the best thing we can do for each other.

Because it works out so well for us. There are things I've never shown anyone before."

It's not just that physical attraction or chemistry can't be judged online; there are also limits to expressing vulnerability in print, and to the acceptance that (if you're lucky) such vulnerability calls forth. The keyboard and screen let you disclose, "listen," encourage, praise, probe, confess, flirt, and seduce, but it's hard to *nurture* an online construct. Talia and Santiago are each amazed to discover a kind of caring in themselves that's lain fallow all those years at the computer. Talia says now she can "save the chameleon for creative writing" and be herself for the first time with a lover.

Their story is extreme but also a reminder that every relationship is a joint delusion. Couples must negotiate a version of reality that's not necessarily everyone else's, and what's an eccentricity in a solo person becomes compatibility when it's shared. Talia tells me that these lines from Simon and Garfunkel's "Dangling Conversation," their song, will be incorporated in their wedding:

> We speak of things that matter
> In words that must be said.

I used to have that album. The next lines mock the sterile bourgeoisie:

> "Can analysis be worthwhile?"
> "Is the theatre really dead?"

I venture to Talia that the lines they've picked may be meant ironically. "We don't care," she answers. Another wedding plan is to have Lone Ranger stand in as father of the bride because he led Talia to Santiago. It's a generous though unorthodox idea, to have the cybersex lover who preceded the groom hand over the bride, but to them it's, as Santiago puts it, "perfectly fitting." All their seemingly arbitrary choices—you could practically call theirs an arranged marriage brokered by blackliripipe and teatime—became a life together when they both accepted them. Another folk-rock quote that would suit their wedding is Dylan's "I'll let you be in my dream if I can be in yours."

CHAPTER 18

Making the Leap

THE FALL OF NERVE

My online dating life, never robust, fell gravely ill in 2005 when my beloved Nerve was sold. Various Inc., the parent company of thirty-million-member FriendFinder, acquired Spring Street and it became FastCupid.com. One September day, I logged on to find the format utterly changed, the number of members increased tenfold, and five years of correspondence wiped out. The changes were all the dumbed-down crap I'd seen on all the other sites.

New Features! included a smiley-face button, presumably for those still mastering the colon/close parenthesis move. I had had sixteen or seventeen credits, now I had 3,400 points. One of the things I liked about Nerve was that you paid one dollar per contact, like a subway card, not by monthly subscription. So if you didn't feel like online dating or there was nobody good to write, you could wait till you did or there was. That was to be phased out in favor of monthly subscriptions. Now there were Silver Memberships (twenty-three dollars a month) and Gold Memberships (thirty-five dollars), explained in the FAQ:

Q: What's the advantage of upgrading to premium memberships?
A: In the past, you've had to search very carefully and try to decide who to spend your precious credits on. Almost hoarding them. You just might have let that special someone slip by. But never again! With our new social networking features, you'll have many more chances to get to know other members and you're going to want to send messages to carry on the conversation. Premium memberships give you unlimited access to all the features on this site, so you never have to think about points again.

Arrggh, it was worse than True.com or eHarmony! The planting of shopper's paranoia: "You just might have let that special someone slip by." The paternalism: "You never have to think. . . ." The assumption that we were carefully choosing whom to contact only because of cheapness, not because we're discriminating or don't want to spend all day online dating! And the grotesque division into classes: it was presumed we all would pony up for the Gold and Silver privilege of lording it over the Standard schlubs.

The membership numbers jumped, but the bachelor quality didn't seem that diluted. If I looked for an hour or two, I could still find a couple of smart, artsy guys in their forties. But it's all so uninviting: the cluttered pages, stupid popularity come-ons, tiny pictures. FastCupid is, as the geeks say, very user-surly, especially for us Standards who didn't want to throw good money after bad. Nobody was writing me, so I searched on my age and zip code and gender, and I didn't turn up in the search! "Heavy drinker" had also somehow become one of my requirements. I could have complained, but apologetic messages were already flashing constantly on FastCupid. They were buried under complaints, and I didn't care enough to get in line. Disgusted friends called and e-mailed throughout the first week of the change. We gagged in particular on this new feature:

> As a Standard member, you have access to many features, such as our chatrooms, and you can respond to anyone who sends you a message, but only our Gold/Silver level members have complete access to member profiles and email functions. Popularity privileges rewards Standard members for having an interesting profile. If a certain number of members view your profile within a three-day period, you'll automatically be given access to fifty member profiles and email privileges to them as well. These privileges typically take effect the day after the quota is made, and elapse after the fiftieth member profile is accessed.

This was the nadir, the antithesis of how Nerve once brought unique people together, letting them decide how to communicate themselves. Now you get paid to advertise to the crowd and rush the popular clique. Nerve abandoned self-expression for complete outer-directedness, following the industry as a whole.

FRIENDSTER "SELLS OUT" TOO

Friendster in 2003 was an exciting moment in Web history. People were connecting in a new way that was intriguing, uncommodified, unhierarchical. Following the friends-of-friends links to new simpatico people inspired optimism about social networking and online dating, but as with all the cool start-ups, reality hit home that Friendster's a business. It had to figure out how to make money connecting its twenty million members, and in 2004 it formed a partnership with eHarmony. When eHarmony's no-matching-gays policy was pointed out, Friendster top brass claimed they hadn't known that.

Another sleazy Friendster development is to disguise ads as profiles—though MySpace is the undisputed master of the celebrity "friends." A 2005 press release announced:

Friendster, the easiest way to stay in touch with your friends, today announced it is working in conjunction with FOX to promote its upcoming series, Stacked, *through the use of Friendster Blogs, a free weblogging service that enables members to create and share online journals and photo albums. More than thirty members of the cast and crew, including* Stacked *star Pamela Anderson, have Friendster profiles and blogs, providing insight and images on the making of the show, and a look at what's going on behind the scenes.*

In only two years, the most unmediated people-connector became another purveyor of corporate fantasy. To stay free, it's taken to offering members fake friendship with Pamela Anderson.

A CLUB I DON'T WANT TO BE A MEMBER OF

There's been no real improvement in ten years over the original technology of anonymous e-mailing and profiles browsable by location, age, and other variables. The twenty-first-century "innovations" of online dating are as insubstantial as cotton candy: pretend friendsterships with celebrities; the science of face-shape preference; the profile advice to "try the Joey"; the multiple-choice test to tell you if you'll want to have sex with someone when you see him. The Web was once a refuge from consumer culture; now the dating sites sell to our fear of not fitting in. And this makes a difference. As much as I want a boyfriend, I wouldn't hang out in a bar I hate—or, more analogously, a mall I hate—to find him.

Individuals still can cut through the sales chatter and find each other, but online dating subtly infects the relations between people. I connect the emotional numbness that follows a run of online dating to the shopper head of "I can do better"; to the glut of dates; to the separation of sex and love; to our tendency to preen and overshare in e-mail. Lying hasn't been a big problem in my online dating (that I know of). But the surveillance-state marketing of sites like True.com has spread the profitable paranoia that anyone *could be* lying. A handful of my dates have opened conversation by damning all the dishonest women online. Crank's-eye view becomes self-fulfilling prophecy when I suddenly "remember" that "thing" I have to "be at in an hour."

Valerie describes "a culture of suspicion" where in order to break through, she overshares, oversteps, pushes too hard. She, like most of us, also overnegotiates. Before they even meet, "couples" e-quibble about expectations and terms ("But your profile said . . ."). They fight for control of a relationship that doesn't exist until one or both walk away in disgust, more annoyed and mistrustful than before. Even my most intrepid online dating friend admits it's surreal to date with "such a radical lack of commitment. Everything is provisional: Will we meet? Will we like each other? Will we be attracted?"

I wrote to that intrepid friend that Nerve's ugly metamorphosis looked like a sign to me. I was coming up on six years of online dating and it was starting to feel insane, according to the insanity definition of repeating the same action over and over and expecting different results. Sixty-five times I've repeated this action without achieving my goal of getting a boyfriend, and the sites alienate me more and more.

My friend e-mailed back,

Yeah, that definition of insanity is fine unless there's no alternative. Does that mean you'd stop dating, give up on men if things didn't go well with them? (I ask rhetorically.) There are certain things one has to keep doing even if it comes out against you 99 times out of 100.

ROMANCE OF BECOMING

Her thought experiment made me realize, no, I'm not giving up. People get married in the nursing home. Letter-writing ladies marry prisoners with long sentences. That German *cannibal* found dinner dates willing to commit. Surely I will find a guy to love for some number of consecutive years, perhaps but not necessarily sharing a roof (the expanded version of my check mark next to "Serious Relationship"). I'm equally sure my single friends will get some version of the love they want too. Which, I realized, sounds pretty romantic.

I still mistrust "romance" as a mating template; I still think it limits people. But if you're single, you can't help imagining the love you want. Maybe romance isn't just assigning people roles from your fantasies, but rather the hopefulness from which everyone dates. It's a religion to comfort the lonely, but not necessarily a lie. I'm some sort of romantic if I'm still hopeful with a 0-for-65 online record. My vision didn't come from movies or pop songs or perfume ads, or not primarily anyway. I've seen what I want in couples who bring out the best in each other and in my own forays into negotiated intimacy.

What I Want is a guy who makes me better. My dream guy's kindness—to me and to others—inspires trust; and mine inspires him. We believe each other innocent till proven guilty. We like figuring each other out and don't hide or lie. We build understanding to draw upon for when we clash, as complicated grown-ups surely will. I conscientiously sketch in the dreary stuff, the compromising and hearing the same stories over and over and getting bored with the sex and with desultory chat when you'd rather just read the damn paper, the times when you're sick of yourself and are cruel to him. We "work on the relationship" with more curiosity than complaint. I imagine my half of the work as the familiar struggle to expand my patience, empathy, self- and other-understanding.

Because even if you're in a couple, you're still the only one you control.

So, yes, in my dreams I build the Platonic form, the Franken-boyfriend; so I guess I'm no better than any other megalomaniac online fantasist. My only defense is that I'm trying to build me from the same blueprint. It's a leap of faith that's also a practical step in a single life; it works for me even if I never get lucky again. Becoming a better, more tolerant, loving self doesn't guarantee me a boyfriend any more than it secures me a cloud in heaven. But, to paraphrase Gloria Steinem, I become someone I want to marry. Which should steer me toward males similarly inclined, even as it helps me enjoy my own company.

"Loving people makes us better" is the distillation of my romantic beliefs. And for all its wonderful advantages, online dating generally does not make people better. The provisional meeting ground does not encourage humanity, patience, tolerance of differences, kindness, or integrity. It encourages paranoia, pickiness, salesmanship, deception, and flight. It encourages "Next!" That's how it feels to me, at the end of my six-year run, and to Christopher, Alice, Aaron, Abe, Clive, Valerie, and Ellen. It's hard enough being single; do we really need this making us feel worse?

The chances to nurture, trust, know, and be known are painfully narrowed outside a couple or family (and the getting of sex never unproblematic either). But openings to love, no matter how quick or small, are more important for single people. Love does seem mythical when you can't see it somewhere—in your friendships or family relationships or even in vague sympathy with humankind. I don't often feel unreasoning love for my six and a half billion brothers and sisters when I'm sitting at the computer. But I do glimpse our connectedness out walking in the city, sometimes clear and sharp enough to bring tears. As my Brooklyn homeboy Walt Whitman knew, "There is something in staying close to men and women, and looking on them, and in the contact and odor of them, that pleases the soul well."

So, despite the dip in my numerical chances, walking away from the computer feels better, more self-respecting, happier than forcing myself out on another stranger audition. It feels like a choice to engage with people the way they are instead of measuring them against a checklist. It's a refusal to live in a starvation economy, no matter how many magazine articles or eHarmony ads tell me I better start scrounging.

Declaring that I won't be online dating's slave isn't the same as a blanket condemnation. I can't write off a technology that's brought so many people love and me my sixty-five chances with mostly good guys. Maybe I'll just take a long break, which I've learned is essential whenever misanthropy creeps in. It's easy to get so focused on the insta-relationship goal that you don't see the impatience clouding your view of your fellow man. I've also learned that you can make the best of online dating if you (1) disregard all pressure to present yourself as you are not. People resent those they lie or conform to, so be yourself. (2) Only use sites that let you search the profiles and contact whom you want. The scientific matching is a crock and keeps you from learning about what you want. Most important, (3) stay connected to the people you already care about. Don't let the virtual world and marriage fantasies and the fear-of-ending-up-alone industry carry you off out of your real life.

Right now, the pages of profiles look to me like a catalog of disappointment. But if I stay away long enough to replenish optimism, they can look like possibility again. If I go back, I'll also be buoyed by Beth and Vivian, Hans and Emily, Lila and Scott, Talia and Santiago, Rachel and Kevin, Michele and Benton. They're all part of my romance script now, especially the stories that include the grateful phrase, "It's the first time I asked for what I wanted." The e-daters who found new integrity or a mate or both didn't demand generic hotness or a compatibility quiz type. Instead, they untangled Who I Am and What I Want from the desires pushed at them by the sellers of things. They asked for what they needed to be a better half, and they became.

ACKNOWLEDGMENTS

For reading drafts, discussing, advising, and bucking up, I thank my agent Beth Vesel; Carolyn Weaver; Daniel Weiss; Pagan Kennedy; my writers group Janice Erlbaum, Anne Elliott, and Emilie McDonald; my mom Marcella Miller and my brother Tom Vitzthum; my editor Judy Clain; Jim Smith; Wesley Yang; Keith Gaby; Dana Hull; Marie Mundaca; Steven Funk; Kenneth McLeod; Jennifer Block; Lisa Dierbeck; Beth Segal; Lisa Selin Davis; Francesco Casini; and Alexander Russo. (It takes a village!) I also want to thank the online daters who generously shared their stories with me.

ABOUT THE AUTHOR

Virginia Vitzthum is a journalist and former sex columnist for Salon.com. She has written for the *Village Voice, Elle, Ms., Time Out,* and many other publications. She grew up near Washington, DC, and lives in Brooklyn, New York.